Traditional cultures:
and the impact of
technological change

Traditional cultures: and the impact of technological change

GEORGE M. FOSTER
University of California at Berkeley

HARPER & ROW · PUBLISHERS

New York, Evanston, and London

For Mary LeCron Foster

TRADITIONAL CULTURES: AND THE
IMPACT OF TECHNOLOGICAL CHANGE
Copyright © 1962 by George M. Foster
Printed in the United States of America

Harper & Row, Publishers, Incorporated,
49 East 33rd Street, New York 16, N. Y.

C-1

Library of Congress catalog card number: 62-8880

Contents

v

Preface

My interest in applied anthropology, and the experiences on which *Traditional Cultures* is based, began in 1951 when Charles J. Erasmus, Isabel Kelly, Kalervo Oberg, Ozzie Simmons, and I analyzed some of the social and cultural factors which seemed to us to affect the functioning of public health centers in several Latin American countries. As Smithsonian Institution teaching and research social scientists stationed in Latin America, we had carried out cultural anthropological studies in Mexico, Colombia, Peru, and Brazil; now, we felt, we should try to determine ways in which this basic knowledge might be used to help solve contemporary problems. With the cooperation of the United States Government's Institute of Inter-American Affairs and the *Servicio* health organizations of the nations involved, we were able to observe behavior and interview personnel and patients in new public health centers in which American cooperation had played a role. Our very modest report, "A Cross-Cultural Anthropological Analysis of a Technical Aid Program," attracted surprising interest, and on the basis of this preliminary applied research we were asked to participate in a major evaluation of the first ten years of bilateral cooperative health programs between the United States and Latin American countries. In this capacity we were members of a public health team sent to the field by the United States Department of Public Health and the Institute of Inter-American Affairs. This experience taught me much about the relationships between social science and newly developing health programs, and it gave me the opportunity to know many people working in international health programs. Among these was Dr. Henry van Zile Hyde, at the time Director of the Health and Sanitation Division of the Institute; his interest, support, and friendship then and over the years have meant much to me both personally and professionally.

In May, 1952, I had the good fortune to be named an adviser to the American Delegation to the Fifth World Health Assembly in Geneva, an experience which enormously broadened my comprehension of international health work. From 1953 to 1955 I served as a member of the Technical Cooperation Administration's Health Committee, which met periodically in Washington. This and the Geneva assignment brought me in contact with additional American and foreign leaders in the field of public health.

During the summer of 1955 the Community Development Division of the International Cooperation Administration sent me to India, Pakistan, and the Philippines to observe American contributions to national community development programs. Again in the spring of 1957 the same organization sent me to Afghanistan for three months. I am deeply indebted to Mr. Louis Miniclier, Director of the Division, for the opportunity to add to my experience through these unusual assignments and particularly to become familiar with the rapidly developing field of international community development.

In 1945-1946, while I was teaching in Mexico under the auspices of the Smithsonian Institution, Dr. Gabriel Ospina (of Colombia) and I carried out a major anthropological study of the Mexican mestizo village of Tzintzuntzan, on the shores of Lake Pátzcuaro. Six years later, in 1952, UNESCO established CREFAL (Regional Center for Fundamental Education for

Latin America) in the nearby town of Pátzcuaro to train community development workers from Latin American countries and to carry out pilot developmental projects in small communities surrounding the lake. Tzintzuntzan was one of the villages that received major attention, and much of this work was directed by Dr. Ospina, who served eight years on the CREFAL staff. Beginning in 1959, aided by grants from the National Science Foundation and the Research Committee of the University of California, I returned each summer to Tzintzuntzan to learn of the changes that had occurred since my initial studies and to attempt to assess the impact of a village program of directed culture change. This research, which continues, has helped me greatly in understanding the mentality of traditional villagers, their world outlook, and the social, cultural, and psychological problems they face in a rapidly changing environment. My students (who have worked in several CREFAL-aided villages) and I have received many courtesies as well as substantial material help from CREFAL. It is a pleasure to acknowledge the friendship and assistance extended by such men as Professor Lucas Ortiz Benítez, Director, Dr. Aníbal Buitrón, Sub-Director, Dr. Ospina, and the other members of the CREFAL staff.

In 1954, after coming to the University of California, I joined informally with a small group of professors and students in the School of Public Health, nearly all of whom had had overseas or cross-cultural experience, in pooling knowledge to delineate some of the general patterns that underlie changing health practices and attitudes that follow the introduction of new and improved health services. In subsequent years, building upon this experimental workshop, I developed a body of theory, ideas, and examples dealing with the wide field of directed culture change, which have been drawn upon for a rather flexible seminar-type course which has been given in the School of Public Health as "Problems in Inter-Cultural Health Programs" and in the Department of Anthropology as "Anthropology in Modern Life" and "Applied Anthropology."

In 1958 a small number of University of California professors established an informal interdisciplinary faculty seminar in community development, under the guidance of Professor Paul S. Taylor, Director of the University's Institute of International Studies. As a result of the success of this seminar, the University in 1960 signed the first of a series of contracts with the Community Development Division of the International Cooperation Administration to provide, through the cooperative efforts of the participants in the seminar, a semester of training for community development officers sent from countries in which the United States supports such programs. To date three groups, collectively representing about twenty-five countries, have come to Berkeley.

During the past seven years professional specialists from most of the countries of the Free World have taken part either in the special community development seminars or in the regularly scheduled University courses. They have brought rich experiences from such fields as public health, nursing, community development, education, and engineering, and through association with them I have had unusual opportunities to develop ideas and test hypotheses. Only because of space limitations have the examples cited in the following pages been restricted to those of Dr. Adeniji Adeniyi-Jones (Nigeria), Dr. Fawzy Gadalla (Egypt), Dr. Henry Renteln (Germany), Dr. Deolina da Costa Martins (Portgual), Dr. Garegin Saroukhanian (Iran), Mr. Mehdy Soraya (Iran), Dr. G. S. Seghal (India), Dr. Y. Subrahmanyam (India), Dr. Y. S. Kim (Korea), Dr. Derek Taylor (New Zealand), Miss Merle S. Farland, R. N. (New Zealand), Miss Mary Hopkirk (New Zealand), Dr. Carlos Alfaro (Peru), Dr. Victoria García (Chile), Dr. Carlos Canitrot (Argentina), Arquitecto Bención Tiomny (Brazil), and Drs. Mary Fox Arnold, Hazel I. Blair, and Franz Rosa, and Mr. Franklin Bumps (all from the United States). I use the expression "newly developing" rather than "underdeveloped" countries at the suggestion of Mr. Akimemi Akapo, a community development officer in Nigeria. The former term is much more acceptable to citizens of countries where the industrial and social revolutions are just getting under way since it implies progress and action rather than a static condition.

This book, then, represents the fruit of a decade of various experiences and interests and the stimulation and aid of hundreds of friends from all parts of the world. I hope they will be reminded of our pleasant associations if they read this book and will feel that I have indeed learned much from them.

GEORGE M. FOSTER

Berkeley, California
November, 1961

Introduction

Once upon a time a monkey and a fish were caught up in a great flood. The monkey, agile and experienced, had the good fortune to scramble up a tree to safety. As he looked down into the raging waters, he saw a fish struggling against the swift current. Filled with a humanitarian desire to help his less fortunate fellow, he reached down and scooped the fish from the water. To the monkey's surprise, the fish was not very grateful for this aid. Don Adams, in a perceptive article about the cultural problems that face an educational adviser in Korea, uses this oriental fable to illustrate the unsuspected pitfalls that await the poorly oriented technician who practices his trade in a society other than his own. "The educational adviser, unless he is a careful student of his own culture and the culture in which he works, will be acting much like the monkey; and, with the most laudable intentions, he may make decisions equally disastrous."[1]

The fable of the monkey and the fish illustrates equally well the problem that has plagued many of the American technical aid programs of the postwar period: Americans wear cultural blinders, of which we usually are ignorant, which prevent us from fully understanding the needs and desires of the people

[1] D. Adams, 1960, p. 22. (For complete bibliographical information on the works cited, see pp. 271-284.)

1

we wish to help, and which make us insensitive to the full range of economic, social, and cultural consequences resulting from narrowly conceived developmental programs. Yet, since the help is offered in a humanitarian spirit, we find it difficult to understand why recipient peoples are often less grateful than seems reasonable to expect.

The peoples of newly developing countries recognize that the world is changing rapidly; they want and need economic and technical help of many kinds. American technical experts in such fields as public health, agriculture, education, and community development are as well trained and professionally competent as any in the world. They know how to do a first-rate job. Consequently, at its best American technical aid has demonstrated how cooperative international programs can ameliorate social and economic problems that, if allowed to run unchecked, would threaten the peoples of all nations. Yet, in spite of the recognized need, the desire for help, and the ability of the technician, the fact remains that our aid programs have fallen short of the goals set for them. Sometimes we have urged programs which recipient peoples did not really want and for which perhaps they were not ready. On other occasions our technical advisers have made poor personal adjustments to living and working in exotic societies, and this has affected the quality of their work. In still other situations imperfectly recognized barriers in the nature and structure of the host society have prevented the achievement of goals sought both by Americans and their local counterparts.

Technological development is a complex process, imperfectly understood even by specialists. The expression itself is misleading for, strictly speaking, there can be no such thing as technological development in isolation. Perhaps the use of the term *sociotechnological development* would clarify our thinking, for development is much more than the overt acceptance of material and technical improvements. It is a cultural, social, and psychological process as well. Associated with every technical and material change there is a corresponding change in the attitudes, the thoughts, the values, the beliefs, and the behavior of the people who are affected by the material change. These nonmaterial changes are more subtle. Often they are overlooked or their significance is underestimated. Yet the eventual effect of a material or social improvement is determined by the extent to which the other aspects of culture affected by it can alter their forms with a minimum of disruption. In newly developing countries, for example, the introduction of factory labor brings changes in family structure. If the workers and their families can accept these new social patterns and reconcile their attitudes toward traditional family obligations with new conditions, industrialization need not be disruptive. But, as we will see, such reconciliation is often difficult, and the process of development is accordingly slowed.

At present we know much less about the cultural, social, and psychological aspects of development than about the purely technological. A public health physician knows he can successfully plan the clinical aspects of a campaign to stamp out smallpox. The problems of the production of vaccine and its storage and transportation to the places needed have long been solved. But the physician does not know how he can induce everyone in a village to come forward willingly to be vaccinated. The use of force, frequently against the will of terrified people who do not understand, often has been the rule in such campaigns. An agricultural extension agent can analyze soil conditions and prescribe a hybrid seed and modified cultivation practices that will vastly increase production. But he cannot be sure that farmers will see the benefits he is sure lie in his improved methods; often he is puzzled by lack of interest in "obvious" advantages. It is a simple technical problem to teach an adult to read, but it is quite another matter to make the adult want to know how to read or to create an environment in which it is to his continuing advantage to do so.

We who, through education and opportunity, share the

values of the complex civilizations of the West, tend to think of development (which we equate with progress) as manifest in science and technology: better automobiles, faster airplanes, finer buildings and more comfortable homes, hybrid seed and larger crops, and miracle drugs and better health. The ingenuity of scientists and technicians captures our imagination; it is hard to doubt that the innovations they produce are good, and it is easy to assume that these contributions to better living must appear equally desirable to people in every part of the world, once they are aware of them.

It sometimes comes as a surprise, then, to find that many people in technologically less advanced lands are reluctant or unable to accept change with the same ease we do. The wisdom of tradition carries more weight among them, and the cries of "new" and "better" may set people on guard rather than stimulate their desire to experiment. The urge for development and the willingness to change are not equally present in all peoples. What may seem desirable to one person may seem undesirable to another, and what may be good for one may be bad for a second. In all of us, motivations to change are opposed by resistances to change. The factors that determine these motivations and resistances are cultural, social, and psychological. They may be rooted in the value system that characterizes our culture; they may be associated with the nature of relationships among the members of our group, with problems of status and role; they may lie in faulty communication within a group or between members of different groups (as, for example, between technical advisers from one country and villagers of another), or they may be found in any of a vast number of other nontechnical contexts.

In recent years the existence of human factors in technological development has been increasingly accepted. It has been generally recognized that technical experts who work in programs of international aid do better if they understand something about the cultural and social forms of the groups to which they are sent. Lip service, at least, is commonly paid to this axiom in briefing specialists for field work. On this level the human problems generally are thought of as falling in two categories: (1) the need to acquaint the technician with the language and culture of the country to which he goes, so that he will know the correct forms of social intercourse, so that he can play the role of a gentleman and avoid giving offense through ignorance; (2) the need to know basic social and cultural forms so that the technician will understand why villagers may fear vaccination, why they often resist new agricultural programs, why literacy campaigns sometimes fail to attract them. With this information the technician can seek ways to overcome resistances.

This is good, and correct, as far as it goes. But a thorough understanding of the cultural forms and values of the people of another nation is not in itself sufficient to eliminate human problems. In developmental programs representatives of two or more cultural systems come into contact. Sometimes the differences are major, as when an American physician works in India. Sometimes the differences are less pronounced, as when a city-bred-and-educated Indian physician is charged with health operations in a rural area of his country. But whether the gulf separating the two worlds is full-cultural or subcultural, it is significant. In either case, the technician shares the cultural and social forms not only of the country from which he comes, but also of the professional group he represents. *His* basic attitudes and beliefs, the things he takes for granted, stem from his cultural conditioning, in the same fashion that the behavior of the people he hopes to influence stems from their cultural conditioning. Whether he is a doctor, an agricultural extension agent, or an educator, the specialist is profoundly—and often unconsciously—influenced by the value system of his professional subculture. From his student days he has been indoctrinated with the motivations, the goals, the ideas about the right ways to work, and the ethics of his field, and he has learned a particular role in the bureaucratic hierarchy through which his profession is organized for action. The technician's uncritical acceptance of his professional point of view, as well as the underlying assumptions of his culture, can be as much a barrier to change as can the cultural forms of the target group.

There is still a third type of human problem in technological development: the ethical one. How far, if at all, is it right to go in deciding what is good for someone else? Do education and technological competence confer wisdom upon the technician to decide what other people should have? Does the state, through its professionally oriented technical services, have the right or obligation to make basic decisions that will profoundly change the lives of its citizens? Or—to take a real problem in developmental work—should villagers in newly developing countries remain untouched until they decide, by democratic processes, that they are ready for change? There is no easy answer to the ethical question, and certainly no answer that can claim to be scientific. But wide recognition of the ethical problems inherent in developmental work and discussion of their implications will help in guiding the decisions that must be made in every specific program.

Thousands of American technical specialists, some well oriented and others less well oriented in the meaning of human factors in technological development, have been sent overseas during the past fifteen years. Thousands more will be sent in the future. Their numbers are being swollen by the hand-picked young men and women of the Peace Corps. For all of them there will be, in the words of Norman Cousins, "the dramatic discovery of conspicuously different cultures."[2] This is a heady experience and it is also an unsettling one. Peace Corpsmen work shoulder to shoulder with the citizens of coun-

[2] Cousins, 1961, p. 30.

tries in all parts of the world, in villages, in towns, and in the slums of large cities. They can be powerful agents for international understanding, but it is also easy to see them as enthusiastic young bulls in a china shop, unaware that their normal way of life may spell disaster for those around them. Peace Corpsmen and new technicians alike will be beset by doubts. The basic values and the implicitly accepted assumptions of American life will not give answers to all the dilemmas that face them. In the words of a young American doctor in a Bombay hospital, "I just wasn't psychologically attuned to the problems I would have to face. Back in the United States a doctor never has to ask himself: 'Why try to keep this baby alive?' He concentrates all his knowledge and will power on the need to save a child and give him a chance for a normal life. But here, in India, maybe two or three hundred million people will never experience a single day free of hunger or sickness in their entire lives."[3]

This book deals with the cultural, social, and psychological sides of technical assistance and technological development, particularly as it occurs in traditional rural communities which have been the targets of developmental programs such as those of the specialized agencies of the United Nations, the United States bilateral aid programs, and private organizations like the Rockefeller and Ford foundations. It attempts to place the phenomenon of planned technological change in the broader perspective of the underlying processes of culture change which occur at all times in all parts of the world. Reflecting the academic bias of the author, the interpretation is narrowly anthropological and more broadly sociological. The nontechnical barriers to change found in all societies are discussed at length, as are the factors that stimulate change. Then the focus is shifted to the American technician, his professional culture, the relationship of his training to the task at hand, and the experience

[3] *Ibid.*

of "culture shock" which all of us undergo when first working abroad.

I believe that many of the difficulties that plague technical specialists in overseas assignments and prevent the most effective developmental programs can be ameliorated by an understanding and a better utilization of social science, and particularly anthropological knowledge. Accordingly I devote the final chapters to a discussion of how the social scientist works in an applied setting and of the kinds of administrative relationships which make possible the best teamwork between program administrators and social scientists. Finally, I touch briefly upon some of the factors that seem to me to be involved in the problem of the ethics of developmental work.

This book is not intended as a handy pocket guide to successful technical aid work, and it contains no formal lists of do's and don'ts. It is my hope, however, that the ideas and the evidence presented will contribute to a better understanding of the implications of planned technological change and the role of the personnel who participate in such programs, and that the practical hints given from time to time will prove useful.

1 . . . . The cultural context of technological development

When we speak of "technological development" in newly developing areas, what exactly do we mean? It is clear that the recipients of public health aid, agricultural extension projects, and community development programs are learning novel techniques, acquiring facility in the handling of new tools, and changing attitudes and customs that impinge on many areas of their lives. But technical specialists differ from social scientists in the frame of reference they use to interpret what is happening. The technical specialist, with the goals and values of his professional subculture, sees developmental work as the successful diffusion of scientific knowledge and of behavior based on scientific knowledge to areas where they previously existed in slight measure or not at all.

The social scientist, on the other hand, as a product of his academic subculture, looks upon technological development as change in the patterns of culture and society. To him, successful technological programs simply constitute a special case in the whole broad process of cultural and social change. He describes what happens as "planned" or "directed" or "guided" cultural and social change, to distinguish the process from the evolutionary or spontaneous or unplanned changes which constantly occur. Since the purpose of this book is to examine technological developmental problems within the frame of reference of the social scientist, rather than of the program specialist, it is important to understand something about culture and society and how they change.

Anthropologists, whose work focuses on culture, and sociologists, whose work focuses on society, have coined elaborate definitions for these two words. In a recent review of the concept of culture more than one hundred and fifty definitions are given, culled from the writing of anthropologists over three-quarters of a century.[1] Some of these statements are descriptive, stressing content; others are psychological, emphasizing symbolism and the learning of symbols; still others are structural, dwelling upon "configurations," the patterns of action delineable in human behavior. Sociologists, in dealing with society, have been equally ingenious.

We need not linger over shades of distinctions. For our purposes we can illustrate culture and society sufficiently well by considering the people with whom we work in developmental programs. Technical specialists direct their efforts toward groups of people; they work in communities, often as easily recognizable as a village or small town. These communities are not simply crowds, agglomerations of people who chance to be physically close to one another. They are "societies," organized groups of people who have learned to live and work together, interacting in the pursuit of common ends. In order to live and work together people require formal rules for defining their relationships one to another. We say that a society has a "struc-

[1] Kroeber and Kluckhohn, 1952.

ture," or an "organization," a patterned arrangement of relationships which social scientists discern in the behavior they observe, a system which is seen to define and regulate the mode of everyday intercourse among the members of the group. Social structure usually is studied by breaking down its parts into "institutions" such as the family, religion, political and economic systems, and the like, each of which harbors a great number of "statuses"—the positions people occupy vis-à-vis each other, which in turn have a corresponding "role," the behavior forms deemed appropriate to each status.

A particular society is a going concern—it functions and perpetuates itself—because its members, quite unconsciously, agree on the basic rules for living together. "Culture" is the shorthand term for these rules that guide the way of life of the members of a social group. More specifically, culture can be thought of as the common, learned way of life shared by the members of a society, consisting of the totality of tools, techniques, social institutions, attitudes, beliefs, motivations, and systems of value known to the group. Or, to put the distinction in a different way, society means people and culture means the behavior of people. The terms are interdependent, and it is difficult to speak of one without relating it to the other. Social scientists often use the terms interchangeably, or they use the compound "sociocultural" to indicate that the phenomena dealt with partake of both society and culture. To illustrate, we can say that "in peasant society prestige is an important motivation in bringing about change," or "the prestige motivation is recognizable in peasant culture as an important factor in change," or yet again, "among the sociocultural factors which explain change in peasant communities, the desire for prestige is high on the list." All three sentences convey essentially the same idea.

The words culture and society have both specific and generic meanings. We speak of "a society," a particular, recognizable, delineable, finite body of people; it may be a primitive hunting band, an agricultural village, a market city, or a modern nation. And we speak of "a culture," which, of course, is the particular way of life of a specific society. We also use the terms, sometimes in the adjectival forms of "social" (or "societal") and "cultural," in a nonspecific, generic, pan-human sense. We can speak of social and cultural forms of mankind without reference to specific groups, and we can study the evolution of culture and the development of society in an equally generalized sense.

For the sake of simplicity, let us say that technological development programs represent planned culture change, recognizing that social change, always present, is subsumed under this definition. As technical specialists, then, we intend to help specific groups of people change some of the aspects of their culture. In the process, and as a result of this experience, some of our own cultural forms will change; we are all quite different beings after a two-year assignment abroad. If we are helping to change culture, and are changing ourselves, it is wise to have a pretty good idea of what it is that is changing. We have already had a definition of culture. Now let us examine the concept in greater detail, particularly with respect to those points that relate directly to the process of change.

1. *Culture is learned.* The behavior patterns that constitute a specific culture are not genetically or biologically determined. Every normal infant has the potential to learn any culture. The one that he comes to share is a matter of chance, the accident of his place of birth. Through the process of socialization, or enculturation, as Herskovits calls it, the child acquires the prevailing attitudes and beliefs, the forms of behavior appropriate to the social roles he occupies, and the behavior patterns and values of the society into which he is born. Because culture is learned rather than transmitted biologically, it is sometimes called man's social heritage.

If culture stemmed from race, change could occur only as

biological forms change; for practical purposes, directed progress would be impossible. But because of the innate potential of the human infant and the inherent plasticity of the human mind, man not only learns a culture, but he can also forget or cast aside parts of a culture and adopt in their place new and often radically different behavior forms.

Although everyone learns the culture into which he is born, the human environment and life experiences of no two people are absolutely identical. The chance that determines one's society also determines one's statuses within that society, and these in turn affect the individual learning process. Consequently, although a culture/society produces similar products, these products are not absolutely uniform. No two people act and react in exactly the same way. Each person has a unique personality—"the organized aggregate of psychological processes and states pertaining to the individual," to quote Linton[2]—and this personality, in relation to the society and culture that goes with it, will determine the specific behavior of its owner. The fact of individual variation among the members of the same social group has important implications for planning change. Some people will be psychologically more disposed to try new things than will others. Depending on life experiences, there will be differences in the ease and ability with which villagers continue to learn and in their flexibility in casting off old forms of behavior that conflict with new forms. A technical expert quickly learns that his first practical task in a new setting is to identify the relatively few individuals in the community whose personalities predispose them to sympathetic consideration of his program.

2. *A culture is a logically integrated, functional, sense-making whole.* It is not an accidental collection of customs and habits thrown together by chance. If the analogy is not carried too far, a culture may be compared to a biological organism, in

---

[2] Linton, 1945, p. 84.

that each of its parts is related in some way to all other parts. Each fulfills a definite function in relation to the others and is essential to the normal functioning of the culture as a whole. Each part, in turn, draws upon all the other parts in some way for its own continued existence, and its growth and development are dependent upon corresponding growth and development in the culture as a whole. To put the matter another way, each institution—religion, for example—reflects the dominant values of the total culture, and the beliefs and activities that constitute religion articulate with other aspects of culture at a thousand points. Social, economic, and juridical phases of a culture cannot be fully understood without an understanding of religious forms which, in turn, are expressed through special speech patterns, social rites, mythology, music, and material culture.

To say that a culture is a logically integrated, functional entity does not imply that its parts interact in perfect harmony, without stress or strain. In an absolutely static community this might be true. But cultures change, and the parts of a culture change at different speeds; consequently, perfect integration and perfect fit are impossible. Varying degrees of disorganization and apparent logical inconsistencies will be found in any specific situation. Every culture, therefore, represents something of a compromise, an attempt to strike a balance between the stresses and strains that are inevitable consequences of unequal rates of change and the forces which work toward the unattainable goal of perfect harmony. Pre-existing relationships between culture elements are constantly disturbed by normal change processes, and, just as constantly, the affected areas of culture strive to adjust themselves to new circumstances and to reach a new stable relationship which may endure until still other steps forward are taken.

The importance of an understanding of culture as a functional, sense-making, logical whole to the practitioner or student of technological change should be apparent: significant change in any social institution or phase of a culture cannot occur without accommodation in those institutions or phases that impinge upon it, and the degree of possible change is limited by the extent to which these accommodations occur. Conversely, any change in one institution produces secondary and tertiary changes in others, of a nature and extent that cannot always be foreseen.

An example from the field of public health illustrates this principle. The keystone of community environmental sanitation is a potable water supply. During recent years sanitary engineers in many countries have designed and built hundreds —perhaps thousands—of water supply systems in villages and small towns previously served only by wells, streams, or lakes. Unfortunately, many of these projects have functioned at less than top efficiency: breakdowns are frequent and repairs are slow in coming; mudholes sometimes develop around broken taps and flies and mosquitos breed. Whole systems have fallen into disuse for one reason or another. These failures can be understood and some provision made to prevent them, if it is recognized that a water supply system is not simply a problem in engineering design, but rather a function of the total way of life of a group. A successful water installation requires a whole series of preconditions, and if these preconditions do not exist, or cannot be created, failure is probable. If water in quantity is to be brought into a community, simultaneous provision must be made to carry away waste; this usually means a sewer system, or at least septic tanks or soakage pits. Trained personnel to maintain pumps and other mechanical components are essential; provision must be made for stocking spare parts in case of breakdown; transportation must be such that chemicals and other supplies will arrive regularly; an administration capable of collecting water bills or taxes is essential; the layout of water lines and outlets should conform to local architectural forms and be in harmony with the social needs and desires of the people. Users must have the will to turn water off when it is not in use rather than to leave taps running.

To the extent that these, and many other, conditions do not exist or cannot be created a water supply system will fall short of perfection. If disposal means are lacking or if people refuse to keep taps closed when not in use, mudholes will appear and breed disease; without trained personnel, machinery will fail and the town will be without water; without spare parts and the regular arrival of chemicals and supplies, trained personnel will be unable to work efficiently; without money to maintain the system, personnel cannot be hired and supplies cannot be purchased; if outlets are planned according to the standards of other cultures, violence will be done to many social customs: women may be deprived of their social opportunities over washtubs or youths may be deprived of courting opportunities at village wells.

3. *All cultures are constantly changing; no culture is completely static.* Although every culture produces inventors and discoverers, who are the ultimate sources of change, no group would progress rapidly if change could come about only through the ingenuity of its own members. If the opportunity for change were so limited, we should still all be in the Stone Age. As far as a particular society is concerned, its proneness to advancement is the result of its members' exposure to the tools, techniques, and ideas of other groups, their readiness to recognize advantages in ways and forms not their own, and their opportunity to accept these ways and forms, should they wish to do so. The complexity of our modern civilizations is due only in small part to the geniuses each has bred. It is due rather to the willingness of our ancestors, over countless generations, to see merit in the ways of other people and to adopt these ways as their own when they saw advantage in so doing. Linton's classic passage should remind the American of his debt to world

cultures and perhaps restore a bit of humility that is not always present.

Our solid American citizen awakens in a bed built on a pattern which originated in the Near East but which was modified in Northern Europe before it was transmitted to America. He throws back covers made from cotton, domesticated in India, or linen, domesticated in the Near East, or wool from sheep, also domesticated in the Near East, or silk, the use of which was discovered in China. All of these materials have been spun and woven by processes invented in the Near East. He slips into his moccasins, invented by the Indians of the Eastern woodlands, and goes to the bathroom, whose fixtures are a mixture of European and American inventions, both of recent date. He takes off his pajamas, a garment invented in India, and washes with soap invented by the ancient Gauls. He then shaves, a masochistic rite which seems to have been derived from either Sumer or ancient Egypt.

Returning to the bedroom, he removes his clothes from a chair of southern European type and proceeds to dress. He puts on garments whose form originally derived from the skin clothing of the nomads of the Asiatic steppes, puts on shoes made from skins tanned by a process invented in ancient Egypt and cut to a pattern derived from the classical civilizations of the Mediterranean, and ties around his neck a strip of bright-colored cloth which is a vestigial survival of the shoulder shawls worn by the seventeenth-century Croatians. Before going out for breakfast he glances through the window, made of glass invented in Egypt, and if it is raining puts on overshoes made of rubber discovered by the Central American Indians and takes an umbrella, invented in southeastern Asia. Upon his head he puts a hat made of felt, a material invented in the Asiatic steppes.

On his way to breakfast he stops to buy a paper, paying for it with coins, an ancient Lydian invention. At the restaurant a whole new series of borrowed elements confronts him. His plate is made of a form of pottery invented in China. His knife is of steel, an alloy first made in southern India, his fork a medieval

Italian invention, and his spoon a derivative of a Roman original. He begins breakfast with an orange, from the eastern Mediterranean, a canteloupe from Persia, or perhaps a piece of African watermelon. With this he has coffee, an Abyssinian plant, with cream and sugar. Both the domestication of cows and the idea of milking them originated in the Near East, while sugar was first made in India. After his fruit and first coffee he goes on to waffles, cakes made by a Scandinavian technique from wheat domesticated in Asia Minor. Over these he pours maple syrup, invented by the Indians of the Eastern Woodlands. As a side dish he may have the egg of a species of bird domesticated in Indo-China, or thin strips of the flesh of an animal domesticated in Eastern Asia which have been salted and smoked by a process developed in northern Europe.

When our friend has finished eating he settles back to smoke, an American Indian habit, consuming a plant domesticated in Brazil in either a pipe, derived from the Indians of Virginia, or a cigarette, derived from Mexico. If he is hardy enough he may even attempt a cigar, transmitted to us from the Antilles by way of Spain. While smoking he reads the news of the day, imprinted in characters invented by the ancient Semites upon a material invented in China by a process invented in Germany. As he absorbs the accounts of foreign troubles he will, if he is a good conservative citizen, thank a Hebrew deity in an Indo-European language that he is 100 percent American.[3]

4. *Every culture has a "value system."* All of us, to a greater or lesser extent, react emotionally to our culture. We are not neutral in our attitude toward most of its elements. We classify the phenomena of our existence into good and bad, desirable and undesirable, right and wrong categories. The particular way in which we, as individuals, classify, reflects the cultural orientation of the group in which we have been socialized. Toward some things we react strongly, with approval or dis-

---

[3] Linton, 1936, pp. 326-327. From *The Study of Man*, by Ralph Linton. Copyright, 1936, D. Appleton-Century Co., Inc. By permission of Appleton-Century-Crofts, Inc.

approbation. The typical American anticipates a good beefsteak with pleasure, but reacts with revulsion to the idea of eating rattlesnake meat, snails, or grasshoppers. To the Chinese a near-petrified egg is an attractive delicacy, but the thought of drinking a glass of cow's milk fills him with horror.

A value system gives stability to a culture. It can be thought of as a balance wheel or a mechanical governor. It justifies us in our actions or thoughts and reassures us that we are behaving as our society expects. The rightness of our way of life is thereby validated. We know that behavior which significantly deviates from the norms established by our value system will be met by threats and punishment, both legal and supernatural, and that behavior that conforms to the norms will be rewarded in a variety of ways. Most individuals find security in conforming to the standards of their culture's value system. In an analytical sense a value system plays an important role in preserving a society. Values seem to change more slowly than other aspects of culture. Although this reluctance to change in the face of rapid technological advances often induces serious stresses, at the same time this essential conservatism of values serves as a brake on uncontrolled change, usually slowing the process to the point where a society can assimilate innovations without threatening its basic structure. The tenacity of value orientation, we will see, is one of the points to which greatest attention must be paid in planning and executing programs of technological change.

5. *Culture makes possible the reasonably efficient, largely automatic interaction between individuals that is a prerequisite to social life.* Through language and other symbols, it provides for the communication and understanding that is essential to the on-going activities of daily living. Culture may be thought of as a memory bank where knowledge is stored, available immediately and usually without conscious effort, to guide us in the situations in which we routinely find ourselves. Culture

supplies us with the "tips" or "cues" that enable us to understand and anticipate the behavior of other people and to know how to respond to it.

When a person goes to live and work in a society other than his own, even though he understands the language, he will not work effectively until he learns the tips and cues that reveal the true significance of language and behavior. J. B. Adams describes how, in an Egyptian village, it is not always easy for an individual to determine at a given moment who his friends and who his enemies are. Overt relationships between people are always structured through elaborate but completely stereotyped expressions of esteem and respect which need have no bearing on the underlying feeling. When two persons exchange greetings, they look to subtle qualities of tone, pitch, and melody in speech for signs of friendliness or enmity, since the verbal expressions themselves are always the same, and hence are no guide. Certain melodic patterns denote sincerity, others sarcasm, others irony, and still others hostility. Ways of accenting, abbreviating, or elongating words, and the tones in which they are uttered, convey similar meanings. "These qualities, in their different modes, are interpretable to one who is acquainted with their culturally defined meanings."[4] An American unfamiliar with these cues may find himself confused when working in an Egyptian village, for the speech melody and rhythm that sound cross and belligerent to him in fact connote sincerity. Conversely, the Egyptian interprets as hostile and vengeful the melody and rhythm that to the American mean righteous indignation.

The function of culture as a shorthand device to facilitate interpersonal relations can perhaps be made more clear by returning briefly to the concepts of status and role. The term status, as previously pointed out, refers to the positions or places of an individual in his society; not simply his social position,

[4] J. B. Adams, 1957, p. 226.

but all of the positions he may occupy from time to time, such as child, parent, buyer, seller, boss, worker, health educator, professor, club president, and so on. Role refers to the sum total of behavior patterns, including attitudes, values, and expectations associated with a particular status. For example, the status of father in American society correlates with a particular role exemplified in more-or-less stereotyped behavior forms toward his children. Allowing for great individual differences, the American child learns to expect certain forms of behavior on the part of his father that are vastly different from the paternal behavior expected by a Hopi child. Conversely, the American child soon learns general forms of filial behavior that his culture tells the father he may reasonably expect from his offspring.

All of us, in the course of the day, occupy a series of statuses for which we have learned the proper role, the customary behavior patterns. When we know the behavior expected of us by our culture for each status we occupy and the behavior associated with the statuses of the people with whom we interact, we achieve a psychological security otherwise unattainable. We feel at home in the situation, we can pretty well predict what we are going to do, and we know in a general way how others will respond to our actions. It is this ability to know how to act and to predict how others will act that makes it possible for members of the same society to function together.

Let us illustrate this point with an example from the United States. As adults we frequently purchase food, often buy clothing, occasionally acquire an automobile, and perhaps once or twice in our lifetime invest in a home. In the four situations we play the role of buyer, a spender of money, but our behavior will be quite different in each situation, as will that of the seller. When purchasing food we pay the asking price without question, usually immediately and in cash, and we accept the product just as it is. When buying clothing we also pay the asking price, but perhaps insist on certain alterations as a part of the bargain. We may also reserve the right to pay until a few days or a few weeks later. When shopping for an automobile we would not think of paying the asking price, and in all likelihood we will insist that the seller accept in part payment a partially worn-out specimen of the very thing we want. The remaining payments may be stretched out over a period of two and even three years. In buying a house we also do not expect to pay the asking price, and we know we can reasonably expect terms over a period of twenty or more years. On the other hand, unlike the example of the automobile purchase, we probably cannot trade in our old home in part payment on the new.

The behavior of buyer or seller that is appropriate to any one of these situations would appear ludicrous in any of the others. But since both buyer and seller have learned the same rules of the game as sharers of the same culture, each transaction need not be preceded by lengthy palaver to establish common meeting ground.

Kluckhohn was thinking in these terms when he compared culture to a map: "If a map is accurate and you can read it, you won't get lost; if you know a culture, you will know your way around in the life of a society."[5] But, however efficient the socialization process, the fact that societies and cultures change means that no culture, however well learned, is a completely satisfactory device for preparing people to live together, just as no map can remain completely up to date. For the stereotyped behavior appropriate to a particular role must change as the nature of the role itself changes. Consequently, in a rapidly changing society it is difficult to update role behavior previously learned to fit the contemporary scene exactly. To illustrate, the past generation has brought striking modifications in the roles of parents and children in the United States. The be-

[5] Kluckhohn, 1949, pp. 28-29.

havior patterns for children and parents learned by young adults in their childhood are only partially useful today. Today's parents must continually adjust their attitudes, make concessions, and tolerate filial behavior unacceptable in their childhood if they are to avoid complete frustration and possible breakdown.

If this is true for reasonably well-adjusted members of a single society in which major changes are internally generated, think of the problems facing individuals experiencing a wide variety of strange behavior forms not indigenous to their previous way of life. The immigrant father in the United States, for example, is confronted not only with the evolutionary changes in parent-child role behavior of his own culture, but also with the very much greater differences he finds in his adopted country. Frequently he has been brought up to feel his role requires authoritarian attitudes that are at variance with modern American practice. He expects degrees of obedience and respect normally absent in today's children, and when the behavior of his offspring, conditioned by that of their schoolmates, does not conform to his expectations his security is threatened, he feels his children are running wild, and he functions less effectively as a father than he or his children wish.

Disparate conceptions of appropriate role behavior characterize many of the situations in which planners and practitioners of directed culture change work. The patient in a peasant community has a vastly different idea of the correct comportment of the curer than does the individual who since childhood has been familiar with scientific medical practice. And when the physician finds himself in a setting where his patients' concepts of respective roles and associated behavior are very different from his own, he will experience some of the same sense of bewilderment and frustration as does the immigrant father in the United States. The practice of medicine in such situations is carried on under considerable handicap.

Today's peasant farmers often find themselves in similar, and in some ways more extreme, situations. Not only do they have no idea of the appropriate behavior associated with the role of the agricultural extension agent; they don't know, until the agent arrives on the scene, that there is such a role. What they have learned is that the role of traditional government officials, vis-à-vis their welfare, has been prejudicial to their interests. It takes some time before peasant farmers can develop faith in a different type of relationship with this new government official, who says he has come to help and not to take away.

In subsequent chapters the strategic importance of a clear understanding and perception of role and role behavior by both initiators and recipients of programs will become apparent.

2 . . . . *How cultures change*

Notwithstanding the importance of local invention and discovery, as we have indicated, the major force in culture change is borrowing; members of the group appropriate forms of behavior they first encounter in alien societies. Consequently, it logically follows that societies that afford their members ample contact with other societies may be expected to change more rapidly and to become more complex than societies whose members have little contact outside their local groupings. The greater the range of novelty to which people are exposed, the greater the likelihood that they will adopt new forms. Contact between societies is the single greatest determinate of culture change.

During the early 1930's the term "acculturation" came into general use among anthropologists in the United States to describe the processes that occur when two or more previously separated cultures come into contact with each other to a degree sufficient to produce significant changes in either or both. Since that time a loose but useful body of theory has developed for the analysis of contact situations, and this acculturation theory affords a convenient backdrop against which to view processes of directed culture change. In the narrow and literal sense, the cultures that come into contact and change as a consequence of this contact are national political units: for example, England interacting with India. But in the broad sense of contemporary technological development the cultures are not national, and they are not even ethnic. What actually is happening is the impingement of twentieth-century scientific culture upon traditional, prescientific cultures. Clinical medicine struggles with folk remedies; the results of experimental agriculture are carried to custom-bound farmers; and literacy is brought to nonreaders. In other words, in the wider sense acculturation phenomena are manifest particularly in the universalization of scientific and technical knowledge across ethnic and political boundaries in all parts of the world.

One of the major factors determining whether people will accept or reject novelty across ethnic or scientific-nonscientific boundaries is how they perceive and interpret the new phenomenon. Depending on cultural conditioning, people may perceive the same phenomena in very different fashions. In studying this process Barnett deals with the concepts of form, function, and meaning, and he points out that form, "the overt expression" of a trait, appears to take precedence over the other two qualities as determinates of change. Among the Indians of northwestern California, for example, the American hair-bobbing rage of the early 1920's never took hold. Traditionally a mourning Indian widow cut her hair short; a hair style interpreted as the latest mode in American culture was perceived as a symbol of death in Indian culture, and for this reason it had no appeal.[1]

Conversely, an overt form from one culture often is not perceived in the same fashion by members of another, but is perceived in such a way that it can be reinterpreted to conform

[1] Barnett, 1940, p. 31.

to their own patterns of meaning and yet retain essentially its original function. This process of reinterpretation with retention of original function is called "syncretism." Religion provides many examples of syncretism. Herskovits has pointed out that, in parts of Catholic Negro America, African deities have become identified with Catholic saints. Legba, the trickster of the Dahomeans and Yorubans, is identified with St. Anthony in Haiti, and Damballa, the Dahomean rainbow-serpent, appears as St. Patrick.[2] The pagan Zulu of Natal held a feast a year after the death of a family head to propitiate his spirit. An ox was slaughtered, incantations were made over the intestines, the kin group and neighbors drank beer and ate the meat, each person taking a prescribed part of the animal according to age, sex, and relationship. Choice bits of meat were laid out as an offering to the spirits. Because missionaries banned the feast, Christian converts hold a "remembrance feast" a year after the death of a family head. An ox is slaughtered, its intestines are blessed, choice bits are laid out for the spirits, and people eat according to age, sex, and relationship. Now, however, they sit at tables instead of on the ground and sing Christian hymns to the greater glory of God.[3]

As a dynamic process of change such misinterpretation, or reinterpretation, is far older than these examples. Greenfield tells of a little church above Paestum (an ancient Greek city in southern Italy) where an image of Aphrodite has been worshipped for centuries as the Virgin Mary, and of the Palio fiesta at Siena, on the occasion of the Feast of the Assumption, which appears to be the modern form of the ancient Ferragosto held in honor of the Emperor Augustus.[4] Runciman also has noted the process of syncretism in Christian Byzantium where belief in the miraculous powers of portraits, emblems, bones, and

[2] Herskovits, 1948, p. 553.
[3] Cassel, 1955, p. 19.
[4] Greenfield, 1947, p. 47.

belongings of God and the saints was widespread. "The thau-maturgy that had characterized the last centuries of pagan Rome survived in a Christian form in Byzantium. The sick went now to be healed to the Churches of Saint Cosmas and Saint Damian or the Archangel Michael, as once they had gone to the temples of Asclepius; and miracles still saved holy fortresses, though the Palladium was now the Virgin's Cloak or the bones of some saint."[5] A significant part of the success of primitive Christianity was due to its members' ability, both accidentally and consciously, to work out a formal identification of Christ's teachings with pagan custom.

The lesson of syncretism is important to the strategy of planned culture change: the probability of acceptance is increased to the extent that innovations are susceptible of reinterpretation in the conceptual framework of the recipient group. Aspirin tablets, for example, are easily incorporated into folk medical pharmacopoeias, which also include pain killers. The practice of vaccination is much more difficult to sell, however, because preventive medicine plays a relatively less important role in most peasant groups. There are societies, however, in which tattooing, cicitrization, and scarification are done in the belief that this will ward off illness. Where this is true, it is quite possible that a good-sized vaccination scar might be interpreted in the same fashion, and if so, the probability of success in a campaign would be enhanced. In such societies it is likely that the modern, almost invisible pockmark handicaps vaccination programs and that the old-fashioned, big scar might be much easier to sell.

Acculturation studies have revealed that change does not take place in a quixotic and unpredictable manner. Like all social phenomena, the events of culture modification are patterned. Although we no longer accept the cultural evolutionary axiom of psychic unity in all mankind, it is apparent that similar re-

[5] Runciman, 1936, p. 132.

actions to common cultural stimuli occur time after time in parts of the world that have had no significant historical relationships. That is, the change processes are independent of specific cultural forms and are functions of similar circumstances. The identification of these cross-cultural regularities, the similar patterns of change through time, is basic to developmental work, for they set outer limits within which programs can be carried out, and they permit a degree of prediction that is essential in all planning. These regularities are not experimentally verified; they are empirically derived from the comparison of large numbers of cases. Hence, they are only as good as the data from which they are drawn, and there are always exceptions. The examples that follow do not constitute a catalogue of all the regularities that anthropologists have suggested but they do illustrate a level of theory with practical implications for developmental work.

1. *Cities are focal points of change.* Most social and economic change begins among the upper classes and then spreads downward to the traditionally inarticulate lower classes and outward to the countryside. The cultural innovations of urban areas have prestige attached to them. This prestige is the motivation which produces the outward and downward diffusion of ideas and behavior forms. Thus, Hoselitz speaks of the "primate" cities of Asian countries where the intellectual, political, and economic elites have their headquarters and where new ideas of government and economic policy are evolved. These cities, he finds, are the most important centers of cultural change, particularly in the fields of education, new forms of business organization, new administrative practices, and new techniques. "Their intermediate position between East and West, their contact with world markets of commodities and ideas, their lack of many traditional bonds make them into eminently suitable vehicles for the introduction of new ideas and techniques."[6]

6 Hoselitz, 1957, p. 43.

Ginsburg speaks of southeast Asian port cities as having acted as catalysts for social and economic change and as channels through which the material goods and ideas of the West have increasingly penetrated inland. In Thailand, for example, the indigenous capital of Bangkok acted as a revolutionary medium for socioeconomic change through which Western influences filtered into the entire country.[7] Davis, contrasting rural and urban India, points out that cities are the centers whence Western traits are diffused and social change begins.[8]

Crane outlines the mechanism of transmission as follows:

> Because the city is a diffusion center for Western ways and because life there is relatively free from the tight social controls of the rural villages, the volume of transient labor in the large cities has special significance. Sojourners from the village carry back home with them new ideas, new attitudes, and new skills. These innovations, allied with other circumstances making for change and dislocation of the traditional ways that have for long characterized village life in India, stimulate the slow diffusion of elements of a different way of life from the cities out into the countryside. Just as the economic tentacles of the city spread out to the hinterland, so too do the intellectual and cultural influences.[9]

The process is the same when looked at from the village. The Indian anthropologist, S. C. Dube, finds that the presence of a nearby big city is an important factor in determining the degree of acculturation that will take place in rural areas. "The inspiration and lead for modification in the traditional ways definitely come from the urban areas, brought into the village community by semi-urbanized people or inspired by the example of urban relatives. . . . The rural communities clearly take the lead from the urban areas, although not without hesita-

[7] Ginsburg, 1955, p. 461.
[8] Davis, 1951, p. 127.
[9] Crane, 1955, p. 467.

tion, misgivings, doubts and an initial resistance."[10] The same
pattern appears in Brazil, where Hamburger, studying the town
of Itapecerica da Serra near São Paulo, found that the direct
influence of this metropolitan center was an important factor in
speeding change from rural to more urban ways.[11]

The practical implications of this theoretical generalization
are clear: technicians working in rural areas cannot ignore the
nature of the relationships of small communities with larger
centers. The nature and kinds of relationships that exist between the village and the city may well hold the key to successful innovation. Friedl has pointed out that in Greece there is a
good deal of upward mobility, and peasant sons educated in the
city enter medicine, law, and other high-prestige professions.
These men and their families maintain contact with their native villages and visits back and forth are frequent. Many new
ideas and attitudes and changes in style of life are brought to
village families by city relatives.[12] Village sons who have acquired the knowledge and sophistication of cities might very
well prove to be among the most effective allies of developmental workers in rural areas.

Yet current community development methods almost ignore
the presence and influences of cities. The strategy is phrased in
terms of "local initiative," "self-help," "community organization," "identification of felt needs," "mobilization of local resources," and so forth. A hard look at the nature and implications of village-urban relationships probably would inject more
life into community development programs than would any
other single act.

2. *Major shifts in the economic basis of livelihood are almost
always followed by significant changes in the nature of family
organization.* Among preindustrial peoples some kind of large

10 Dube, 1955, pp. 230-231.
11 Hamburger, 1954, p. 287.
12 Friedl, 1959.

or "extended" family is often the functional unit of social and economic interaction. Obligations and expectations of reciprocity extend to distant uncles, cousins, and nephews and nieces, and social gatherings may embrace scores of related people. Frequently the social, psychological, and economic security of the individual stems from membership in an extended kin grouping. The individual is tied to his family, but it is also his source of strength.[13]

Today, however, the growth of a world-wide monetary economy is drastically changing these patterns. Cash crops for sale in cities are replacing subsistence crops, and increasing opportunities for wage labor on plantations or in factories are the rule. Greater independence is thus possible for those who wish to break away from family ties. The mutual security functions of the extended family are less important than formerly—at times, as we will see, they are a positive handicap—and so the functional family group shrinks in the direction of the Western nuclear biological family of parents and children.

This trend is reflected in preindustrial societies of all degrees of complexity. In the American southwest Hamamsy finds that among the Navaho Indians at the Fruitland Irrigation Project wage labor is causing the importance of the independent biological family to increase, whereas the influence of the extended family and of larger tribal units lessens.[14] In nearby Cochiti pueblo Lang discovered that clan organization is breaking down in functional importance, and looking forward he predicts that it will disappear from general Cochiti consciousness, to be replaced with kinship concepts and terminology from Spanish and Anglo cultures.[15]

At the level of the peasant village the process is the same. In

[13] For reasons that cannot be discussed here the importance of the extended family in southern European and Latin American rural communities is somewhat less than in many other parts of the world.

[14] Hamamsy, 1957, p. 105.

[15] Lange, 1953, p. 693.

Itapecerica, Brazil, the extended family is rapidly giving way to the conjugal one, family ties grow weaker, and the trend is toward "individualization."[16] In village India Dube writes that family ties have weakened under the impact of new socio-economic factors, and that the kin-group has lost some of its characteristic strength.[17] The process is also clear in the Muslim cities of North Africa, where in the country and small towns the family continues to be very strong and widely extended, while "in all the big cities it tends to be replaced by the small-family unit."[18]

At a more advanced stage of change—in Japan, for example—the same trend continues. There, as in other nations which have undergone industrialization, ties of kinship have diminished rapidly. "In the period of less than a century since the opening of Japan to the West, changes in kinship have followed a familiar pattern. The nuclear family is displacing the extended family and has come to be the dominant form in the cities of Japan. Where the extended family exists, it has everywhere diminished in size and functional importance."[19]

These world-wide changes in traditional kinship patterns do not represent a simple case of the diffusion of Western forms. Rather, we are dealing with a cause-and-effect situation. The demands of urbanization, industrialization, and a monetary economy usually are uncongenial to the extended family group-ings of subsistence peoples. Where these changes come about, we can predict that traditional family forms almost certainly will be modified in the direction of the nuclear biological family. Gough is describing a world-wide phenomenon when, in speaking of the Nayars of Malabar, India, she writes,

> Kinship change among the Nayars is not explicable in terms of the concepts of "culture contact" or "cultural borrowing,"

16 Hamburger, 1954, p. 287.
17 Dube, 1955, p. 229.
18 LeTourneau, 1955, p. 534.
19 Norbeck and Befu, 1958, p. 116.

but rather in terms of growth in the social structure as a whole, stimulated by external economic factors. Changes in the Nayar kinship system, correlated with changes in local organization, appear to have taken place in response to changes in the technology and economic organization of the society as a whole. They can therefore only indirectly be attributed to European contact. . . . It appears that the stage of disintegration of the traditional lineage system and of development of the modern bilateral system depends on the degree of absorption of the inhabitants into the modern economy of cash crops, cash wages and urban occupations, and on the consequent degree of social and spatial mobility.[20]

In Chapter 5 we will see that the traditional obligations inherent in large family groupings are often strained to the breaking point by this process of transition. At a particular point in the sequence, before a final break, they constitute a serious deterrent to the introduction of new and improved production techniques, since a progressive individual's greater income may be drained away in maintaining traditional forms of hospitality and help to relatives. The technician who is familiar with traditional family forms, and who has some idea about how far changes have gone, will be well prepared to decide whether his program is going to encounter difficulties because of conflicts in family organization. The technician who is ignorant of such factors will move blindly.

3. *The introduction of cash crops and the increasing use of money tend to destroy traditional rural cooperative work patterns.* Anthropologists have noted the existence of cooperative work groups in village cultures in many parts of the world. In West Africa and in Haiti large numbers of field hands may often be seen working to the accompaniment of music and drums in reciprocal activities known as the *dokpwe* (in West Africa) or the *combite* (in Haiti). Other less colorful, but none the

[20] Gough, 1952, p. 86.

less important, reciprocal forms have been found in most of Latin America and in much of Asia as well. Analysis has revealed that some of these groups have significant economic functions and that total productivity is increased as a result of their role. But perhaps more often the social functions outweigh the productive functions, and in a "rational" sense, the activity is uneconomic. Erasmus, surveying the evidence from Latin America, found a high correlation between the commercialization of agriculture and the use and availability of money on the one hand and the decline in the frequency and intensity of reciprocal agricultural work patterns on the other hand.[21] With the attraction of a market, a peasant farmer usually becomes quite "rational." When he finds it is cheaper to hire a few hard-working peons instead of paying for food and drink for a larger number of fiesta-minded friends, he is ready to let this aspect of tradition slip into the past. Some cooperative forms do continue, but usually because of the social values that still exist and only rarely because of economic values.

An understanding of the relative importance of cooperative work forms is important to developmental workers because of the frequent, but often erroneous assumption, that village people are "naturally" cooperative, and that if they prove reluctant to give the outsider the degree of group support he expects, something must be wrong with his presentation of the program. Reasons are given in Chapter 3 which show why villagers often are not basically cooperative, and such degrees of reciprocal services as have been evidenced in the past are, in most cases, rapidly disappearing. When the technician is familiar with traditional cooperative work forms and knows to what extent they still exist and what social functions they serve, he will be less likely to jump to the easy conclusion that his new friends obviously like to work together. On the other hand, if the agent is familiar with the process of syncretism, he may be able to build

21 Erasmus, 1955.

new cooperative units on the basis of near-extinct traditional groupings by identifying past values with present goals.

4. *Dietary deterioration frequently follows a shift from a subsistence to a monetary economy.* Primitive and subsistence peoples, through long experience, usually have learned to exploit their environment in such fashion that a relatively balanced diet is available to them. Chronic malnutrition, barring exceptional starvation periods, is not characteristic of natural man. Primitive man makes use of many items that the European or American would not recognize as food: insects, wild seeds, fruits and berries, herbs and leaves, and so forth. Some years ago professional nutritionists became interested in Mexican Indian diets. By American standards there appeared to be serious deficiencies: little citrus fruit for vitamin C and no milk for calcium. But investigation proved that the lime water in which maize was soaked before being ground and made into tortillas provides a good substitute for milk calcium, and vitamin C exists in abundance in the hot chile peppers eaten by many Indians. Small amounts of meat cooked with beans releases vegetable protein, providing sufficient protein with less meat than required by American standards. Wild herbs, grasses, and other items often added only for seasoning, also contributed to the balance. In short, Indian diets proved to be surprisingly good. Subsistence people are not aware that they have a balanced diet, or even that there is any such thing. They do not understand that they are making daily decisions that have an important bearing on their health.

When, however, such people are in situations in which a major part of their diet must be purchased, tradition and experience no longer serve them. They must learn anew to develop a balanced diet, this time by allocating their food budget wisely. This is not easy. It requires education and understanding. Only in recent years in the United States, with almost universal literacy and abundant food supplies, has real progress

been made in improving food habits of people. Previously subsistence people, when faced with a variety of new foods, are, in
a sense, starting out to invent a dietary culture. Guides are few,
and the factors of taste and prestige tend to be dominant in
determining new habits. Sugars and other items with attractive
sensory qualities increase rapidly in consumption. Processed
and packaged foods, because of the prestige attached to them,
become more important than formerly, even though in process-
ing much of the natural nutritional value has been removed.
Desired and desirable foods such as meat, eggs, butter, and
fruits often are obtainable only in small quantities because of
high costs. Since malnutrition develops slowly, peoples in the
process of learning new dietary patterns usually are not aware
of the relation between their health and their food.

The evidence for the downward dietary trend is striking.
Richards writes that it is an unfortunate fact that the diet of
many primitive peoples has deteriorated in contact with white
civilization. In much of Africa, including Northern Rhodesia,
where she worked among the Bemba, the colonial administrator
is hard put to ensure that his wards have as good a diet as
formerly, let alone a better one. Medical officers, she says, report
that the physique of natives, whether in the country or in
towns, is deteriorating, and that signs of malnutrition are on
the increase.[22] Hunter, writing of the Pondo, in Cape Province
in South Africa, notes the same thing. Of the patients admitted
to Victoria Hospital, Lovedale, in 1915, 7.2 percent were suffering from diseases due solely to malnutrition; by 1926 the
figure had risen to 13.9 percent.[23]

The Eskimo village of Kaktovik, 400 miles north of Fair-
banks, Alaska, has enjoyed unparalleled prosperity since 1953,
when its men were recruited to help build and maintain a
DEW Line radar station. These Eskimos have adapted to West-

[22] Richards, 1951, p. 3.
[23] M. Hunter, 1936, p. 546.

ern culture more easily than many native peoples, but their diet has suffered. During the summer of 1958, for example, they imported watermelon by air from Seattle, but, over the long run, says Chance, "While there has been an increase in the variety of food consumed, its nutritional quality has definitely deteriorated."[24] Under Japanese rule villagers in the Marshall Islands acquired a great liking for store food, especially polished rice, sugar, biscuits, and white flour, the consumption of which had increased to the point where beriberi—a previously unknown disease—appeared. Conditions improved after World War II, when imported foods were not generally available and people were forced to return to their earlier diet. But Spoehr, who studied the Islands shortly after the war, fears that deficiency diseases will reappear if imported foods are allowed to supplant, instead of supplement, the indigenous diet.[25]

Diet deterioration is not due simply to the fact that people do not know how to chose wisely or that they are attracted to foods with a high sensory value. Wilson, writing particularly of the mining town of Broken Hill, Northern Rhodesia, points out the adverse effect of the increasing availability of products of industrial countries. These items now compete with food for the limited resources of the individual. "The new ambitions of the country dwellers have reduced the proportional significance of food to them; they still want food, but, wanting clothes, saucepans and bicycles too, they would rather go hungry than do without them . . ."[26]

Knowledge of this common dietary sequence in newly developing countries can be of much help to public health workers. It should be clear that in areas still producing a high percentage of their food and where industrial products are not yet easily available, environmental sanitation and basic immunization

[24] Chance, 1960, p. 1030, and n. 5, p. 1042.
[25] Spoehr, 1949, pp. 150-151.
[26] Wilson, 1941, p. 52.

should take precedence over dietary programs. But where cash crops have become important, where wage labor also gives monetary income, and particularly among detribalized natives working in mines and factories, nutrition education is at least as important as any other health measure.

5. *Rapid acculturation frequently promotes village factionalism, and divisive tendencies become more apparent than when tradition alone is the controlling factor in community cohesiveness.* Peoples who are exposed to limited outside influences are faced with few alternate choices about which they cannot decide on the basis of past experience and custom. Opportunities for disagreement on major issues are rare. But in contact situations where people are faced with many new alternate choices, tradition and custom do not provide all the answers. Opportunity for disagreement is heightened, and such disagreements may erupt in the form of bitter feuding between factions. Frequently the division is between conservative and progressive factions, one group that wishes to be guided by tradition and another that wishes to embrace more of the new.

J. B. Adams has described the effect of the Nasser-led social revolution in an Egyptian village he studied. Although the philosophy and aims of the revolution were but imperfectly understood, the men had formed two factions each composed of several cliques. "One of the factions accepted and supported the proposals of the revolutionary government to effect changes in some of the traditional ways of the village. The other, though it accepted the revolution as a *fait accompli,* opposed changes that seemed to threaten traditional values and institutions. The several cliques within each faction differed in the degree to which they found the proposals threatening or attractive, and in the methods by which they hoped to oppose or implement them."[27]

A similar division in Badaga tribal society in the Nilgiri Hills

[27] J. B. Adams, 1957, p. 225.

of southern India occurred when a progressive group, desiring to emulate Hindus in the caste system, tried to dispense with the traditional services of Kota musicians in ritual performances because musicians rank very low in Indian caste structure. The more conservative Badagas saw this move as a threat to the whole tenor of tribal life and stubbornly clung to their old relations with the Kota. The conflict crystallized factional differences, and a fight between the promusic and the antimusic parties resulted in several deaths.[28] In earlier years of less contact with Hindu culture, the alternate choices that led to the tragedy did not exist.

In Chapter 6 examples are given of how factionalism threatens developmental programs. In one case a social worker was completely unaware of the fact that there were major divisions within the village in which she worked. By making initial friendships largely—and accidentally—with the members of one faction she automatically set the members of the other side against her program. A cardinal rule for developmental workers is to determine the schisms between community groups, their depth and intensity, the affiliation of leaders and the strength of their followings. When these things are known an approach can be made which will emphasize the impartiality and lack of favoritism of the outside technician.

6. *Nationalistic movements may be thought of as one phase of the acculturation process.* In acculturation situations, ranging from primitive tribes in fresh contact with more advanced peoples to newly developing countries with a flood of new relationships with the industrial world, there seems to be a sequence through time in the form of a series of stages of contact. This sequence was outlined by Elkin in 1936,[29] and more recently Margaret Read, speaking of European education in Africa, has described the same phenomena.[30] In the initial period of contact the recipient people may be antagonistic to

[28] Mandelbaum, 1941, p. 19.
[29] Elkin, 1936–1937.
[30] Read, 1955, pp. 105-110.

changes suggested or imposed by outsiders, other than in the field of material goods of obvious utility. Adults are fearful of the changes they realize will come.

Subsequently there is increasing acceptance of the outsiders' ways, particularly by the younger generation, and growing enthusiasm to learn more. This leads to the rejection of a great deal of indigenous culture, to scorn for traditional ways, and to disregard of the advice of elders. The validity of earlier customs is denied, and people who cling to old ways are taunted as old-fashioned. In much of Africa, traditional songs, dances, and folklore were put aside, and hymns, drill, and school readers took their place. As a paramount chief told Dr. Read, "The white teachers taught us to despise our past,"[31] and for a time educated Africans did just this. There is a headlong rush to acquire foreign culture, and a desire on the part of the local elite to become like the economically dominant outsider.

This is followed by a period of disillusionment. It soon becomes apparent that the members of the less complex society cannot participate fully in the society of the more complex group. Restrictions imposed by the dominant power are part of the cause, but other deeper cultural and psychological causes are also involved. The dominated group feels that its own culture is threatened, but it has nothing to substitute; feelings of insecurity result. In some regions, in parts of Oceania, for example, depopulation followed, but more often, among tribal peoples the common reaction is the nationalistic manifestation of nativism. Several forms may occur, but the common element is a partial or complete rejection of the culture of the foreigner and an attempt to return to or restore the fundamental values of earlier days. The Ghost Dance of 1890 of the North American Indians is one classic example of a nativistic movement. The Cargo Cult reactions of Melanesia in the first half of the twentieth century is another.

The same general sequence is apparent at the level of modern

[31] *Ibid.*, p. 108.

states. Newly developing countries which, in the twentieth century, are anxious to assimilate the material techniques of the West but, at the same time, to maintain indigenous "spiritual values" find themselves frustrated in that changes do not come as easily as they wish. The elite, who a few years earlier eagerly sought to identify themselves with the ways of the West, in dress, education, food, and politics, and who often deprecated their own culture and its achievements, now lead their people in a search to discover the essence of their traditional cultural forms. The values inherent in ancient ways are recognized, and attempts are made to restore and perpetuate them. Identification of a way of life as peculiarly one's own and as a positive creation of the local group—the essence of successful nationalism—is accomplished through symbols. These symbols must have a high degree of visibility, and they must stem from the traditional culture. They are focal points around which people rally, both to be convinced of and to reaffirm their faith in the vitality and uniqueness of their own culture.

The symbols of nationalism that reappear time after time, in Latin America, Africa, India, and Southeast Asia, are surprisingly similar: language, costume, dietary patterns, fiesta celebrations, an interest in archaeology (which gives the best possible evidence of past greatness) and folklore (to reconstruct music, dance, and popular arts), humor, and sometimes folk medicine, sports, and religion. Symbols of nationalism are important because pride in one's culture and belief in its ability to progress are essential in developing strong states. But excessive symbolization of nationalistic forms can also hinder development as, for example, when folk medical practices are elevated to the status of a different but also valid system for coping with illness.

The technical specialist who is aware of the course of nationalism and who knows the local symbols of primary importance can avoid mistakes as well as capitalize on opportunities which would otherwise be missed. Such knowledge will explain, for example, why the people of a village may be more interested in a new mosque or church than in a community reading room. If the symbolic needs of religion are adequately satisfied, then perhaps people will be ready to move on to other things which are, by definition, not parts of the traditional culture. Or, to cite another example, a specialist familiar with local nationalistic symbols may see ways to arouse enthusiasm for a community project by organizing it around a traditional fiesta, or by using puppets who, in language, costume, and wit, epitomize the group's self-image. When a specialist knows what people are proud of and understands why, he sees innumerable ways for using this knowledge to help them through the process of change.

3 . . . . *The traditional rural community*

Despite the rapid urbanization of the twentieth century, more than half of the world's population dwells in villages. Indian demographers estimate that in their country alone there are nearly 600,000 small rural communities. These communities—peasant villages, to use the historical term—have in recent years drawn the particular attention of specialists in public health, education, agriculture, and community development, because their inhabitants are less well situated to know about and participate in technological and social development than are their city cousins.

Peasant communities have also drawn the attention of anthropologists in recent years, both because the field methodologies of research first worked out in primitive tribes are applicable to such groups and because they afford important new knowledge about the total culture patterns of man. During recent years, and especially since World War II, a series of fine reports has appeared, so that we have a fairly good idea about peasant communities in most parts of the world. No two villages in different countries are the same. Matters of language, religion, political organization, and social structure determine the unique qualities of the communities of every major area. The technical specialist who familiarizes himself with the reports on the country in which he works is in a better position to work effectively than if he simply assumes that people are basically the same everywhere and what worked at home will work equally well here.

At the same time, it is abundantly clear that, although the content of peasant society—the cultural details—are infinite, the forms are astonishingly similar. Peasants in Mexico face economic problems very like those confronting the Hindu farmer; the Peruvian villager looks upon illness, and reacts to it, in a way that would be familiar to the Egyptian *fellāhīn;* the Chinese village family is rent by inheritance squabbles in the same fashion as its Italian counterpart.

The similarities in peasant life the world around are so marked that we are justified in sketching an "average" community to serve as a guide to what characteristics one may reasonably expect to find when attempting to introduce innovation. This is important, because even among people who have worked a good deal in such situations, there are often misconceptions about some very fundamental qualities of village life. For example, as earlier mentioned, it is often assumed that villagers, not too much influenced by the individualism of city life, are essentially cooperative in spirit. Action programs sometimes rest on this assumption. Yet in fact, and for reasons I will try to make clear, cooperation in peasant society occurs only in rather special situations, and it is usually not a sound basis on which to build new programs.

The "desirable" qualities in village life are often overestimated by action workers; so are the "undesirable" qualities. We wonder why the peasant is skeptical of what we say, why he often doubts us. We marvel at his fatalism, while bemoaning its hold on him. We puzzle at his apparent reluctance to take advantage of new techniques, the advantages of which must be obvious to him. But whatever the nature of peasant society, and however it may affect us in our work, there is good reason underlying it. In this chapter I try to analyze some of the characteristics of peasant society which seem to make more understandable the problems that face developmental workers.

In analyzing the nature of a peasant community, the first thing to note is that it differs from an isolated Indian tribe, a band of Australian Bushmen, or the people of a Polynesian island before the arrival of the white man in that it is not a self-sufficient unit. Peasant communities exist in an intimate relationship with cities and towns. Peasants are primarily farmers, and sometimes artisans as well. They produce much of their food and are able to make many of the material items they need for life such as clothing and tools. But they depend on town markets to sell surplus produce and to buy items which they cannot make themselves. Kroeber aptly characterizes them as "part-societies" with "part-cultures," forming a class segment of a larger unit of civilization.[1]

The North American Indian, the Australian Bushman, and the Polynesian islander was self-sufficient with respect to his religion, his philosophy, and his government. But the peasant depends on the city for this kind of nourishment. His religion represents a simplified form of what Redfield has called the "Great Tradition" of his society; it comes to him from the outside and is not a product of his own creation. Many of his values likewise represent diffusion from urban centers. Politically, the peasant has little independence. Since time immemorial he has been governed from the city; his own community has but weakly developed leadership patterns.

Peasant communities represent the rural expression of large, class-structured, economically complex, preindustrial civilizations, in which trade and commerce and craft specialization are

[1] Kroeber, 1948, p. 284.

well developed, in which money is commonly used, and in which market disposition is the goal for a part of the producer's efforts. The city is the principal source of innovation for such communities, and it holds the political, religious, and economic reins.

Peasant communities should not be thought of as a "way station" midway between civilization and primitive tribal communities. They appeared with the first civilizations between five and six thousand years ago, and they have been an enduring way of life ever since, as essential to the city as the city is to them. Modern primitives who have found themselves in contact with an industrial world in this century will never be peasants —an industrial civilization requires adjustments that do not include a peasantry. Similarly, modern peasant communities represent a cultural lag from a preindustrial period, and ultimately they will disappear, simply because a peasant component is logically inconsistent with an industrial age. The fact that the peasant way of life ultimately will disappear, however, in no way lessens the present problems of such peoples.

Now let us look at the implications of the peasant communities' ties to urban centers. It is clear that *the basic decisions affecting such villages are made from the outside* and have always been so made. For generations the villager has been able to show initiative only in the most limited areas. Small wonder that he often has trouble in making up his mind about something new. Moreover, not only does the villager have little or no control over the basic decisions made from the outside, but *usually he doesn't even know how or why they are made.* The orders, the levys, the restrictions, the taxes that are imposed from the outside have for him the same quality of chance and capriciousness as do the visitations of the supernatural world. And the peasant feels much the same toward both the authorities of the city and the supernatural: he can plead, implore, propitiate, and hope for a miracle, but in neither case can he expect by his own action to have any effective control. A fatal-istic attitude toward life? It is hard to imagine more favorable circumstances in which it can develop, and hard to understand how it can be lessened until these circumstances are changed.

The villager has been victimized by persons more knowledge-able than he since the beginning of time. He knows he is a rustic, a country bumpkin who, in his necessary trips to town, will be taken advantage of by men without conscience. He needs the city, but he hates and fears it. He fumes at humiliation and imagines slights even when they are not intended. The Wisers, in the last chapter of their wonderful little book, *Behind Mud Walls,* sensitively put into words the Hindu villagers' feelings about their helplessness.

> In the cities they devise ways of exploiting us. . . . When we get our money and want to take home some cloth, the shop-keepers get out the pieces which they have been unable to dis-pose of, and persuade us to buy them at exorbitant prices. We know that they are laughing at us. But we want cloth, and the next shopkeeper will cheat us as badly as the last. Wherever we go in the town, sharp eyes are watching to tempt our precious rupees from us. And there is no one to advise us honestly or to help us escape from fraudulent men.

> You cannot know unless you are a villager, how everyone threatens and takes from us. When you [the Wisers] go any-where, or when a sophisticated town man goes anywhere, he demands service and gets it. We stand dumb and show our fear and they trample on us.[2]

In the mestizo village of Tzintzuntzan, Mexico, in which I have done research for many years, I know an intelligent and imaginative young man, a pottery merchant. He buys the lovely ware made by his fellow villagers and delivers it on commission to stores in Mexico City. At least once a month he climbs into the bus for the overnight run to the capital, his crates of pottery

[2] Wiser and Wiser, 1951, pp. 163, 167.

strapped to the roof. Upon his arrival he makes his deliveries, admires the city, and climbs on the bus for the return trip. The bus is like home; it is known, and safe. He has never spent a night in the big city, and he tells me he wouldn't know how to go about it.

Another villager in Tzintzuntzan, recognizing a need for better bus service to the nearby market town of Pátzcuaro, bought a second-hand bus from an official of a local line. He was delighted, and so were his neighbors. Now it would not be necessary to wait on the highway while bus after loaded bus passed without stopping; Tzintzuntzan would have its own service. Then our entrepreneur began learning about the outside world. A franchise? Bus drivers unions? The official who sold the bus fought him on both scores, and won. Sadly he sold the bus back to the same man, at a fraction of its cost to him.

The peasant has learned that the outside world is fraught with dangers, that it is unpredictable and cannot be understood. Is it surprising that he has come to value his traditional ways and the predictable quality of life within this microcosmic world, his village?

With so much of the world not subject to control and not even understood, it is not surprising to find that the critical sense of the peasant operates within narrow limits. In my experience, and that of others, the peasant is able to believe the most improbable things. R. N. Adams found in Guatemala that blood withdrawn in health surveys was rumored to be a test to see if children were fat enough to be sent to the United States where children were delicacies for the tables of epicureans.[3]

Goswami and Roy found in India that an agricultural program in which land was being cleared and improved gave rise to the rumor that the local people would be cleared out after they had done the work and an American colony would move

[3] R. N. Adams, 1955, p. 448.

50 · Traditional cultures

in.[4] Philips, describing the Rockefeller Foundation antihook-worm campaign in Ceylon many years ago, tells how coolies distrusted medicine in capsule form: a highly successful whispering campaign warned that capsules were time bombs that would explode after months or even years.[5]

This lack of a critical sense, one of the most difficult things to deal with in working with villagers, is seen even in areas where it would appear that experience would have taught better. I have often listened to villagers in Tzintzuntzan tell stories of buried treasure. The fact that within living memory no one has ever found treasure in no way decreases the faith in its existence. One just needs luck, as in all other things.

With the outside world a constant threat, it might seem logical to expect a high degree of cooperation among villagers as a defense mechanism. Should not common adversity draw people together in the pursuit of common ends? Cannot a village find strength in unity? However natural this might seem, the evidence indicates that villagers frequently are suspicious of each other, filled with envy, ready to suspect the worst about their neighbors, distrustful in the extreme. The quality of interpersonal relations appears to be bad, and true cooperation is largely limited to certain traditional types of labor exchange in agriculture and house building.

Oscar Lewis' findings, in his classic account of the Mexican village of Tepoztlán,

> emphasize the underlying individualism of Tepoztecan institutions and character, the lack of cooperation, the tensions between villages within the municipio, the schisms within the village, and the pervading quality of fear, envy, and distrust in inter-personal relations.

> Gossip is unrelenting and harsh. . . . Facts about people are unconsciously or maliciously distorted. . . . Relatives and neigh-

4 Goswami and Roy, 1953, p. 305.
5 Philips, 1955, p. 287.

bors are quick to believe the worst, and motives are always under question. . . . Successful persons are popular targets of criticism, envy, and malicious gossip.[6]

The readers of accounts of Italian peasant life will not find this description surprising. Friedmann's superb analysis of the "world of *'La Miseria'*" in Calabria and Lucania dwells upon the peasants' "mentality of mutual distrust," their inability to work cooperatively and to collaborate for the common good; *La Miseria* is a "world in which to love one's neighbors, to let down one's guard in the face of the relentless struggle for existence, would simply mean to commit suicide."[7] Banfield found, in the south Italian village of Montegrano, that friends and neighbors are considered potentially dangerous. No family can stand to see another prosper without feeling envy and wishing the other harm; beyond the nuclear family, he finds, concerted action for the common good is impossible.[8]

The physician-psychiatrist Carstairs found a similar picture in a Rajasthan village in India. Villagers often made enthusiastic plans to work together for the mutual good, but these plans were rarely carried out. "Within an hour or two, one of the group would warn me that someone else was only in the scheme for his own advantage. . . . From the beginning to the end of my stay, my notebooks record instances of suspicion and mutual distrust."[9]

The list of illustrations could be extended, but the point should be clear: to a greater or lesser extent peasant life is characterized, within the village, by a bitter quality of mutual suspicion and distrust which makes it extremely difficult for people to cooperate for the common good. With this mentality, a new technical aid program which presupposes a high degree of village cooperation is obviously headed for trouble.

[6] Lewis, 1951, pp. 429, 294.
[7] Friedmann, 1958, pp. 21, 24.
[8] Banfield, 1958, pp. 10, 121.
[9] Carstairs, 1958, p. 40.

Why is the quality of village interpersonal relations often so poor? If we dig into the reasons, we find that quarrels about property, and particularly land ownership, are most frequently mentioned. For example, Simmons writes that in the Peruvian south coastal village of Lunahuaná the characteristic reaction to even those one knows well is suspicion and distrust; everyone is presumed to be out for himself and will use the most unscrupulous methods in pursuing his self-interest. "Sibling relations," he says, "after the abdication or death of parents, are characterized by disputes and feuds arising from conflicts over the division of land and the other goods of inheritance.[10] The Italian novelist Ignazio Silone describes village life in Fontamara in this fashion: "In bad weather months they arranged family affairs. That is, they quarreled about them. . . . Always the same squabbles, endless squabbles, passed down from generation to generation in endless lawsuits, in endless paying of fees, all to decide who owns some thornbush or other."[11] Adamic describes how the "seemingly perfect village life" of the Slovenes every once in a while is "shaken by fierce quarrels among peasants over the possession of a few feet of ground or a tool or a beast. . . ."[12] And in China, Smith tells how the division of land following the death of the owner almost always results in bitter feuds, even between brothers.[13]

If we look beneath these overt expressions of competition and bitterness, we see a second basic characteristic of peasant life (the first is impotence in the face of the outside world) which makes behavior more intelligible. This is, *peasant economy is essentially nonproductive;* peasants ordinarily are very poor people. Their resources, particularly land, usually are absolutely limited, and there is not enough to go around. Productive techniques, based on human and animal power and the simple

10 Simmons, 1959, p. 104.
11 Silone, 1934, p. ix.
12 Adamic, 1934, p. 97.
13 Smith, 1899, p. 328.

tools first used before the time of Christ, are essentially static. Consequently, production is constant (except as affected by weather), and perhaps it declines over the centuries, as the result of erosion, deforestation, and other consequences of man's exploitive activities. That is, the total "productive pie" of the village does not greatly change, and moreover, *there is no way to increase it however hard the individual works,* unless new land and improved techniques become available.

In each village tradition has determined approximately what a family may expect as its share of this small productive pie. It can expect no more, and it zealously watches to make sure it receives no less. The consequences of this situation are apparent: *if some one is seen to get ahead, logically it can only be at the expense of others in the village.* The traditional division of the pie is being upset, and the rights of all are potentially threatened. Even if an individual cannot see that he is suffering as a consequence of another's progress, he knows that he must be; the logical premise on which his society is based tells him it *has* to be so.[14]

Looking at peasant economy in this fashion helps us to understand why the successful person invites the suspicion, the enmity, the gossip, the character assassination, and perhaps the witchcraft and physical attacks of his fellows. Any evidence of a change for the better in his situation is proof of guilt, all that is needed to show that, in some fashion, he has taken advantage of his neighbors. The villagers not unnaturally react in the most effective way known to them to discourage a neighbor from tampering with the traditional division of the pie. The force of public opinion in peasant society, through its very bitterness and mercilessness, is thus seen as a functional device

[14] Banfield (1958, pp. 115-116), noting the absence of a feeling of charity or even justice in the Italian village of Montegrano, comments that any advantage given to another is thought to be at the expense of one's family, and that all people outside the nuclear family are potential competitors, and hence potential enemies.

whereby families protect themselves from economic loss through the real or imagined chicanery and dishonesty of their friends.

This economic focus also explains why peasant families usually attempt to conceal their economic improvements. Visible evidence of fortune will be interpreted as an open confession of guilt, and the lucky or hardworking family will be subject to slander and gossip and perhaps economic blackmail as a consequence. Again it is the Wisers who make so clear the villagers' attitude toward display of wealth.

> Our walls which conceal all that we treasure, are a necessary part of our defence. . . . they are needed against those ruthless ones who come to extort . . . our fathers built them strong enough to shut out the enemy, and made them of earth so that they might be inconspicuous. . . . But they are a better protection if instead of being kept strong they are allowed to become dilapidated. Dilapidation makes it harder for the covetous visitor to tell who is actually poor and who simulates poverty. When men become so strong that the agents of authority work with them for their mutual benefit, they dare to expose their prosperity in walls of better materials and workmanship. But if the ordinary man suddenly makes his wall conspicuous, the extortioner is on his trail. You remember what a short time it was after Puri put up his imposing new verandah with a good grass roof, that the police watchman threatened to bring a false charge against him. He paid well for his show of progress. Old walls tell no tales.[15]

In many peasant communities wealth can be displayed only in a ritual context—a church fiesta, for example—in which the pious individual may in fact go deeply into debt. So we have the striking contrast of poverty-stricken people spending enormous (for them) sums of money to maintain their standing in the community. And the individual who does not, at least once in his life, carry such a religious obligation, will be scorned by

[15] Wiser and Wiser, 1951, p. 157.

the traditionally minded. It is almost as if the society requires him to say, "Look, I have in no way consciously improved my position at your expense, and if I have had advantages about which I have not known, I want no part of them. To prove my sincerity, I am giving away most of what I have so that you can feast and enjoy yourselves, and we can worship our God. You will see that I do not even want to keep that which is rightfully mine."

Peasant culture places heavy burdens on those who wish to live by its rules. Yet it also provides the devices whereby, within the traditional framework, the individual is able to reach out and achieve some degree of security, however modest the level may be. Opposing the centrifugal forces which are constantly tearing at peasant societies are centripetal forces which hold it together. In some places—the Indian village is a good example—a strong feeling of unity marks the extended family and the caste, and mutual and reciprocal obligations mark the behavior of people bound together in such units. The Wisers, again paraphrasing the villagers, write,

> No villager thinks of himself apart from his family. He rises or falls with it. . . . we need the strength of the family to support us. . . . That man is to be pitied who must stand alone against the dangers, seen and unseen, which beset him. Our families are our insurance. When a man falls ill, he knows that his family will care for him and his children until he is able to earn again. And they will be cared for without a word of reproach. If a man dies, his widow and children are sure of the protection of a home.[16]

Sometimes the *ideal* of familial unity is extended to the village, even reaching across castes and in the face of real schisms and divisions that make village cooperation difficult. McCormack describes how in a Mysore village "The ideal of village unity emerges as an important element in the villagers' own

[16] *Ibid.*, p. 160.

interpretation of proposals for village improvement," and it is strongly felt that a unanimous vote is a precondition to going ahead.[17] In spite of the real picture, conflicts and notorious examples of lack of cooperation in families and within village groups are considered as "shameful," and an important task of hereditary leaders is the arbitration of disputes to restore what is imagined to be a normal village unity.

In other parts of the world—the Italian and Latin American data come to mind—the extended family is sometimes less strong, but its place is taken by a godparenthood system, tying individuals and families together with sacred sanctions which give them something of the group strength and social security afforded by an effective family unit. Formalized friendship, again, often functions to tie together the loose strands occasioned by the divisive forces extant in peasant society. In both formalized friendship patterns and the godparenthood system, we note the element of individual reciprocity based on a sense of *contract,* in contrast to the *ascriptional* basis of the kin-based group. The prevalence of these and other similar types of "fictive kinship" (the anthropological expression for godparent, blood brother, best friend, and similar kin-like relationships) in peasant society helps to explain one of the most important things an outsider must understand in working in such a community. A contract is a bargain between two or more people. It is *personal,* entered into freely by the participants. It implies both obligations and expectations. One must help a friend or a co-godparent (a *compadre,* to use the Spanish terminology) when such help is requested and to the best of one's ability. Conversely, aid and succor may be expected when needed. Relationships are *personalistic* in a society in which the individual contract is the only effective nonfamilial basis for social intercourse. One achieves through having the right friends with effective obligations toward one; conversely, one

[17] McCormack, 1957, p. 257.

often does things for these friends, even if the reasons are not fully understood. Not infrequently community development workers have found that villagers have cooperated with them, not because they understood or desired the innovation, but because they felt they had established a friendship relation with the outsider which required that they do what the new friend asked, in return for previous or subsequent favors which he would bring.

It is for reasons like this that an effective worker must thoroughly understand the social structure of a community, the forces that divide people, and the forces that draw them together. The behavior of a peasant villager, however stubborn and unreasoned it may seem to an outsider, is the product of centuries of experience. It is an effective protective device in a relatively unchanging world. It is less effective in a rapidly industrializing world, and ultimately it becomes a serious hindrance. But the peasant is pragmatic; he is not going to discard the clothing that has served him well until he is convinced that he will profit by so doing. He sees that the future holds new things, but he remembers the past: "Our lives are oppressed by many fears. We fear the rent collector, we fear the police watchman, we fear everyone who looks as though he might claim some authority over us, we fear our creditors, we fear our patrons, we fear too much rain, we fear locusts, we fear thieves, we fear the evil spirits which threaten our children and our animals, and we fear the strength of our neighbour."[18]

It is against the background described in this chapter that the processes of social and cultural change which follow will be described.

[18] Wiser and Wiser, 1951, p. 160.

4 . . . . The dynamics of change: culture, society, psychology, and economics

All societies are constantly in a state of relative tension. Each society can be thought of as a host to two kinds of forces: those that seek to promote change and those that strive to maintain the status quo. These forces are locked in perpetual combat, the former trying to throw the latter off balance, to gain the ascendency, and the latter trying to prevent this from happening. Since a tendency to change is fundamental in culture, it is obvious that, in the long run, the forces that promote innovation will have the edge over those that strive for conservatism. But the degree of ascendency that change-making forces achieve is not often, and perhaps never, a constant, for the tempo of culture change varies with time. The forces for change will predominate for a considerable period, and rapid alterations in the nature and structure of a society will occur. Then there may follow a period of relative quiescence, in which the unusual stresses and strains occasioned by rapid change are relieved, and the elements of the culture regroup and accommodate themselves in a more harmonious fashion. Hence, at a particular moment in time, the relative stability of a culture, or its proneness to change, reflects the extent of the balance between the opposing forces.

The most successful guided technological development occurs when program planners and technical specialists are aware of the struggle between the forces for change and the forces for stability found in all cultures. Not only must the presence of the forces be recognized, but in a specific situation they must be identified and related one to another. The strategy of promoting change is then relatively simple—in theory. The strength of the conservative forces must be weakened, or their results neutralized, while simultaneously the change forces must be strengthened. The following four chapters call attention to the more common forces promoting the status quo and those promoting change.

For expository purposes I have found it helpful to think of the change-inhibiting factors in all societies as "barriers." There is no equally good word for the change-promoting factors; sometimes I refer to them as "stimulants" to change, sometimes as "motivations" to change (when the phenomena are largely psychological), and at other times, simply as "factors promoting change." Some barriers can be conceptualized primarily in cultural terms: the basic values of the group, its conception of right and wrong, the nature of the articulation of the elements of the culture, the "fundamental fit" or integration of its parts, and the overriding economic limitations that can be identified. These barriers are "culture-based"; for simplicity's sake they are called "cultural." Other barriers are found in the nature of the social structure of the group: the prevailing type of family and the relationships of its members, caste and class factors, the locus of authority in familial and political units, the nature of factions, and the like. These barriers can be called "society-based," or simply "social." Still other barriers are most easily comprehended if phrased in psychological terms: individual and group motivations, communication problems, the nature of perception, and the characteristics of the learning process. These are "psychologically based," or "psychological" barriers.

The factors that facilitate change, the stimulants, can also be examined in cultural, social, and psychological terms. They are the antithesis of barriers, the opposite side of the coin, and only in an analytical sense can they be separated from them. Barriers and stimulants are part and parcel of the same process, and they must be manipulated simultaneously. To illustrate, the values of a culture may be such that an energetic farmer easily perceives advantages to him in adopting new cultivation practices. Whether he actually adopts these practices may be determined by familial structure and traditional reciprocal relationships within the kin group. If he is a member of an extended family in which the fortunate share generously with the less fortunate or improvident, he may feel that increased income will mean no personal gain, but rather will mean only increases in familial obligations. In this circumstance he is apt to reject the proferred aid. On the other hand, in a changing society in which such mutually accepted responsibilities are losing weight, the farmer may decide that enough of the increased income will remain with him to justify changed practices.

Cultural, social, and psychological barriers and stimulants to change exist in an economic setting. In a more comprehensive analysis, economic factors should receive extensive treatment, for they seem to set the absolute limits to change. As will be seen, people often are unwilling to change their ways because of cultural and social and psychological factors. But equally as often, they are quite aware of the value of change and anxious to alter their traditional ways, but the economic sacrifice is too great. If an economic potential does not exist or cannot be built into a program of directed change, the most careful attention to culture and society will be meaningless. Several examples will illustrate the relationships between economics and other aspects of culture change.

In Tzintzuntzan, Mexico, a government-operated public health clinic is beginning to attract patients, particularly for pre- and postnatal services and for the dressing of injuries and other similar ailments. Service is either free or offered at a nominal cost, depending on type. The cultural, social, and psychological barriers which are involved are, little by little, being overcome. In addition, a variety of private medical services are available 10 miles away in the town of Pátzcuaro. Frequent bus service permits increasing use of these services. But many people who are convinced, or nearly convinced, of the value of medical care, hesitate to take the plunge because of the cost, or the fear of the cost, which is unknown and unpredictable. An infant falls ill and does not respond to folk medical care. This presents a dilemma. The parents know that the town physicians sometimes have cured children when local curers failed. But the cost is certain to be high by their standards: perhaps 50 pesos, perhaps 200 pesos. There are other small children who are not yet economically contributing members of the family. They require food, clothing, and many other things. Their well-being, and that of other members of the family, may be jeopardized if the parents undertake an unknown and potentially costly treatment for the critically ill infant, who perhaps, because of age, is hardly yet considered to be a real member of the family. The social cost of trying to save the tiny infant is weighed against the total family welfare, and it may be deemed too great to be justified. Furthermore, in addition to money costs, the parents will lose much productive time by the bus rides, long waits in the doctor's office, and perhaps the necessity to remain for several days or longer in a hospital.

A similar example has been described in Ceylon where, from 1916 to 1922, the Rockefeller Foundation carried out a demonstration hookworm-eradication program. Although a considerable measure of success was ultimately achieved, unforeseen cultural, social, and economic factors greatly handicapped the work. Hookworm treatment is not particularly painful, but the purges weaken the patient for several days, and it was found that in the more isolated villages a major resistance to treatment arose out of poverty. "It took some time for the field doctors doing the village work to understand the basic poverty. They struggled to overcome the evasions and refusals, and finally learned that the real trouble was that the villagers felt they could not afford the time away from work for treatment and recovery from treatment. Usually they were too weak to work for a day or two after taking the medicine."[1] Loss of this income counterbalanced the little-understood advantages of freedom from hookworm.

Oberg and Rios have analyzed a community development project in a small Brazilian village and have shown how social and, particularly, economic factors have affected adversely the generally sound planning. To illustrate, a latrine program was instituted as the keystone of environmental sanitation. Slabs for the pits were cast and given free to villagers, who then had to dig the hole and erect the shelter. Few people, however, took advantage of this aid, and most of the latrines eventually were installed by project workers. Analysis revealed the reasons for this puzzling lack of interest. A census was taken, which showed that the village was highly unstable in terms of social organization. Half the inhabitants had lived there for less than five years and did not really consider themselves permanent members of the community. After saving a little money they hoped to migrate to other parts of the country where better opportunities might exist. Consequently they felt little attachment to the village, no stake in its future, and had no interest in making capital improvements in something they didn't expect long to enjoy.

[1] Philips, 1955, pp. 288-289.

Many people lived rent-free in their shacks, simply caring for them for absent owners. Since they might be evicted at a moment's notice, they saw little advantage in working on property that, by virtue of improvement, would be more attractive to the owners or to someone who might pay rent. The owners themselves, since they were away and since they received no income, had no incentive to make improvements in their homes. So the failure of this program lay not so much in the inability of the people to understand and appreciate the hygienic advantages of latrines as in social and economic factors that the planners had not understood.[2]

In the discussion that follows, then, the essential neglect of economic factors does not mean I consider them unimportant. They are enormously important. The apparent neglect stems from my feelings of inadequacy in this field and from my inability to weave the economic factors into the exposition of cultural, social, and psychological factors.

[2] Oberg and Rios, 1955.

5 . . . . *Cultural barriers to change*

Within the major categories of barriers to change—cultural, social, and psychological—the specific examples fall in subgroupings. There is no magic or inner logic in the system of classification used in this and the following chapters. It is simply one author's attempt to group examples in a sufficiently clear fashion so that the underlying themes will be apparent to the reader. Cultural barriers, for example, seem to fall easily into the groupings of "values and attitudes," "culture structure," and "motor patterns."

VALUES AND ATTITUDES

Tradition

Some cultures value positively novelty and change for their own sake. The fact that something is new and different is sufficient reason to examine it and perhaps to try it. Americans, we know, are attracted by the new. Advertisements play upon the theme of "new," "better," "improved," and the customer buys.

In general, the positive attraction of the new and novel seems to be associated with industrial societies. Whether peoples with the most interest in novelty became the first industrialists because of this interest, or whether an industrial system produces these values, we cannot be sure. I suspect the latter—that aspirations are developed through the opportunity to satisfy them. In any event, the relationship between a productive economy and a tradition for change is so close that it cannot be thought of as being due to chance.

In contrast, in most nonindustrial parts of the world, novelty and change have less positive appeal. Rather, the individual is conditioned to view new things with skepticism and, if he is uncertain, not to be tempted. The great Spanish lexicographer Covarrubias, for example, defined *Novedad* ("novelty") in 1611 as "something new and unaccustomed." Then, unconsciously injecting the value judgment of his society, he added, "characteristically it is dangerous because it sullies traditional usage."[1] And nearly one hundred years earlier, in 1531, Guevara admonished the President of Granada: "Do not attempt to introduce new things, for novelties bring in their train anxieties for those who sponsor them and beget troubles among the people."[2]

In peasant society conservatism appears generally to be culturally sanctioned. In *The House by the Medlar Tree* the Italian novelist Verga describes a Sicilian fishing village in the later half of the nineteenth century. 'Ntoni, the patriarch of his family, was old, wise, and respected; he embodied the folk wisdom of his group. "Old Master 'Ntoni remembered many sayings and proverbs that he had learnt from his elders, because, as he said, what the old folks said was always true. One of his sayings was . . . 'Be satisfied to do what your father did, or you'll come to no good.' *And he had many other sensible sayings as*

[1] Covarrubias, 1611, p. 831.
[2] Quoted from Menéndez Pidal, 1950, p. 133.

well."[3] Recently the Indian anthropologist Dube described life in a small village in his country. Here he found the forces of conservatism to be enormous. Persons having too many novel and original ideas come under the suspicious eye of the group and invite criticism.[4] In the same country Goswami and Roy report that because of past exploitation and ignorance the villager is conservative, and "fights shy of anything new."[5]

It is clear that in societies where the positive strictures against being tempted by novelty are strong—where aphorisms and maxims are quoted to validate tradition and where fear of criticism haunts the would-be innovator—a fertile field for a broad program of social change does not exist until after a good deal of preliminary cultivation has been done.

Fatalism

The attitude of fatalism is closely allied to the forces of tradition and constitutes a barrier of equal strength. In industrial societies people have proved to their satisfaction that a high degree of mastery over nature and social conditions is possible. An undesirable situation is not a hopeless block, but rather a challenge to man's ingenuity. In industrial societies people have come to believe that almost anything can be achieved; at least, any reasonable plan is worth a serious try.

But in nonindustrial societies a very low degree of mastery over nature and social conditions has been achieved. Drought or flood is looked upon as a visitation from gods or evil spirits whom man can propitiate but not control. Feudal forms of land tenure and nonproductive technologies may condemn a farmer to a bare subsistence living. Medical and social services are lacking, and people die young. Under such circumstances it is not surprising that people have few illusions about the possibility of improving their lot. A fatalistic outlook, the assumption that

[3] Verga, 1955, p. 3. (Italics mine.)
[4] Dube, 1955, p. 182.
[5] Goswami and Roy, 1953, p. 306.

whatever happens is the will of God or Allah, is the best adjustment the individual can make to an apparently hopeless situation.

The Colombian anthropologist Virginia Gutiérrez de Pineda studied cultural factors involved in the high rate of infantile mortality in rural areas of her country, and she points out in poignant fashion the lethargy that social and economic conditions have forced upon the countryman. When an infant dies, the parents say, "It was his destiny, not to grow up." In Santander province it is often said of an unusually beautiful child, "This child is not for this world," and thus the parents prepare themselves for the 50 percent probability that the child, in fact, "is not for this world." On the other hand, when an ill child recovers, the parents say, "See, he recovered without medical attention; God did not intend him to die." In the face of such attitudes, Mrs. Pineda found that the trained physician had a difficult time in gaining the confidence of the people. When she would urge parents to take an ill child to see a doctor, often they shrugged their shoulders and replied, "The rich also die, in spite of having so much money for medical care."[6]

A fatalistic attitude is widespread in rural Latin America. In the Brazilian village of Cruz das Almas, near São Paulo, described by Donald Pierson, it is commonly believed that illness comes from God, having been sent, often, as punishment for sins, and that it is "He who either cures or 'takes you away to the other world,' . . . In the event of illness or death, one often hears the phrase, *'Deus quis'* (God willed it). If the illness is prolonged, this fact is considered a part of the person's *sina* (destiny)," and characteristically one asks the rhetorical question, "what is there to do about it?"[7]

In Egypt death is perceived as Allah's will, and no one can extend life because the Koran says "Wherever you are, death

---

6 Pineda, 1955, pp. 18-19.
7 Pierson, 1955, pp. 281-283.

will seek you, even if you are in strongly built castles." This attitude is one of the reasons for high infant mortality in that country.[8] In India the attitude is similar. Carstairs tells how in a village he was called to the bedside of a child dying of diphtheria. Although he saw the case was hopeless, he gave the patient an injection, so the parents would feel that something was being done. When the inevitable happened, he feared the parents' anger, that he would be blamed for the death. To his surprise and great relief, this was not true. "After the first outburst of grief, the family repeated the traditional formula: it was his fate, his day had come; he was a loan from God, to whom he had returned."[9]

Cultural Ethnocentrism

We Westerners, proud of the achievements of our science and technology, often believe that this implies our total culture is the most advanced and therefore superior to the cultures of simpler peoples. Our conviction of superiority and our belief that we have knowledge of truth make us anxious to "share" this superiority with other peoples whom we believe to be less fortunate. It sometimes comes as a surprise to us to discover that the members of all cultures believe that basically their way of doing things is natural and best. Primitive peoples are quite willing to acknowledge the superiority of a steel knife over a stone knife, and sometimes an aluminum kettle to a pottery vessel. But these are peripheral and inconsequential areas of culture. The real essence of culture, all of us believe, lies in what we think and do, our attitudes, our social forms, and our religious beliefs. The question of superiority in such things is, of course, harder to measure or prove. Begging the question of absolute values, it is apparent that the universal belief in the superiority of one's culture is a powerful force for stability.

[8] Communicated by Dr. Fawzy Gadalla.
[9] Carstairs, 1955, pp. 114-115.

This is as true of the American as of the Australian bushman.

The anthropologist studies ethnocentrism in terms of what he calls "cultural relativism." By this he simply means that the values of all peoples are a function of their way of life and that they cannot be understood out of context. The point of view of relativists is not that all ways are equally good—they do not endorse slavery, murder, and other conditions or acts in which the individual is deprived of rights or opportunities to realize his full potential—but they hold that it is wrong to condemn the ways of others simply because they differ from those of the person who is passing judgment.

Ethnocentrism is so deeply engrained in all of us that even when we are sensitive to the philosophy of cultural relativism we may easily fall victim to evaluating others in terms of our own views. It is Mrs. Pineda, again, who so clearly points out this danger. Her field work in Colombia has included study of the lives of the cattle-raising Guajiro Indians of the Guajira Peninsula.

> I remember when once I spoke with an Indian woman of high social class about marriage, and the Indian custom of giving money and cattle to buy the wife. I had not yet come fully to understand the Indian culture, and while the woman spoke of her price I felt terribly sad that a Colombian woman could be sold like a cow. Suddenly she asked, "And you? How much did you cost your husband?" I smugly replied, "Nothing. We aren't sold." Then the picture changed completely. "Oh, what a horrible thing," she said. "Your husband didn't even give a single cow for you? You must not be worth anything." And she lost all respect for me, and would have nothing further to do with me, because no one had given anything for me.[10]

Pride and Dignity

Anthropologists have noted that an innate dignity in personal bearing and a pride in their way of life characterize the peoples

[10] Communicated by Virginia Gutierrez de Pineda.

among whom they work. This correlates with the ethnocentric position of most people vis-à-vis their cultures, and it is reflected in a strong—not to say rigid—belief about the behavior appropriate to recognized roles. Many technically well-designed aid programs have run into trouble because culturally defined forms of pride and "face" which express these strong feelings about role have not been recognized. Desire to avoid humiliation as a result of being cast in an inappropriate role seems to be universal. But what determines propriety is determined by culture. In the United States, for example, the idea of "life-long learning" is deep-rooted, and adults do not hesitate to take correspondence courses or attend night school if they feel they will profit thereby. The role of student is one which the individual may occupy at any time during his life without fear of ridicule.

But in much of the world schooling is associated with childhood. The role of student is all right for youngsters, but it is inappropriate to the adult state. Dube points out that in India, where the Community Development Programme stresses adult literacy projects, adults often quickly drop out of night classes, even though literacy and education are highly valued. Since only children are supposed to attend schools, the adult exposes himself to general public amusement when he starts to school with pencil and slate.[11]

Fear of loss of face can threaten agricultural programs also. One phase of the Indian agricultural program includes selling improved seed to farmers at moderate cost. Curiously, the best and most progressive farmers often are the most resistant to this aid. In one village the wealthy and able farmers neither purchased nor used this seed. "It has long been thought a disgrace and a sign of failure or poor management to be forced to borrow or buy seed. The village farmer takes special pride in being able to raise enough food to maintain his family and in having

11 Dube, 1958, p. 122.

enough left over to use as seed."[12] The able farmer does not wish to be cast in the role of the incompetent agriculturalist.

Isabel Kelly tells that in parts of Mexico it has been difficult to persuade people to use a yellow maize which is superior nutritionally to the local white variety. The explanation is found in the locally accepted evidence of good cooking. The tortilla, the staple of life, is made by soaking hard maize grains in lye water, grinding a dough, patting out thin circular cakes, and baking them on a clay griddle. Tortillas made with white maize are white when cooked, unless too much lye has been added, which turns them yellow. In the villages described, yellow tortillas resulting from the use of yellow maize were identified with careless cooking, and housewives did not wish to be stigmatized as careless or incompetent cooks.[13]

Fear of loss of face has handicapped maternal and child health programs in Taiwan. There, where the extended family is still strong, the older women, in whom much familial authority is vested, feel that it reflects on their ability and judgment if young pregnant women in their families attend prenatal clinics or seek the aid of trained midwives. Young women who have been convinced by visiting public health nurses of the value of new practices have been prevented from adopting them because of the authority of their elders.[14]

The barriers of pride and fear of loss of face are not limited to primitive and peasant societies alone. A recent study at Harvard University revealed that, in spite of stiff language requirements for the Ph.D. degree, many graduate students would not enroll in language courses, preferring the less efficient method of self-study. When asked why they shunned such courses they commented that "enrollment in an elementary course seemed degrading . . ."[15]

[12] Opler and Singh, 1952, p. 7.
[13] Kelly, 1958, pp. 205-208.
[14] Communicated by Miss Merle S. Farland, R. N.
[15] Elder, 1958.

In the preceding chapter it was said that part of the strategy of directed culture change consists of identifying barriers and then seeking ways to weaken them or neutralize their effect. The two following examples show how different problems were successfully attacked.

The Organization of American States operates the Inter-American Housing Center near Bogotá, Colombia. Young architects and other potential urban planners come from many countries to learn the new science of city and regional planning. First-hand knowledge of materials is believed by the staff to be an important part of the training, and students are asked to mix mortar, lay bricks, and otherwise engage in manual labor. Most Latin Americans, however, have doubts about the dignity of working with one's hands. A professional man uses his mind, not his brawn; hired peons do the menial work. For this reason the work part of the curriculum was not successful in the early stages. Then someone hit upon the idea of supplying white laboratory coats to the students, with their names embroidered over the pocket. In the new and acceptable professional status of laboratory technicians they now happily went about the chores they formerly had resisted.[16]

The other instance comes from Chile where public health centers, modeled after United States patterns, were introduced beginning in the 1940's. The prenatal mothers' "class" taught by a public health nurse was a part of the introduced pattern. But the new program was only partially successful; expectant mothers balked at being taught in classes like children. Consequently it was decided to represent the classes as short-lived "clubs," which met for the prescribed number of weeks, usually in the homes of the mothers. The health center provided tea and cakes, and the meeting thereby became a social affair, in which the discussion of prenatal care was only an incidental event. Since club life is associated with the upper and middle

16 Communicated by L. Currie, former Director of the Center.

classes, the women from low-income brackets who were health center patients were delighted to be asked to participate in such activities, and the program, as a health measure, has been highly successful.[17]

Norms of Modesty

Like feelings about dignity and pride, the ideas as to what constitutes modesty are instilled in the members of all societies by their cultures. These ideas are culturally defined and differ greatly from one community to another. Proper behavior in one group may be shockingly improper in a second. But no culture is without the concept of modesty. Most often such ideas seem associated with dress and decorum in behavior. Modest dress more often than not is associated with covering of the sex organs, but this is by no means universal, and among many peoples nudity or seminudity is taken for granted. Travelers returning from the Amazon Basin tell of the embarrassment of Indian women who were observed at close range in a state of nature. This embarrassment usually disappeared when the women had retired a moment to reappear wearing a string of beads or some other simple ornament. In Mexican villages a housewife is greatly upset if a caller surprises her without her apron, even though she is wearing a skirt and numerous petticoats. And older men, at least, are most uncomfortable if seen without a hat.

In programs of directed culture change, ideas of modesty often constitute serious barriers to some kinds of programs. Medical and public health workers, for example, have been seriously handicapped in their efforts to reduce infant and maternal mortality by widely prevalent ideas about female modesty and the proper relationship of a physician to a pregnant woman. In Moslem countries, in Latin America, and in many other areas, it is quite unthinkable that a man other than

[17] Author's field notes.

a woman's husband should have the degree of intimacy with her required by a gynecological examination. The impersonality of modern medicine, largely taken for granted in Western countries, is not a part of the understanding of most of the rest of the world, and many women prefer to avoid scientific prenatal care rather than to submit to examination by a male physician. Often, too, it is the husband who objects to this routine (to Westerners) treatment. This difficulty usually can be overcome by utilizing female physicians, but here again the problem is great. Until very recent years women have not been permitted to study medicine in most of those countries in which this resistance is found, and it will be many years until there are sufficient female physicians to meet the demands of adequate prenatal services.

Although female physicians probably are the answer in most parts of the world where modern medicine in all its aspects has not been accepted, this is not a blanket rule. Schneider points out how, on the island of Yap in Micronesia, women are resistant to genital examination by a male physician, but they are even more resistant to examination by a female. Yap women regard all other women, regardless of age, as potential rivals for men's attention and, at the same time, they believe their own genitals are their strongest power over men. Exposing their source of power to potential rivals, they believe, weakens their competitive position and threatens them with loss of masculine attention.[18]

Among the Navaho there is not too much resistance by parturients to male physicians; male assistants have long helped with childbirth under native conditions, and it is not thought particularly shameful for men to be present at such an event. But resistance to hospitalization for delivery is strong, largely because of the customary short hospital gown. Navaho modesty requires good coverage from waist to ankle for women, and the

[18] Schneider, 1955, p. 231.

American hospital gown is offensive in the extreme.[19]

Relative Values

There is a tendency for specialists who work in technical aid programs to assume that the people with whom they are working, and whom they hope to help, are essentially rational, however uneducated they may be and however simple their way of life is. It logically follows that if the technician has difficulty in putting his program across, either the people are unusually stupid and can't see the obvious (to the specialist) advantages of change, or the technician has not been as skillful as he should be in the presentation of his case.

In fact, people often understand the message perfectly, but they have weighed the relative value to them of the alternate forms of behavior and have decided against the new program, or some part of it, however compelling the evidence may seem to someone with a different point of view. The technician, frustrated by some example of irrationality on the part of the people he wishes to help, may attempt to relieve his tension by furious chain smoking, even though he knows the medical evidence for a correlation between the use of cigarettes and lung cancer is pretty convincing. He has made a value judgment and prefers the satisfaction of smoking to the probability of lessening his susceptibility to cancer.

The satisfactions of life are many and varied, and economic rationality, though very important, is far from being the only determinant of value judgment. The agricultural extension agent, struggling to solve problems of food shortage, often wonders why people are reluctant to grow more nutritious and higher-yielding strains. One of the most striking examples of this situation has been summarized by Apodaca. In a community of Spanish American farmers in the Rio Grande Valley of New Mexico, a Department of Agriculture county extension

[19] Bailey, 1948, p. 1120.

agent succeeded in 1946 in introducing hybrid corn that produced three times the yield of the traditional seed. After participating in initial test demonstrations, a majority of the growers adopted the innovation. Yet four years later nearly all farmers had reverted to the old corn. Investigation revealed that the farmers' wives had complained about the texture of the dough used to make tortillas, about the color of the finished product, and about the taste. In the system of values of this community, corn quality turned out to be more important than corn quantity; people were willing to sacrifice economic gain for something they esteemed, in this case traditional food characteristics.[20]

This is not an isolated example. Eating habits are among the most emotionally based of all activities, and unfamiliar taste often turns out to be a reason why new foods are rejected, unless they can be cloaked with even more powerful counter arguments, such as prestige value. In India a village worker asked a farmer about his reaction to a new wheat that had been tried experimentally for several years. The villager replied that it was better in appearance, brought a higher price, and was more resistant to rain and frost. Then he added, "But the local variety is better in taste," and concluded, "From the point of view of health there is nothing like it."[21] In 1957 I encountered the same story in the Helmand Valley in Afghanistan. Improved maize seed had been introduced which, when planted in rows (rather than broadcast) and cultivated with improved techniques, produced up to three times the yield of local varieties. Although the new seed was slowly making progress, resistance to it was surprisingly strong. One of the principal reasons given by farmers for their lack of interest was that bread baked from the new maize compared unfavorably in taste with bread made with the traditional maize.

[20] Apodaca, 1952.
[21] Dube, 1958, p. 196.

Apparent economic irrationality is no more limited to folk and peasant peoples than is the fear of losing face or dignity, and comparative values may go just as far in explaining behavior among Westerners as among peasants. In 1953 the British love of birds constituted a considerable threat to increased egg production, an increase badly needed in view of food rationing. The uproar was set off when the Ministry of Agriculture encouraged chicken farmers to adopt the battery system in which hens are placed in cages just big enough to hold one roosting bird. Enclosed in this cage with a light burning eighteen hours a day to encourage overtime, a hen spends the rest of its life of about nine months eating, sleeping, and laying eggs. Battery hens average about 20 percent more eggs than free-roaming barnyard fowl. Although the battery system was partially responsible for an increase in egg production that ended egg rationing, many Britishers objected strenuously, and the Society for the Prevention of Cruelty to Animals demanded an end to the system, even though this meant a loss of 150 million eggs a year. The Ministry won the battle, but obviously many Britishers were willing to forego badly needed food rather than be guilty of possible cruelty to hens.[22]

CULTURE STRUCTURE

Logical Incompatibility of Culture Traits

Not all culture elements or institutions can be easily combined. Between some there is a logical compatibility, between others, a logical incompatibility. When logical incompatibility exists, change comes about with difficulty. The contrast between a monotheistic and a polytheistic religion illustrates this point. Peoples who practice polytheism often are not unreceptive to Christian missionaries. God is obviously a powerful deity, or

[22] *Time* Magazine, *62* (7) 28: (August 17, 1953) .

his representatives would not be so far from their homes; he appears powerful also, because of the power he has delegated to his lieutenants. When these lieutenants ask the natives to accept Him, often they are able to do so with great ease and a clear conscience, because no serious violence is done (at least in the early stages of Christianization) to their basic religious beliefs. They already pay homage to a number of deities with special attributes; they have added deities from time to time in the past, and it is the most natural thing in the world to add a new one who obviously possesses special merit.

On the other hand, proselytizing among monotheistic peoples offers a much more difficult problem. Monotheistic peoples can accept a new deity only by rejecting the previous incumbent, or by completely identifying the new god with the old one through the process of syncretism. This is asking a good deal more of people than is necessary with polytheistic groups.

The contrast between autocracy and democracy is similar. By definition, autocracy cannot permit important divergences of opinion, but democracy does not exist unless these divergencies are present. The two forms are logically incompatible and cannot be reconciled.

On a less sweeping level, logical incompatibility of culture elements is seen as posing barriers to change. For example, the Navaho Indians have resisted both Christianity and pagan nativistic movements because their religious beliefs are incompatible with those offered by the alternate forms. They were immune to the Ghost Dance movement of 1890, which swept many western reservations and which taught the resurrection of the Indian dead, the removal of the whites, and the reestablishment of the old order. Hill suggests that "For the Navaho with his almost psychotic fear of death, the dead and all connected with them, no greater cataclysm than the return of the departed or ghosts could be envisaged. In short, the Navaho were frightened out of their wits for fear the tenets of

the movement were true."[23] Reichard believes the Navaho ab-
horrence of death made it very difficult for them to comprehend
Christianity, which is based on the concept of death and resurrection.[24]

In some recent instances agricultural extension programs in
Buddhist countries have encountered problems in pest control:
the religious prohibition against taking life in any form is
logically incompatible with the direct approach to the problem
through insecticides. A convenient rationalization sometimes,
but not always, helps people overcome the dilemma posed by
apparent logically incompatible goals. I recall the example
given in lecture by the late Professor R. H. Lowie, who pointed
out that Buddhist fishermen in southeast Asia do a thriving
business: they are doing the poor fish a favor by drying them
out after their long soaking in water! At times a technical expert will go farther with a reasonable rationalization than with
a convincing demonstration.

Unforeseen Consequences of Planned Innovation

No change can occur in isolation. Any induced change will
produce secondary and tertiary changes over a wide area. It is a
little like throwing a pebble into a pond. The effect of the blow
on the water will extend in ever-widening circles until the impact loses its force. In the same way, the impact of an introduced trait will extend in widening circles until its effect is felt
in areas of culture far removed from the point of contact. Conversely, the extent to which changes can be introduced depends
on other changes that are taking place, or that can be made to
take place, which will influence the reception accorded the
innovation.

Of all of the practical guides anthropology can offer to technical specialists, none exceeds in importance the necessity to

23 W. W. Hill, 1944, p. 525.
24 Reichard, 1949.

consider carefully all possible consequences of a new program. Most culture change involves a social cost. However logical and desirable an innovation may appear to the scientifically trained technical specialist, some of its secondary and tertiary consequences may be highly undesirable from the standpoint of the people affected, and apparent advantages must be weighed against possible disadvantages. Dr. Hazel I. Blair has told me of two dilemmas she faced while working with the Eskimo of Alaska. Echinococcus disease (the cystic larval stage of a small tapeworm) is prevalent on St. Lawrence Island in the Bering Sea. It is transmitted through sled dogs, and effective control of the disease means extermination of the dogs. But what substitute is there for the traditional means of transportation? Again, says Dr. Blair, "an interesting decision the doctor may have to make in areas where people subsist almost entirely on fish is whether it is better to have fish tapeworms from eating raw fish or to run the risk of a vitamin deficiency by cooking the fish." Also, in fuel-short areas, how is the cooking to be done?[25] Obviously, a straightforward, single-minded answer to these questions may do as much harm as good.

One of the primary tasks of the anthropologist working with developmental teams is to follow through on the possible consequences of a proposed change, to analyze the factors involved, and to attempt to predict what will happen. If he knows the culture well and if he is familiar with the general processes of culture change, he should be able to anticipate unforeseen reactions which can seriously affect the outcome of planned change. Often, if these critical points can be dealt with in planning, they can be neutralized; if they are ignored, failure is apt to result. The following examples show how proposed innovations must be appraised in broad perspective rather than in terms of a single goal.

In village India, cooking is traditionally done over an open

[25] Communicated by Dr. Hazel I. Blair.

dung fire in the kitchen. There is no chimney, and there are few windows, so the room fills with choking smoke which gradually filters through the thatch roof. Cooking is unpleasant under such conditions, and respiratory and eye ailments are common. The Community Development Programme has recognized this situation as a serious threat to health, and has developed an inexpensive pottery stove, a "smokeless chula," which maximizes the efficiency of fuel and draws smoke off through a chimney. It is sold at very low cost to villagers. Yet the smokeless chula has had limited success. In much of India woodboring white ants infest roofs and if they are not suppressed they ruin a roof in a very short time. The continual presence of smoke in the roof accomplishes this end. If smoke is eliminated roofs must be replaced far more often, and the expense is greater than farmers are able to support. So the problem of introducing the smokeless chula—at least in many areas—lies not in the villager's addiction to smoke-irritated eyes, nor in his love of tradition, nor in his inability to understand the cooking advantages of the new stove, nor in the direct cost of the stove itself. He has simply added up the total cost and found that the disadvantages of the new stove outweigh the advantages. In this case the critical area of resistance has nothing to do with cooking at all.

Dr. Henry Renteln describes a similar example in Iran. On the south shores of the Caspian Sea, smoke-filled houses cause health problems similar to those found in India. Yet resistance to better cooking methods was found to be intense. Here, too, smoke has its positive side. The area is heavily infested with anopheles mosquitoes and malaria is widespread. A high level of smoke in the house is the only way the villager can obtain relief from bites.[26]

These examples illustrate an important point in the strategy of directed culture change. If the reasons for resistance are

[26] Communicated by Dr. Henry Renteln.

analyzed, it may be found that a series of innovations which tie together and mutually reinforce each other will make success possible, where single innovations will fail. The Indian villager probably did not know, before he tried the smokeless chula, that smoke preserved his roof. He discovered it when smoke was removed. If the roof can be preserved by other methods, the threshold of his resistance to improved cooking methods will be greatly lowered. Malaria eradication with regular DDT spraying is one of the main projects of the Community Development Programme. If spraying is coordinated with the demonstration of the smokeless chula, white ants as well as mosquitoes will be eliminated, and one of the costs—economic in this case—that constitutes a barrier is eliminated. Similarly in Iran the same double program should go far in solving the problem of the villagers' resistance.

Other examples illustrate barriers which may be lessened if they are approached not in isolation but as part of a cultural complex which must be examined as a unit. Good animal husbandry practices require the castration of many male domestic animals: pigs and sheep so treated grow fatter, and oxen are larger and stronger. The scientifically minded animal husbandryman sees these advantages as functions of farming practice in his own country, and the advantages seem to far outweigh the disadvantage of an occasional infection or lost animal. Yet this practice often meets strong opposition in newly developing areas. In 1957 I found great resistance to castration of young bulls in the Helmand Valley of Afghanistan. The principal reason was entirely logical from the standpoint of the farmer: fields are tilled with a crude wooden plow fastened to an equally crude yoke which rides on the neck of the pair of oxen. The yoke is held in place by the large hump that develops on the shoulder of the mature animal. If bulls are castrated while young, the proper time if maximum benefits are to derive from the operation, this hump does not develop, and the animal is useless for traction. Dr. Y. Subrahmanyam tells me that among the Koya hill tribes of southeast India he encountered similar resistance, and for the same reason.[27]

It is obvious that if castration of bulls is to be a serious part of a livestock program in these areas, a new type of yoke must be introduced. This should not be too difficult. The Mediterranean and Latin American yoke is quite similar, and no more difficult or costly to manufacture. It is lashed to the horns of the oxen, thereby eliminating the need for a hump.

In recent years, as a part of the United States technical aid program, attempts have been made to introduce the native American bean *(Phaseolus vulgaris)* into the Helmand Valley. This crop often proves to be an inexpensive and effective way to introduce needed protein into a diet marked by meat deficiency, and it appeared to be a logical step in Afghanistan. Although the local people like the new food, and it grew well, resistance ran high. It was then discovered that a shortage of fuel places a premium on quick-cooking dishes; the bean was uneconomic in this sense. Subsequently, the black-eyed pea, which has high nutritive value but cooks in much less time, has been rather successful.

In villages in the high Andean area of South America a fire smoulders in the middle of the floor of one-room houses night and day. In programs of home improvement attempts have been made for sanitary reasons to get housewives to use a raised fireplace.These attempts have been largely unsuccessful. The Ecuadorian anthropologist, Aníbal Buitrón, points out that in these home betterment programs the fire is viewed simply as a cooking device, whereas it serves the equally important function of affording warmth to householders, who sleep around it at night and huddle around it when they come indoors on cold days. A sanitary, raised hearth appreciably reduces the value of the fire for heating. Dr. Buitrón suggests that the dual function of

[27] Communicated by Dr. Y. Subrahmanyam.

the fire might successfully be met by introducing the corner fireplace of the pueblo Indians of southwestern United States. This would reflect heat into the room, and at the same time give some degree of protection to food and dishes.[28]

An immediate answer to all linked problems is not always apparent. Another example from the Helmand Valley points up the sensitivity of culture to a single change. The local oxen are thin and scrawny and have relatively little strength. The traditional plow merely scratches the surface of the earth to a depth of a few inches and does not turn a furrow. Mold-board plows which cultivate much more effectively have been tried, but the animals are too weak to pull them. In some of the newly irrigated areas of the Valley better pasture has made possible fattening of oxen, which would seem to meet this drawback. But the fattening introduces still another unforeseen difficulty. The well-fed animals are much less docile, don't obey commands well, and are generally unmanageable with customary control techniques. Consequently, many local farmers are not anxious to feed their animals too well. A weak, tractible draught animal is preferable to a strong, uncontrollable one. More perfect domestication, or better methods of harnessing and driving oxen must be developed before this problem can successfully be met.

In Haiti, Taylor has pointed out still another example of unforeseen consequences of cultural innovation. A major dam and irrigation works, which can provide increased food production desperately needed in Haiti, has been built in the Artibonite Valley. But the social costs are high. The present farmers have a low level of living, but they own their small plots of land and have at least a minimum degree of security, as well as equality with their fellows. As the land improves it becomes increasingly attractive as a capital investment for city dwellers. Illiterate peasants, dazzled by what seem like fantastic offers for their

[28] Buitrón, 1959.

land, sell and are quickly reduced to the status of landless proletariat. Although they may continue to work for wages, high land capitalization places a premium on larger units that can be farmed with machinery, reducing the demand for hand labor. So, from the point of view of the Artibonite Valley dwellers, this improvement may well turn out to be an unmitigated disaster.[29]

Two final examples, one from South America and the other from Africa, illustrate how strikingly similar unforeseen consequences may result when all the implications of an innovation have not been thought through. In 1951 a yellow Cuban maize was introduced into the eastern lowlands of Bolivia in the Santa Cruz and Yungas regions. It had many apparent advantages: it grew well in the tropics, matured more rapidly, had more fat content than local varieties, was less subject to insect attack, and produced a higher yield per unit of land. The new maize seemed to be an excellent device to improve the diet of both people and animals, and it was for this reason that it was introduced. It has proved very popular, but not for the reasons anticipated. Its very hardness, desirable from the standpoint of storage, makes it difficult to grind, and people are unwilling to take the time and trouble to haul it to commercial mills in towns. But it makes an excellent commercial alcohol and prices are high. Thus, a seemingly desirable innovation has promoted alcoholism instead of improved diet.[30]

Annette Rosentiel tells how attempts to substitute cassava for millet in Northern Rhodesia have had undesirable results. Millet is not a very satisfactory commercial crop in Rhodesia. It is attacked by locusts and is easily affected by changes in the weather. Cassava is easier to grow and more profitable. But the economic basis is not the only one to be considered in attempting a simple substitution. In South Africa millet is essential for

29 Taylor, 1954.
30 Kelly, 1959, pp. 9-10.

beer, which plays a vital role in the social and religious life of the people. Further, however unsatisfactory it may be as a cash crop, it is important in diet. Since it is rich in fat content it is an important substitute for meat and milk, unprocurable because the tsetse fly makes it difficult to raise cattle. Compared to millet, cassava is deficient in fat content, so nutritional standards were lowered by this enforced change. Perhaps worse, with the prohibition of millet beer, drunkenness increased; the natives substituted a concoction called *skokian,* composed of methylated spirits, calcium carbide, molasses, sugar, and other ingredients. The new drink was not satisfactory as a social or ceremonial substitute for the old; it was dangerous; and it aroused great hostility toward the administration.[31]

MOTOR PATTERNS AND CUSTOMARY BODY POSITIONS

It is apparent to all of us that we learn speech patterns with ease in childhood, but that as adults it is far more difficult to duplicate exactly the sounds of a foreign language. Motor patterns and customary body positions can also be thought of as a way of expressing ourselves, easily learned in childhood, but modified only with difficulty when we are adults. Culture determines the positions in which we sleep, stand, sit, and relax. Culture determines what gestures we use, how we hold and use tools, and how we manipulate our bodies in an unlimited number of situations. In Negro Africa, field workers stand with straight legs, bending almost double at the waist, to work with short-handled tools. The Mexican Indian also uses short-handled tools, but he squats close to the earth. American craftsmen usually work on an elevated bench, and dexterity with toes and bare feet is not essential. In many places—I have noted it both among the Popoluca Indians in Mexico and in Hindu vil-

[31] Rosentiel, 1954.

lages—work is done on the ground and the feet are almost as important as the hands. Americans hold a knife so that the blade projects on the side of the thumb and forefinger; Eskimos and northwest coast Indians prefer a knife blade to project from the opposite side of the clasped hand. American carpenters draw a saw toward them; in Latin America carpenters push a rip saw away from them.

In childhood we acquire all the patterns characteristic of our culture in the same unconscious fashion that we acquire the speech of our society. And, just as the necessity or desirability of utilizing a new language may confront the adult with difficulties, and perhaps induce him to avoid or reject the situation in which the new language would be advantageous, so the necessity or desirability of modifying motor patterns may cause the adult to reject new ways which would be of advantage to him.

To illustrate, Mexican potters utilize a variety of techniques in forming vessels. The most advanced is, of course, the wheel. There are many skillful potters, however, who use hand modeling methods or who form pots in molds. In the State of Michoacán most of these molds consist of two halves with a vertical division so that each half is a mirror image of the other. The potter places a thin sheet of clay in each half, trims the edges, and joins the sections, rubbing the weld with her hand to seal the joint. When the molds are removed the pot is perfectly formed and needs only a little polishing before firing. In this work there are few rotary or revolving motions made with the hands.

In other parts of Mexico the potter places the clay over a mold which is like an upturned bowl. This forms the bottom of a vessel. Then the sides of the pot are built up with coils or daubs of clay, by pinching, and by turning the developing vessel round and round. Then the potter takes a wet piece of leather, and with a circulatory motion smooths the outside and inside. Thus, motor patterns differ substantially from those of

Michoacán in that the pot rotates, even though very slowly, and the potter smooths the vessel in much the same way that a wheel-using potter smooths a vessel.

In the 1930's the Mexican Government, desiring to improve the quality of pottery made in the country and to increase the income of certain villages, established trade schools in which master potters taught more modern techniques, including the use of the wheel. Research some years later revealed that in Michoacán villages, where vertical-halves molds were used and where few rotating or circulatory hand motions were customary, the wheel was not adopted. Apparently traditional motor patterns of adult potters were so rigid that they could not or would not take the time to master a radically different technique. But in those villages using the second type of mold—the upturned bowl—in which rotary and circulatory motions were involved, the wheel was often accepted. Old motor patterns were speeded up, but basically new forms did not have to be learned.[32]

To have to change customary motor patterns is both difficult and tiring. As part of a community development program in the Cook Islands, a raised cooking stove was developed so food would be protected from dirt and animals and women wouldn't have to stoop continually in doing their work. The raised stove generally was rejected. The complaint: it was so terribly uncomfortable to have to stand on one's feet while cooking.[33] Dube tells how an Indian village well was cleaned, bricked, and provided with a waist-high protective wall to reduce the danger of contamination. At first the villagers' enthusiasm was great, but shortly their interest waned. The high protective parapet required the use of pulleys (an innovation), thus necessitating a change in the traditional bending posture for drawing water. The women found the new set of motor patterns more exhausting than the old ones.[34]

[32] Foster, 1948.
[33] Communicated by Miss Mary Hopkirk.
[34] Dube, 1958, p. 134.

Comparable lessons have been learned in environmental sanitation programs, where the sanitary latrine has been introduced. American technicians have played a major, although not a dominant, role in popularizing the latrine in many newly developing countries. The outhouse at first thought may not seem to represent modern technology, but it constitutes an enormous advance, from the standpoint of health, over the ways of disposing of bodily wastes traditional in many places. Not surprisingly, the American technician thinks of the latrine in terms of the style formerly prevalent in this country: a square wooden structure with a raised seat perforated by one or more holes. Yet this type of latrine has had limited acceptance. An incident in El Salvador illustrates the problem. Several years ago a coffee planter, interested in the welfare of his employees, built a latrine for each house according to the standard American model. He was upset when his employees refused to use them. Finally an old man offered a suggestion. *"Patrón,* don't you realize that here we are squatters?" The planter ripped out the seats, replaced them with a perforated slab floor, and was gratified to find that public acceptance was much greater.[35] He had learned what has had to be learned independently, time after time, in many parts of the world: latrines with raised seats, for psychological or physiological reasons, seem to cause constipation among people who customarily defecate in a squatting position.

When new tools and technical innovations can be adapted to traditional motor patterns, the probability of acceptance is greater than if no attempt at accommodation is made.

[35] Foster, 1952, p. 13.

6 . . . . *Social barriers to change*

The traditional patterns of interpersonal relations between people in a community have a great deal to do with whether certain innovations are possible. In all societies time has sanctioned the social institutions that exist and has validated the ways in which these institutions and the individuals involved articulate with each other. In all groups we find the family, and often important forms of fictive kinship and formalized friendships as well. People have an idea how their community functions, or should function, and they bring public opinion to bear to attempt to maintain these norms. Authority exists within families, in the form of political structure, and in reciprocal relationships which may exist across caste and class lines. Whatever the village ideal of harmony may be, conflict is always present in the form of factions, vested interests, and other rivalries. Some social structures are rigid, others are more "open." The quality of hardness of a given society again has important bearing on the ease with which change may be accomplished.

In this section I consider the evidence of barriers in social structure under the principal headings of group solidarity, conflict, loci of authority, and rigidity of social structure.

GROUP SOLIDARITY

In examining peasant and folk communities, one is impressed by the way in which people hold to an ideal of how they ought to behave toward their fellows. This ideal is reflected in a strong sense of mutual obligation within the framework of family and friendship, a general preference for small-group identification, and a willingness to criticize anyone who deviates greatly from these customary norms.

Mutual Obligations Within the Framework of Family, Fictive Kin, and Friendship Patterns

Much of the success of peasant society appears to lie in the fact that the obligations and expectations associated with individual roles are social imperatives. They are not optional, at the convenience of a person; they must be recognized and accepted without question. As long as this attitude is held to, in spite of factions and interest conflicts, a community will have a high degree of integration. I recall the case of my friend, Vicente Rendón, and his wife, Natividad, in Tzintzuntzan. I had asked them to join me on a trip to Mexico City, 250 miles away. Neither had ever been there, and the event was talked about with much excitement for many days. Then, the night before we were to depart, the father of Vicente's compadre, Salvador Villagomez, died. This posed what to me would have been a real conflict: the obligation to help with the funeral and the keen disappointment at seeing a plum slip through my fingers. After all, Salvador had other compadres who might help. But there was no problem for Vicente and Natividad. Their duty was clear to them, and they fulfilled it without apparent regrets or questions as to whether alternate behavior would have been possible.

This type of reciprocal behavior, whether between members of an extended family, friends, or fictive kin, fulfills a number of functions. In times of food shortages, lack of money, life crises such as death, and in many other situations, economic, spiritual, and physical support is provided. The mutual obligations of these relationships take the place of many of the activities of more highly developed state forms: social security and welfare, an effective police system, cooperative and credit facilities, and the like.

This reciprocal pattern, however, tends to be incompatible with the trend toward individualization that characterizes urbanization and industrialization and with the increased use of money in place of subsistence activities and barter. When societies in which reciprocal obligations are so important are in transition, their very strength constitutes one of the most serious brakes on change. Many instances have been noted in which able individuals have refused proferred technical and monetary assistance that would have greatly increased their productive capacity—and hence their value to their developing homelands.

An American fisheries expert once told me of an experience in Peru. The Peruvian developmental unit to which he was adviser was interested in modernizing coastal fishing techniques by motorizing launches, increasing the size of nets, and establishing a low-interest credit system. A promising young fisherman living in a north coast port was offered such aid. Rather to the surprise of members of the mission he did not jump at the chance, but asked time to think it over. The next morning he declined. When asked his reason he replied that if he made more money it would simply mean that he would have more relatives to take care of; it was doubtful that he would be any better off, for he would have greatly increased responsibilities.

Dr. Derek Taylor tells of a similar experience. Among the New Zealand Maori the extended family continues to be strong, and traditional obligations are still respected. The Department of Maori Affairs, recognizing that substandard housing constitutes a health hazard in some areas, has a special housing fund to help people build homes with low down payments and favorable interest terms. "I recall one family," writes Dr. Taylor, "in a community called Tokomaru Bay that lived in a house that was substandard in almost every respect. The husband was earning a good wage at the local freezing works and could well afford the monthly outlay necessary to enable him to build a home under this plan. He gave as his reason for not doing so that if he built a house all of his relatives would move in and live with him!"[1]

Individuals like the Peruvian fisherman and the Maori wage earner are faced with a cruel dilemma: if they are to enjoy the fruits of their greater initiative they must be prepared to disregard many of the obligations that their cultures expect of them, or they must expect to support an ever-increasing number of idle relatives and friends with little or no profit to themselves. Often people solve this dilemma by continuing to accept the status quo. Macgregor points out how, among the Sioux

The Indian who amasses a large herd of cattle, builds a good home, and receives an income of a thousand dollars or more but does not distribute his wealth on ceremonial occasions, such as a wedding or funeral in his family, becomes the subject of severe criticism and ostracism by his relatives and friends. This is just what happened to many mixed-bloods who followed the white pattern of accumulating property and thus lost favor and status with the majority of the people in their communities. . . .

To receive and feed all visitors, especially relatives, is still an obligation. It is this custom which undermines economic development of individual families and keeps them poor. When there were greater food resources to be obtained by the skill of the hunter and everyone was close to the same level of wealth, hospitality did not tax the individual family too heavily. . . .

This is not now the case . . . hospitality has become a burden to the few and a strong deterrent to accumulating material wealth. . . .

The man with a regular salary today becomes a target for his

[1] Communicated by Dr. Derek Taylor.

poorer and ne'er-do-well relatives. "He has enough. Why should he not feed us? He is my relative," is the prevailing attitude.[2]

This has been the experience of members of other Indian tribes. Among the Navaho, kinship obligations frequently make it difficult, if not impossible, to conduct a successful business in an area in which the trader's family is concentrated. Relatives importune the entrepreneur to give loans to his kinsmen and gifts from his store, and they expect that loans need not be repaid. Navaho cooperatives have failed because of the dilemma of family solidarity versus the demands of sound business practice. Mary Shepardson tells of a white-owned trading post in a Navaho community in which a Navaho clerk was transferred to a job as driver. When she asked the reason she was told that his many relatives in the neighborhood put so much pressure on him that he could not resist "stealing" from the store to feed and outfit them, even though he was thoroughly honest.[3]

Brown recently compared the common resistance to wage labor that he found characteristic of the inhabitants of American Samoa and of the Hehe people of Tanganyika Territory in East Africa. In both groups a major cause was found to be the high value placed upon the full performance of social and political obligations, the time-consuming nature of which made regular labor impossible.

> In Samoa, social and political obligations are expressed and emphasized by elaborate ceremonial, almost ritual. This takes time, both in preparation and actual performance. It also involves a large display and distribution of wealth, both foodstuffs and less perishable products. This ceremonial life is highly valued by them, both for the social values it expresses and as an end in itself, as something dignified and pleasant. It would be impossible for a people who spend most of their life

[2] Macgregor, 1946, pp. 113-114.
[3] Communicated by Dr. Mary Shepardson.

working such as a European peasant or a plantation wage force.[4]

The Hehe have a less-developed ceremonial sense, but a strong feeling for social responsibility. They must be ready to fulfill obligations to a wide circle of kindred at such times as crop-planting, betrothals, weddings, funerals, and sickness. Moreover, every man, to be respected, must assist at the settlement of legal disputes, an act which, in view of the African fascination with law and legal procedures, often takes much time. "It is obvious that their obligations to their kindred and to the community would both suffer if the bulk of their time were consumed working for money." Brown concludes that neither the Samoans nor the Hehe are good subjects for economic development on Western lines.[5]

Coleman speaks of a process of community disintegration in Nigeria which is accelerated by seasonal or migrant laborers who return to their villages with new tastes and ideas. When they are in cities, where they are physically isolated from their traditional milieu and where they earn their own living quite independently of village support, they are subject to strong individualizing influences which create profound tensions in many of them. "The struggle between the strong urge to cut himself adrift from his family and live his own life, on the one hand, and the wish to sacrifice his own comfort and happiness to fulfill deeply engrained family and communal obligations on the other, has been a painful dilemma every wage-earning Nigerian has had to face."[6]

Small-Group Dynamics

A sense of personal identification with small groups seems to be necessary for most people, to provide psychological security and satisfaction in their daily work. This identification may be

[4] Brown, 1957, p. 13.
[5] *Ibid.*, p. 13.
[6] Coleman, 1958, p. 71.

expressed in the form of a large family, a circle of friends, a cooperative work group, a small village, or any one of many other forms. Part of the importance of the small group lies in reciprocal obligations of the type just discussed, but, quite apart from this, the small group seems to provide a gratifying framework within which to work. Often innovations which upset such traditional groups meet with strong resistance, and again, unless effective small groups can be created, lack of interest and apathy may greet promotional efforts. People, we know, will sometimes forego comfort, convenience, and economic gain in return for more fun out of life. Here again, of course, we are dealing with values and value judgments which are not always rational in an economic sense.

In many of Latin America's villages women gather on a stream bank to wash clothes under conditions that are anything but comfortable. But the pleasures of working in the company of others and of conversation and joking compensate for hardship. The Latin American pattern is duplicated in other parts of the world. Dwight D. Eisenhower is reported as the source for an African example:

> In welcoming the American Council on Education's convention to Washington, the President made a succinct point with a personal anecdote: "I have never forgotten my shock, once, when I saw a very modern-looking village deserted in a far corner of Africa. It had been deserted because the builders put running water into all the houses. The women rebelled because there was now taken away from them their only excuse for social contact with their own kind, at the village well. I had been guilty of the very great error of putting into their minds and hearts the same aspirations that I had. And it simply wasn't so."[7]

Dr. Deolinda da Costa Martins, who grew up in the famous old University town of Coimbra in her native Portugal, told me

[7] *Time* Magazine, 62 (16):26 (October 19, 1953).

a similar and even more graphic story. The town lies along the north bank of the Rio Mondego, rising steeply several hundred feet to the University, which is situated on a plateau. Here, as is so often true, social ecology is reflected in topography and the wealthy families are concentrated near the top, just beneath the University. In these homes clothing is washed by professional washerwomen who come in by the day. Two tariffs prevail: a higher one, if the clothes are washed in the laundry of the owner, a lower tariff, if the clothing is washed in the Rio Mondego. If the latter, the woman goes down the hill with a great bundle on her head and in the evening she struggles up the hill with the still heavier wet wash, at considerable cost in time and effort. Yet, in spite of the added work, most washer-women are willing to accept lower pay in order to have the pleasure of being with their friends, to be able to pass a pleasant day in conversation, rather than to be isolated for a day of hard labor.[8]

Problems of the type illustrated by washing habits often can be solved if they are examined in terms of the values of the recipient rather than those of the donor group. Then it is clear that it is the *social* factor, and not the attraction of the river bank itself, that is important. If the social demands can be met, the rest is easy. In San Salvador I have seen public laundries built by engineers who understood the problem. Here washtubs are lined up in batteries, hot and cold running water flows to each, and there is plenty of space to hang clothes. Washerwomen pay a few centavos a day, and with far greater comfort than on the river bank they accomplish their work and still maintain social ties with their friends.

Recently when Brazilian architects, working as members of a community development project in the State of Minas Gerais, tried to design an economical "improved" kitchen which gave more usable floor space with less over-all area, thus saving con-

8 Communicated by Dr. Deolinda da Costa Martins.

struction costs, they encountered an unexpected social problem. The architects proposed putting the raised cooking hearth in a corner, so good use could be made of wall space, and so the central room area would remain uncluttered. But housewives resisted the new design. This is a rather cold area, and there are few social contacts for women. So when visitors come, they gather in the kitchen, to drink coffee and talk with the housewife as she prepares meals. With the new kitchen design, the housewife had to keep her back to her guests most of the time, an action both rude and socially ungratifying. The architects were forced to accept a larger kitchen in which the raised hearth projected from the wall, in such fashion that the housewife could stand behind it and work facing her guests. Economical architectural planning was not synonymous with good social planning.[9]

The workings of small-group dynamics are revealed in a different context in Spicer's account of the "reluctant cotton pickers," in which Japanese of American and Asiatic birth who had been resettled in World War II in the Colorado River Relocation Center were initially antagonistic but subsequently agreeable to the idea of working out of camp to save a local cotton crop. When the plan was first broached, very few evacuees showed interest. Although the reasons involved are many, an important factor was found to lie in the fact that, to preserve approximate equality of income for all involuntary campers, it had been decided that wages would be put in a Community Trust Fund, for later disbursement as community leaders might determine. But it was clear that the Relocation Authority administrators and the Nisei leaders themselves had overestimated the solidarity of a unit of 9000 people. Some people thought the only solution lay in individual incentive in the form of wages paid directly to the cotton-pickers. The secret, however, was found to lie in considering the barracks "block" of about 300

[9] Communicated by Arquitecto Bención Tiomny.

individuals as the primary social unit. Internees in several blocks suggested that the money earned go into a block trust fund to be used for improvements in the mess hall, for parties, and for other functions with which there was an immediate sense of identification. This was tried and found to be quite successful. Increasing number of internees went out to pick cotton, relations with the local Anglo towns improved, and a spirit of competition developed among blocks. Little by little chance aggregates of people were welded into societies. "This case illustrates," says Spicer, "the strength of local group or neighborhood as a social unit focusing the interests and activities of its members. It demonstrates the greater strength of the local group over that collection of local groups which constituted a community."[10]

Sasaki and Adair describe another example in which the nature and role of the primary group has been critical in hindering desirable culture change. In the early 1930's the U.S. Bureau of Indian Affairs began to settle Navahos on the Fruitland Project, an irrigated tract along the San Juan River in northern New Mexico. In spite of the technical excellence of the irrigation system and a good deal of attention over the years to helping the Navahos settle and work, the level of production has remained low. The authors trace much of the problem back to the social structure of the primary social-economic-political unit of the Reservation: the "outfit." An outfit is made up of a number of related extended families with common land-use rights in a given area who recognize the authority of an older man as spokesman for their group and in dealing with neighboring Navaho groups. When the first unit of Indians was settled the outfit grouping was maintained to a considerable extent more or less by accident, thus permitting continued cooperation in the new geographical setting. Subsequently, when more Indians were relocated, the unity of the outfit was not

10 Spicer, 1953, p. 52.

maintained. This has meant that the high degree of cooperation and recognition of authority necessary in the successful maintenance of irrigation works has been lacking, and these attempts to better the Navaho's lot have been most disappointing.[11]

Public Opinion

The unity of a small primary social group seems essential to the prosecution of much directed change. At the same time, it provides, through concentrated public opinion, the means for discouraging the innovator who potentially is the most useful man in the group. An example, quoted at length, illustrates the tragic results of unenlightened group pressure in an Indian village subject to the work of the Community Development Programme.

Hukm Singh, a rangy man in his middle 30's with sloping shoulders, a shaggy black mustache, and a perpetually melancholy look, is one of the best farmers I have met in India.

He also is one of the more prosperous, with 50 acres in south central Uttar Pradesh state where holdings average about five acres. When the Akola community project was launched, the village level worker (VLW) singled out Hukm Singh as a natural village leader. He had land, resources and a high school education. Other villagers looked up to him.

Hukm Singh quickly took up improved seed, artificial fertilizer and other agricultural practices suggested by the VLW.

When the project introduced mustard seed, Hukm Singh volunteered one acre as an experimental plot to compare combinations of 10 varieties and three fertilizers.

With VLW's guidance he converted three acres of land near the irrigation canal into a profitable fruit and vegetable nursery.

Then Hukm Singh went too far. Although he was a Jat, a vegetarian caste, he bought some white leghorn chicks from the project to raise poultry and eggs for tourists visiting the Taj Mahal in nearby Agra.

[11] Sasaki and Adair, 1952.

The other Jats were incensed. The caste council ostracized him. His neighbors refused to pass him the hookah—that is, they shunned him in their evening get-togethers over a community pipe.

Hukm Singh held out at first, but eventually he buckled under the pressure. He gave the birds to his Harijan (untouchable) sweeper.[12]

CONFLICT

In folk and peasant communities there is often found an ideal self-image of village solidarity and agreement that in fact does not exist. The reader may recall the illustration in Chapter 3 in which in an Indian village the ideal of family unity is extended to embrace the entire community, and where conflicts and lack of cooperation are regarded as shameful (pp. 55-56). In spite of this not uncommon feeling we have seen that, in fact, villagers frequently are suspicious of the motives of their fellows, they fear they will be outdone by their associates, and they are reluctant to cooperate with others. These fears, as pointed out, are often reflected in factional disputes, in which a village divides into mutually antagonistic power blocks. In other situations, where a community is horizontally stratified economically and socially, some groups will have special powers, prerogatives, and interests best served if a status quo is maintained. Conflict problems are here discussed under the headings of factionalism and vested interests.

Factionalism

Some kinds of culture change may involve only a few people, or even a single person. A man may, without being affected by others, try an improved plow, build a latrine, or learn to read. But most of today's induced change is based on the assumption that groups of people will participate. An agricultural extension

12 Hertz, 1958.

service is uneconomic if it is directed toward a single farmer; demonstrations and follow-throughs require that a number of people develop interest. A single latrine does little to reduce a person's chances of fly-borne illness if all his neighbors continue traditional unsanitary feces-disposal practices. And the literacy efforts, provision for reading materials, and perhaps village reading rooms that are essential to teach adults to read and write, like agricultural extension, are prohibitively costly unless group interest is aroused.

Mass programs, then, must be carried out in such fashion that a significant number of people will wish to participate and vocal opposition will be minimized. But, since societies in transition frequently are plagued by greater-than-normal amounts of factionalism, this often means that if the members of one faction show interest in a new program, the members of another faction immediately declare against it, without logic and without attempting to weigh its true merits. The bitterness and hostility between factions and the lengths to which people will go to humiliate their rivals is difficult to believe. While studying community development programs in 1955 in India and Pakistan, I found that factionalism was one of the greatest problems with which program personnel had to cope.

Dube, with his wide experience in this field, also notes that this is a major problem in India. Village level workers, the technicians with the most direct and immediate contact with villagers, must make friends with the people they hope to influence. But the very success the worker has also jeopardizes his work. Friendly relations and friendships, according to village norms, presuppose mutual and reciprocal obligations. Hospitality is always returned in some way, and one's friends must be supported. The art of establishing friendship with a person also identifies the outsider with his group or faction, and by implication he assumes the villagers' hostility to rival groups and factions. If community development personnel identify too closely with one faction their plans will have only partial success. "The members of the friendly group would support the officials not because they are convinced about the utility or efficiency of the programs sponsored by them, but simply as their part in the obligations of friendship. On the other hand the members of the hostile group would feel it their duty to reject anything offered by officials identified with their rivals, even if they saw merit in the program."[13]

The story from other parts of India is the same. Goswami and Roy write that "The bitterness of the factious spirit often drives out the desire to improve the village. It becomes more important to cause annoyance to the other party than to get something done. Co-operation between the two parties is impossible . . ."[14] McCormack found in spite of the fact that the people of Morsralli believe the cooperation of every family group is necessary for village cooperation, factionalism is rampant, and growing in intensity, a condition making group cooperation increasingly difficult. Leaders of factions feel their honor is impugned and their status threatened if their followers do not support them. Consequently, "personal grievances of factional leaders" are magnified into village-wide issues.[15] Hertz, in his analysis of the Community Development Programme, found that the government plan to use elected village panchayats, or councils, to provide community-wide support was negated in many villages by factional disputes.[16]

Factionalism is not an Indian monopoly; it appears to be panhuman. R. N. Adams found the same picture in Guatemala. There, a village social worker, a member of a nutritional research program, found shortly after going to work that the people in one section of a village resented her activities more than those in the other, and "as she made more friends in one

13 Dube, 1957, p. 136.
14 Goswami and Roy, 1953, p. 307.
15 McCormack, 1957, pp. 258, 259, 261.
16 Hertz, 1958.

barrio [section of the community], she became simultaneously less acceptable to the other."[17] Adams, an anthropologist, studied the social structure of the village and found that the two halves, the barrios, were rather different in customs, religion, economic level, and degree of progressiveness. This pre-existing schism was unwittingly intensified by the presence of an outsider who, quite by accident, made a majority of her friends in only one of the two barrios.

Vested Interests

Many of the social and economic changes that are being promoted in the world today threaten, or are interpreted as threatening, the security of some groups or individuals. Native medical curers and midwives, for example, often resent modern medical programs because they fear the competition will be injurious to them. Large landlords sometimes feel that too much education for their tenants is undesirable because it will promote unrest and, perhaps, demands for land distribution. Village moneylenders are opposed to low-interest government-managed credit programs, and merchants object to consumer cooperatives. These people normally are individuals of power and prestige, and they are able to exploit their position if they wish to hinder change.

In peasant communities means of dissemination of knowledge are few compared to those in urban centers, and rumor is a powerful force in determining action. Untrue rumors are among the most common techniques used by individuals who feel threatened by proposed changes. Particularly where novelty, outsiders, government agents, and free gifts and services are suspect, the word spreads swiftly, no matter how preposterous it may be. Goswami and Roy describe the gullibility of Indian villagers which, combined with their suspiciousness, makes them an easy target for rumor mongers.

[17] R. N. Adams, 1955, p. 442.

Vested interests such as the money-lender or the landlord may deliberately start fantastic rumors. Immediately the Bhadson Extension Project was announced, there were rumors that this was the first step to nationalization of land. When a census of persons was taken, there were rumors that anyone who gave his age as over sixty-five would be killed. When an American Point Four expert appeared on the spot, there were rumors that the villagers would be driven out and all land used for setting up an American colony. These rumors made the task of extension workers hard at the beginning.[18]

In other situations rumors are not necessary. A feudal landlord can decide whether he wishes extension agents or health workers in his villages or not. If he decides against such work, individual decisions on the part of villagers are not involved. Progressive landlords can be and sometimes are powerful forces in promoting change; in Pakistan I have encountered landlords who paid for schools, 4-H club supplies, and other civic improvements. But with greater frequency they, like the midwife and the merchant, are apt to throw their weight against change.

LOCI OF AUTHORITY

Where does authority lie in a family? In a neighborhood group or barrio? In a village? How is this authority manifest in decision making, and what are the processes whereby a group decides on a course of action, or an individual is permitted to take steps he feels are desirable? The way in which these questions are answered in any specific situation will have much to do with the receptivity of a group to suggested change. Within a village, much authority lies in the family, defined and vested by tradition. Other types of authority are found in political structure. Authority may also be thought of as existing in the personality of exceptional individuals who, without formal

18 Goswami and Roy, 1953, p. 305.

powers, influence the behavior of others. Authority likewise exists outside the village; as has been pointed out (Chapter 3) this is a basic truism with respect to peasant society. Such authority often overrides local forms and may be a major factor in the growth of a community.

Authority Within the Family

Individual decision-making is such a part of American culture that it is hard to realize that this is not a world-wide cultural pattern. For example, in middle-class society in the United States the physician's recommendation that an appendix be removed probably will mean consultation with the patient's spouse, but it is not the occasion for a big family council meeting. In many other societies, however, the locus of authority and traditional decision-making processes are manifest in family structure and are quite different. Public health personnel working in intercultural programs have found that, even in small families, a patient often is not free to make decisions that are taken for granted in Western countries. Bailey points out how, among the Navaho, the decision to enter a hospital is reached only after a family conference: a woman and her husband alone are not free to exercise their discretion in this regard.[19] Margaret Clark found exactly the same situation in the Spanish-speaking Mexican enclave of Sal Si Puedes in San Jose, California: hospitalization is a grave and serious step, a family and not an individual problem.[20]

Dr. Y. S. Kim pointed out to me a similar situation in his country, Korea. If, for example, a young wife is found to have active tuberculosis requiring hospitalization, the physician must first explain the problem to her parents-in-law who occupy the position of authority in the family; her husband does not have the right to make the decision. Or, if a mother finds her child

19 Bailey, 1948, p. 1419.
20 Clark, 1959, p. 231.

has malaria, she must first ask her parents-in-law's permission to take the child to a modern health center. If they say no, she is reduced to patronizing an herb doctor.[21] Marriott describes an identical example in the Indian village in which he worked. The father and father's brother of a Brahman girl ill with malaria begged the doctor for quinine, and enough was supplied for a full course of treatment. Three days later he discovered that none of it had been used. "An old widowed aunt who ruled the women of that family had voiced objections, and the whole matter of western treatment was dropped."[22]

The conservative pull of such traditional authority patterns obviously often has sad consequences for sick or injured individuals. Franklin Bumps told me of an experience in Saudi Arabia where he worked for Aramco. A Moslem worker in a machine shop badly injured his right hand in a lathe. The American shop foreman tried in vain to persuade the worker to go to the modern hospital where skilled medical help was available. Instead, the worker fled into the desert. Several days later he returned, with tribal permission for the Western-trained surgeon to repair the hand. By then, gangrene had set in, and although the hand was saved, it was badly crippled, a particularly grave problem for a man who, for ritual reasons, may do certain classes of things only with the right hand. The worker filed charges against the company, and the unfortunate shop foreman languished in jail for a number of months.[23]

The opposite end of the authority spectrum can be just as frustrating. Dr. Blair was surprised to find that, among the Eskimo, a child's opinion was frequently asked about whether certain things should be done to or for him. "After apparently getting all the necessary consents for immunization I have been told, 'but he doesn't want it.' "[24]

21 Communicated by Dr. Y. S. Kim.
22 Marriott, 1955, p. 243.
23 Communicated by Mr. Franklin Bumps.
24 Communicated by Dr. Hazel I. Blair.

The practical implications of evidence of this type are apparent. Technical aid experts, in urging specific courses of action which to Westerners appear to involve only the individual, must in fact find ways to communicate with and gain the support of the individuals and groups in whom authority is vested. Marriott points out how lines of power within families affect utilization of medical treatment in an Indian village.

> Whatever the treatment may be that is suggested by a specialist, it will be mediated and enforced, or perhaps modified or rejected, according to who is most influential in that particular family. The exploratory clinic in Kishan Garhi encountered this problem directly when courses of treatment were thoroughly "sold" to some members of a family but were later rejected by others who had controlling voices in the family. Since families in villages of northern India frequently lack lines of authority that are obvious to nonmembers, and since the social worlds of men and women are sharply divided, authoritative communication by the medical specialist must aim to include all important family members of both sexes, if it is to be effective.[25]

In terms of the way of life of the peoples described in these accounts, these form of behavior are not irrational; they are logical and obvious. This is what makes them so difficult to cope with. Margaret Clark makes clear the conditions which underlie the pattern and reasons for group decisions in cases dealing with medical treatment. She points out that in illness as well as other aspects of life, people are members of a group of relatives, to whom they are responsible for their behavior and on whom they are dependent for support and social sanction. "Medical care involves expenditure of time and energy by the patient's relatives and friends. Money for doctors and medicines comes from the common family purse; many of a sick person's duties are performed during the period of illness by other members of his social group." Illness obviously is more than a biological

[25] Marriott, 1955, p. 251.

disorder; it is a potential social and economic crisis for an entire group of people. Under such circumstances it is not surprising that an individual *cannot even decide unilaterally that he is ill.* Symptoms must be presented to the group, described and observed, and consensus reached. "In other words, an individual is not socially defined as a sick person until his claim is 'validated' by his associates. Only when relatives and friends accept his condition as an illness can he claim exemption from the performance of his normal daily tasks." Since illness directly affects an entire group, it is only logical that the group should be expected to participate fully in decisions that must be made.[26]

Authority in the Political Structure

In the simplest primitive groups, there is no political authority in the usual sense of the word. The simple functions of government are carried out through the family, or perhaps the lineage or clan. In all peasant and folk societies, on the other hand, we find institutions quite properly labeled "political," in which various types of authority, coupled with the right to make decisions, may be distinguished from authority vested in families. The nature of these political systems has much to do with the receptivity of a community to change. Perhaps the problem can be most simply stated by asking questions: In carrying out technical aid programs, how does the technician identify the leaders with whom he must work? Where does he find the people who have the formal or informal power, the prestige and influence, who will be instrumental in deciding whether work is to go forward? Are the obvious political leaders the best bet? What is the role of religious leaders? Are there informal leaders whose power can be known only after familiarity with the community? Is it best to work through established leaders, whatever their position, in spite of the fact that they

[26] Clark, 1959, pp. 203, 204.

are often conservative because of vested interests, or can new leaders be found or created?

There are no simple answers to these questions. We have come to realize that the nature of leadership patterns in a community is one of the most important of all factors influencing cultural change, but we still know much less about the subject than would be desirable. The United States is so organized for activities of all types, with formal and informal, paid and volunteer leaders, that we assume competent and willing people can always be found to do the job. It sometimes comes as a surprise to Americans to find that in many societies leadership, as an institution, is poorly developed and perhaps inadequate to guide the group decisions that must be made in programs of major change. Often an individual who steps forward to volunteer his services for a new project will be criticized rather than praised for his pains; his neighbors suspect that he sees opportunity for personal gain, at their expense. In some societies modesty and self-effacement are the norms of good conduct; the individual who shows interest in leadership is, at best, guilty of bad manners, and hence subject to public disapproval. The problem is highlighted in a report from a community development program in southeastern Nigeria, where Hill found that "in the intensely democratic village society, leadership was lacking and, even where the will for voluntary effort existed, there was uncertainty about how to set about making a start."[27] The New England town meeting, so dear to most Americans as exemplifying simple, uncomplicated democracy in small communities, is just not a common pattern in the world, and programs based on the assumption that this kind of decision-making body exists or can be created will usually fail.

The problem of the locus of political authority is illustrated by Dube in an analysis of a community development program in India. Not illogically—to agents trained in a democratic en-

27 C. deN. Hill, 1957, p. 19.

vironment—it was assumed that persons elected to local offices by popular vote were the proper village leaders with whom to work. The community development workers largely confined their group discussions and individual contacts to this circle and to other obviously important and respected individuals. These leaders responded enthusiastically, and prospects looked bright for successful work.

The basic assumptions about leadership, however, were only partially sound. These people were leaders, but not the only leaders. As is true in many other similar situations, they constituted a group with authority to mediate between the village and the outside world, but there were important areas within the community where they had little or no power. "The village looked to them for guidance in its general relationship with the urban areas and the officials; and their help was sought in legal matters, in contacting and influencing officials, and generally in facing problems that arise out of contact between the village and the outside world. *They were not necessarily looked upon as leaders in agriculture, nor were they in any sense decision makers in many vital matters concerning the individual and his family.*"[28] In fact, although the villagers were dependent on them for some kinds of leadership, they were, precisely because of this dependence, suspicious of them. Dube concludes that undue emphasis in working with traditional leaders was construed by some villagers as an attempt of the government to maintain the status quo, and thus support the domination of the wealthier people. "A closer study of group dynamics in village communities reveals several different levels of leadership, each with somewhat specialized functions." To work effectively in a community, it is desirable to know these several levels and the areas of influence of each. "An excellent village politician" says Dube "is rarely a model farmer; the latter is generally an obscure and apolitical person 'who minds his own business.' In

[28] Dube, 1957, p. 141. (Italics mine.)

112 · Traditional cultures

adopting agricultural practices people are more likely to follow his example rather than that of the local politicians."[29]

An almost identical situation has been described in a Philippine village in which the government-sponsored Community School program of adult education and community development made primary use of schoolteachers as agents of technical change. Teachers occupy a high status in the Philippines because of their education and relatively high salaries, and their leadership in formal schooling matters is unquestioned. But they are not accorded universal knowledge; their area of competence is circumscribed. "To be advised on rice growing and animal husbandry by teachers, who did not themselves participate in such activities, was clearly laughable to a sizable proportion of the adult population."[30]

Authority of the Unusual Individual

Gifted or unusual people who may or may not occupy formal positions of leadership in a community often play decisive roles in bringing about change. If they are looked to by their associates for any reason, and if their actions are apt to be imitated by others, they may be thought of as leaders, regardless of their status in their social group. Two classes of people have been singled out by anthropologists as probably the most significant in bringing about change. Barnett believes that the "marginal man," the deviant who is unsatisfied with traditional ways is most apt to be an innovator.[31] Mandelbaum, although not generalizing, gives substantiating evidence in his description of an unusual Kota tribesman (see p. 114). The other point of view is that the "prestige-laden" individual is more effective as an agent of change. Individuals who, because of social position, wealth, or other reasons, will be followed by others will in fact be more significant in the long run in promoting change.

[29] *Ibid.*, p. 142.
[30] Sibley, 1960-1961, p. 211.
[31] Barnett, 1941.

There is evidence to support both points of view. Barnett thinks of marginal individuals as the "dissident," the "indifferent," the "disaffected," and the "resentful." Such people, he believes, will be more than ordinarily receptive to innovation for a variety of reasons. Dissenters have never accommodated themselves to specific cultural demands, and the more courageous and independent among them are more apt to rebel and withdraw openly and to be attracted by new alternatives to traditional forms, than are persons satisfied with customary ways. The indifferent accept new ways because they are not strongly committed to a custom or an ideal of their society. The disaffected are often those who have been exposed to novel ways, and who, within their own cultures, are denied the satisfactions they have learned to want by alien teachings. The resentful, obviously, are those who cannot accept the inequalities built into their social systems, if they are in an inferior position compared to others more fortunate.[32]

In primitive and peasant parts of the world bicultural half-breeds and natives who have had more than average contact with foreigners are particular candidates for the categories enumerated. Indian widows and half-breed orphans and illegitimate children of white men who lived with Yurok, Yakima, and Tsimshian Indian women are examples of this group. They "had had a taste of the white man's way of life, enough to make them unhappy with the Indian way; and when they were thrown back to feed upon tribal values, they found them tasteless, bitter, or indigestible. Case histories of individuals of this sort are highlighted by rebellious and delinquent trends, which testify to their suggestibility and to their desperate clutching at any new straw which would enable them to fight against or relieve them of the necessity of conforming to native standards."[33]

[32] Barnett, 1953, pp. 378-410.
[33] *Ibid.*, p. 391.

Keesing finds that mixed bloods are frequently prominent in movements for cultural or political nationalism.[34] One of the most interesting examples of this pattern is reported by Mandelbaum. At the time of his field work in the late 1930's, Sulli was the one Kota tribesman in the Indian Nilgiri Hills who could speak English. Through his vigorous personality he was able to bring about a series of significant changes in several villages. His life history showed deviation since childhood: his desire to become educated particularly illustrates the drive of a restless dissident. He had urged his fellow tribesmen to cut their hair, to abandon their traditional calling as musicians for other tribes, to cease eating carrion, and to abolish the menstrual hut.

> Sulli himself has gone beyond the reforms he advocates. The prestige value imparted by contact with an ethnographer and a linguist lent him enough courage not only to cut his hair but also to tog himself out in shorts, topee, and stockings in the style of an Englishman. Although his reforms are savagely opposed by many, some of the younger men have followed his example in cutting their hair and in abandoning other tribal practices. Had Sulli been a weaker personality, he could not have held his followers or himself to his schedule of acculturation. Much of Kota culture change is channelled through and directed by a single individual, the leitmotif of whose personality is deviation from established tradition.[35]

Of course, we are not dealing with an "either-or" situation. Both the deviant and the prestige-laden individual may be important in bringing about change. In spite of the interesting evidence of Barnett, Keesing, and Mandelbaum, I am inclined to believe that the influence of the deviant individual usually is less important than that of the prestige-laden individual—a wealthy and respected member of a community, a member of the privileged class—in bringing about change. If we recognize

[34] Keesing, 1941, p. 289.
[35] Mandelbaum, 1941, p. 26.

the enormous force of prestige in driving people to modify habits (see Chapter 8), it is logical to expect this. Comparative evidence also supports this position. R. N. Adams, directing himself specifically to Barnett's position as originally set forth in 1941, challenges the "marginal man" hypothesis and describes the personality and influence of an innovator in a high Andean Peruvian village he studied, a man of wealth and social position.[36] Wellin's interesting account of attempts to introduce the boiling of contaminated water in a Peruvian coastal town through health education also suggests that the prestige of powerful people was perhaps the single most important factor in bringing about limited acceptance of this innovation.[37]

It should be noted that two distinct but related phenomena are involved here. On the one hand, the dissident or disaffected individual may himself adopt new forms, but it is quite a different matter as to whether his example will be followed by others in the community. Often, I suspect, he is followed only by other dissidents, leaving unaffected the bulk of the population. My guess would be that, as a practical guide to technical aid workers, the really marginal individual is only occasionally a good candidate as an influential local innovator.

CHARACTERISTICS OF THE SOCIAL STRUCTURE

Some aspects of a social structure, and the associated values, seriously inhibit change, in much the same way that family structure may do so. In countries like India and Pakistan a rigid caste organization slows cultural innovation. The prerogatives associated with each group are jealously guarded, and attempts to infringe upon them by members of lower groups are resented and often repulsed. Under the traditional system, for example,

[36] R. N. Adams, 1951.
[37] Wellin, 1955.

members of certain different castes could not draw water from the same well, attend the same schools, eat together, or otherwise mingle. The types of physical labor one could do were rigorously prescribed, and violation of the rules was condoned neither by members of one's caste nor by members of castes that normally would do such work. Almost the same words could be used to describe the position of Negroes in much of the United States. In other situations, where force is not present, the basic configuration of a society will have much to do with the types of innovation that will occur.

Caste and Class Barriers

In stratified societies and bureaucracies, people expect to obey or take orders from those in superior positions of authority or power and, in turn, to dictate to those below them. This limits the free interplay of ideas and opinions that is so important in many change situations. J. M. Hunter describes a case in which an American university technical assistance team of professors was meeting with a local counterpart group in a foreign country to work out a public administration curriculum for a proposed night school. During discussions a junior member of the American group took issue with the senior U.S. team member. The senior foreign professor expressed great surprise that a junior would disagree with his superior's point of view. It turned out that the junior of the two host staff members had never been asked his opinion, nor had he expressed his opinion on any of the several points that had been discussed.[38]

Straus has described a similar situation in Ceylon where the well-developed national agricultural extension service has fallen short of expectations, in part, at least, because of the rigidity of that country's hierarchical, authoritarian administrative system. Extension operates from the top down. The department works primarily through drives to get farmers to grow various crops,

[38] J. M. Hunter, 1959, p. 445.

and little attempt is made to find out what the farmer feels he wants. The local extension worker finds himself in an almost untenable position. Usually he is of higher caste than the farmers he serves, and because of this he (and the farmers) know of no relationship other than that based on subordinate-superordinate patterns. At the same time the agent, since he does a technical job in a society that esteems desk and literary work, occupies a low status in his own bureau. Efficient operations, even with the best technical training in the world, are difficult under such conditions.[39]

A similar situation was found in the Indian Community Development Programme. In theory the traditional "boss-subordinate" relationship within the Indian government was expected to yield to a new concept of democratic teamplay. In practice this did not work out. As Dube describes a particular project, the higher officials were unable to view their role other than as that of inspecting officers, and they continued to supervise and appraise the work of their subordinates in the traditional fashion, thus lending a distinct authoritarian tone to their administration. Furthermore, because of their higher status, many resented any views that departed from or questioned their own policies and work. Although in theory subordinates were expected to express themselves freely, in practice they realized it only exasperated their superiors. Since promotion depended on the goodwill of these officers, the underlings found it desirable to adopt an attitude of compliance and agreement. Consequently, communication was largely one way, and subordinates received and executed orders from their official superiors, without making the suggestions that, from experience, they certainly were entitled to make.[40]

Role conflict, stemming from traditional caste patterns, may also hinder innovation. Dube describes how a village level

39 Straus, 1953.
40 Dube, 1958, pp. 90-91.

worker of the Community Development Programme was able
to persuade villagers of the desirability of constructing compost
pits outside the settlement. In general he had the cooperation
of people, who both for aesthetic and hygienic reasons felt it
best to deposit manure outside the village, and they willingly
dug a number of pits. But, even though the village council
passed resolutions making it obligatory for villagers to use the
pits, under pain of fine, many were not utilized. The reason,
Dube found, was that tradition dictates that women must clean
the house and cattle-shed, depositing dung and refuse privately
on or near the property. Even women of the highest castes can
do this, since they are not publicly visible, but it would be
improper for them to be seen carrying such loads through the
streets to compost pits on the outskirts of the village. And since
this activity culturally is defined as women's work, no man
would wish to do so. The few upper caste families that can
afford to hire a servant for this work do so, but in general the
old, unhygienic practice continues.[41]

Basic Configuration of a Society

A single example will illustrate this point. Brown describes
how in Samoa three churches have done serious missionary
work. The Congregational Church has had most success; the
Methodist and Catholic churches have had much less, in spite
of the fact that the elaborate ceremonial of the latter church
undeniably appeals strongly to tribal peoples. Brown believes
the similarity in sociopolitical structure between native Samoa
and the Congregational Church has been the most important
factor in producing this situation. Village autonomy has long
been characteristic of Samoa; federalization and alliances come
into being from time to time, but they are rarely long-lived, so
that ultimately power and authority reside in each village. "The
Congregational Church fitted into this organization because the

[41] *Ibid.*, 1956, p. 22.

individual church is autonomous. It lends itself to village separatism and enables the Samoans to identify church and village as one. . . . The more rigid central control of the Methodists has less appeal. As for the Catholics . . . its hierarchical organization is a serious handicap."[43]

[42] Brown, 1957, p. 14.

7 . . . . *Psychological barriers to change*

When people are confronted with new opportunities, acceptance or rejection depends not only on the basic cultural articulation, on a favorable pattern of social relations, and on economic possibility, but also upon psychological factors. How does the novelty appear to the individual? That is, how does he perceive it? Does he see it in the same light as the technical specialist who presents it to him? Does it convey the same message? Since perception is largely determined by culture, people of different cultures often perceive the same phenomenon in different fashions. In the Mexican village of Tequila the Indians are reluctant to call the priest for the Last Rites for a sick relative, even though they are Catholics. They have noticed that on entirely too many occasions the patient dies shortly after the priest's visit![1]

What the innovator perceives as a decided and obvious advantage may be seen entirely differently by the recipient. It is for this reason that effective communication is so important in programs of directed change. Communication means much

[1] Soustelle, 1958, p. 166.

more than mastering a language and presenting ideas in simple and clear speech; it means that new ideas and techniques must be presented verbally and visually and conceptually so that the recipient perceives the potential advantages in much the same fashion as does the technical agent. This does not mean that change comes about only when these conditions are met, for sometimes people perceive a program in a very different light from that of the innovator, but they still like it and willingly cooperate. For example, people may build latrines, not because they appreciate environmental sanitation but because they perceive the prestige that will accrue to them for their progressive ideas.

Differential perception and faulty communication may be barriers in situations in which the change agent and the recipient have different expectations of the proper role behavior of the other. When physician and patient meet in a cross-cultural setting, lack of mutual understanding sometimes occurs because each, from previous experience in his own culture, expects a form of behavior from the other which in fact does not occur. Consequently, changes in health practices may be fewer than the physician hopes.

Perception and communication also bear upon the problem of learning. In the final analysis permanent change in an individual's behavior means learning and relearning. There is increasing evidence that the difficulties attendant upon learning, even of simple ideas or operations, are not fully appreciated by technical specialists and that, unless a series of favorable conditions is present, acceptance of new ways will be much slower than anticipated. A clear, simple talk and a sound demonstration are often insufficient to teach even new behavior forms which the recipient is quite ready to accept.

In this chapter the problem of psychologically based barriers to change is examined under the categories of basic perception, communication, and learning.

122 · *Traditional cultures*

DIFFERENTIAL CROSS-CULTURAL PERCEPTION

The Problem in General

Dr. Franz Rosa, while stationed in Tehran as a member of a Point Four mission, once urged his gardener and his wife, recently arrived from a village, to divert themselves by attending the free movie at the United States Information Service. The pair were delighted when they returned. Dr. Rosa asked them what it was about. "Oh," they replied, "it was all about the American dictator. He is a very bad man and very crazy, and he has a little black mustache." The movie was Charlie Chaplin's *Great Dictator,* and since he spoke the language of the gardener's employer, they assumed he was the ruler of their country.[2]

Another story illustrating differing perception has been told for several parts of the world. Possibly some of the stories are apocryphal, but the kernel of the story is true. In one version the U.S. Navy landed on a Pacific island in World War II. The health officer felt that the presence of flies constituted a health problem that, with the assistance of the natives, could be easily conquered. He asked the chief to assemble his people, to whom he gave a health lecture illustrating the horrors of fly-borne diseases with a foot-long model of the common house fly. He believed he had made his point until the chief replied, "I can well understand your preoccupation with flies in America. We have flies here, too, but fortunately they are just little fellows," and he gestured with thumb and forefinger to show their small size and, by implication, lack of menace to health.

Paul Fejos tells how, when working on Soembawa Island, a shaman friend was greatly impressed by the magical power of the letter *B,* the Bayer trademark appearing on all the products in Dr. Fejos' medicine chest. After several months the native doctor asked permission to use this powerful magic. "Less ethi-

2 Communicated by Dr. Franz Rosa.

cally, and without the permission of the Bayer Company, I released the copyright, and the letter B within the circle was em-
blazoned on my friend's chest. It gave him a tremendous additional amount of mana, and *de facto* increased his curative
powers."[3]

Health problems, in cross-cultural perspective, seem to pose
a particularly difficult perception problem, if we judge by the
number of examples that have been reported. In Egypt, as in
much of the newly developing world, hospitals are perceived as
places where people go to die and not to get well; consequently,
there is much resistance to hospitalization because the patient
perceives it as meaning his family has lost all hope for him.
This aversion is expressed in a famous saying about the Kasr El
Eini Hospital, the largest in Egypt: "He who enters it will be
lost [dead] and he who comes out of it is born [as a new man]."[4]

The extent to which well-planned health programs can be
misunderstood is illustrated by an episode told by Dr. G. R.
Ross at the Fifth World Health Assembly in Geneva in 1952.
A smallpox epidemic was raging among tribal peoples in Northern Rhodesia where Dr. Ross worked, and health teams were
sent to vaccinate all people to check the spread of the disease.
But the teams had great difficulties. In village after village the
natives had simply disappeared. One day a team found a small
boy in a village, fortunately well on the road to recovery. During the moment while the vaccinating team tried to question
the boy they were quietly surrounded by a group of spear-
bearing adults. Their leader asked the chief vaccinator what he
planned to do with the boy, to which the reply was given that
the boy was recovering and was free to go his way. Then the
vaccinator started to chastise the adults. "We are your friends,
your people are dying, we can stamp out the disease, and we
have come to help you. Why do you reject our help?" To which

[3] Fejos, 1959, pp. 28-29.
[4] Communicated by Dr. Fawzy Gadalla.

the native leader replied, "Six months ago our cattle were dying of something you called 'hoof and mouth disease.' You came, and you said, 'We are your friends, your cattle are dying, we can stamp out the disease, we have come to help you.' We permitted you to help us, and you killed all of our cattle!"[5]

A high incidence of congenital hip dislocation—1,090 per 100,000 as compared to 3.8 in New York City—afflicts the Navaho Indians. The condition can be treated successfully by nonsurgical means during the first couple of years of life, and surgically during the next several years. But at later ages "freezing" the hip, which eliminates motion, is the only way to prevent probable painful arthritis beginning at the age of 40 or 45. This is the accepted treatment in American culture, and when medical workers discovered the high Navaho incidence, they assumed this was the answer to the problem among Indians. This was not so. The condition was not considered to be really serious, and perhaps it was actually a blessing, since fate, having dealt this minor deformity, was thought less likely to strike a family with greater ill fortune. Among the Navaho, congenital hip is not a barrier to marrying and having children. But, for a Navaho, a frozen hip is a serious problem: he cannot sit comfortably on the ground or on a sheepskin to eat with his family, and he cannot ride horseback. These handicaps more than offset the thought of disability twenty or thirty years in the future, disabilities which may not come anyway. "From the viewpoint of the Navaho . . . the sole contribution of modern medicine to the question of congenital hip disease was to transform something that was no real handicap, and was almost a blessing, into something that represented a very serious handicap indeed."[6]

Differential perception has also affected agricultural programs. In an Indian village the extension agent encountered difficulty in introducing improved seed to be used for new pur-

[5] Recorded by the author May 16, 1952 as Dr. Ross told the story.
[6] McDermott *et al.,* 1960, p. 281.

poses. There the farmers grew a degenerate local variety of pea which they used as animal fodder, but when the agent introduced a superior edible variety, the people continued to view it as a fodder crop, and, being unfamiliar with peas as food, they wondered why they should spend more to buy a seed for a crop to be grown for animal consumption. There was resistance to other vegetables as well. People perceived vegetables as a delicacy, an embellishment to their diet, but not as a staple or necessary item. For reasons of novelty and prestige a few people raised small plots of new vegetables, but because of their traditional attitude toward them as food, little effort was made to extend this cultivation.[7]

Perception of the Role of Government

In the world today a majority of programs of planned change are carried out through government agencies. Yet in many areas, and particularly among the lower classes and rural groups, suspicion of the motives of government and its representatives is widespread. The demands of taxation, of military conscription, and other forms of interference that emanate from cities have taught the villager that the less he has to do with government the better off he will be. An early program of social work in Egypt was hampered by this fact. Getting acquainted with villagers was not easy, ". . . because social work in its modern form was not known even to many well-educated persons in the area, and because of the suspicion of the *fellaheen,* many of whom were doubtful about any move to change or improve the conditions of their life. *Government officials came to uphold the laws, to gather taxes, to follow criminals, or to fine them for their actions, which were usually the result of their ignorance and misunderstanding of state laws*"[8] The anthropologist Ammar has also pointed out how

[7] Dube, 1956, pp. 20-21.
[8] King, 1958, p. 39. (Italics mine.)

Egyptian villagers consider both government and government officials to be agencies of imposition and control, and hence to be feared. "To keep away from governmental institutions was always the safest policy."[9] In similar vein Erasmus describes the reaction of South American farmers. "Generally," he writes, "farmers are suspicious of government authorities and prefer to let someone else try the new technic before they adopt it."[10]

When since time immemorial the presence of a government agent in a village has meant bad luck, it is not hard to understand why villagers are skeptical when an agricultural extension agent, a medical man, or an educator comes and says, "I'm different. I'm your friend. I'm here to help you." Attitudes stemming from the experience of centuries change slowly. Neisser points this out in connection with a community development and mass education program in Nigeria. In the several villages where work was first done intensively results were good, but when the campaign was spread to more distant villages, she found that "it took several years for the people beyond these experimental villages to overcome their deep-seated suspicion that the government was 'playing a trick' on them and would take away all the new buildings sooner or later."[11]

In India the government attempted to combat endemic goiter in the Himalaya foothills by selling iodized salt below cost and below the price of commercially traded uniodized salt. This step, the government believed, would drive the latter salt off the market and medical goals would be achieved. But the fact that the salt was sponsored by the government convinced the people that it was worthless and quite possibly dangerous. To get people to use this salt it was necessary to declare salt a government monopoly.[12]

In much of the world the technical specialist's initial handi-

9 Ammar, 1954, p. 81.
10 Erasmus, 1954, p. 153.
11 Neisser, 1955, p. 355.
12 Communicated by Dr. G. S. Seghal.

cap stems not only from the fact that he is likely to be a government agent, but also from the simple fact that he is an outsider, an unknown quantity. In Sirkanda, a Himalaya village, anything unfamiliar—a person or a program of change—is regarded with suspicion. "To take a stranger's advice and change accepted practices would be foolhardy."[13] Technical aid specialists, with their missionary zeal, sometimes forget how strange they appear to villagers upon first contact, and how long it takes for people to be convinced that they are experiencing something new in human relations.

Suspicion of the government agent and the stranger is not limited to rural areas of newly developing countries. When Margaret Clark began her research among Spanish-speaking people in Sal si Puedes in San Jose, California, and particularly when she took a census, she found much resistance. It took a long time and much hard work before her new friends really believed she was not a government worker in disguise. When Dr. Clark made a list of the strangers who were most likely to appear at the door, the results were startling: truant officer with the news that a child had been playing hookey from school, a deputy sheriff or a representative of the juvenile court informing a mother that her adolescent son was in a scrape with the law, an immigration authority checking on documents, a sanitarian suspecting substandard sanitary facilities, a building inspector wishing to make sure no code was being violated, tax assessors, FBI agents, and many others. All these people, not surprisingly, "are viewed as potential threats to the security of barrio people."[14] Obviously, a major problem of workers in developmental programs is to establish a role as friend and helper in a society which traditionally has had few or none such roles.

[13] Berreman, 1959, p. 605.
[14] Clark, 1959, p. 232.

128 · Traditional cultures

Perception of Gifts

Another aspect of differential perception sometimes not fully appreciated has to do with gifts. In many technical aid programs it has been deemed desirable, because of the obvious poverty of the people, to offer commodities and services without cost. Acceptance of such programs often has been negligible. The reason appears to be that in many situations people interpret a gift as something without value; if something has value, they reason, no one would be so foolish as to give it away. Hence, the mere act of offering something for nothing is interpreted by potential recipients as meaning that the offering is not worth the trouble to collect or use it. But frequently it has been found that if a token price is placed upon services and facilities, people will accept what they otherwise reject.

When the Colombian government, in a program to increase fruit production, gave seedling orchard trees to farmers in one province, few of the trees were planted, and many of those planted died for lack of care. The following year the program was repeated, but this time a nominal charge was made for each tree. Demand was brisk, and the trees planted received much better care. The farmers perceived value in trees that cost something, and therefore felt they were worth caring for.[15]

When powdered milk was first distributed in Chilean health centers, it was given gratis because of the poverty of mothers who attended maternal and child health clinics. But few mothers would use the milk; they suspected it was of poor quality or downright harmful. A free gift, in their experience, was suspect. Subsequently a token charge was made for milk; the mothers then perceived that in the eyes of clinic personnel the milk had value, and shortly the supply could not keep up with the demand.[16] Similarly, in a new health center in San Juan Zacatepequez, Guatemala, no charge was made for visits. Pa-

[15] Communicated by Dr. Charles J. Erasmus.
[16] Communicated by Dr. Victoria García.

tronage was poor and suspicion of the purpose of the center was high. Subsequently a flat charge of 20 centavos was adopted for all patients, regardless of the nature of their visit or its real cost. Health center personnel believe that this act of giving value to services rendered was very important in developing the present high utilization of center facilities.[17]

This same problem aróse in the Rockefeller antihookworm program in Ceylon in the early years of this century: the very fact that the treatment was free was suspicious. A Moorish physician attached to the program countered this suspicion among his coreligionists with what is certainly one of the most justifiable of all white lies: he told them that Mr. John D. Rockefeller had been very ill with hookworm and had been cured, and out of gratitude to Allah he had given all his money to cure everyone else who had the disease. The account concludes, "May Allah and Mr. Rockefeller forgive this deliberate falsehood, if it should come to their attention."[18] This story illustrates, in addition to the perception of free goods, a very important point with respect to planned culture change: the Moslem physician, familiar with the religious beliefs of his patients, was able to answer their doubts and cast his program in terms that fitted the culturally-determined expectations of the people as to why a man would want to give something for nothing.

Most of the examples I have encountered suggest the wisdom of conferring value on goods and services by making nominal charges. In one of the hospitals for children in Alexandria, Egypt, the outpatient clinic was badly overcrowded. The administration suspected that a good many mothers brought their children just to have an excuse to visit with other mothers, or to have a reason to get away from their cloistered homes. Since the services had been free it was decided to collect a small fee

[17] Communicated by Miss Mariana Flores.
[18] Philips, 1955, p. 291.

in the belief that this would limit visits to those children actually in need of attention. To the astonishment of the hospital administration, the number of patients almost doubled. The mothers believed that now that a charge was being made, the services must be much better than when they were free.[19]

Marriott also believes that payment for health services increases rather than diminishes their utilization. In an experimental health clinic in an Indian village where he worked the attempt was made to present Western medicine in the most favorable light possible. The technical quality of services was high; patients were dealt with as individuals of equal worth to personnel; examination, diagnosis, and dressings were given free; and medicine was offered at costs far below market prices. Yet many villagers were disappointed and distrustful when they learned how cheap and simple the physician's treatments were. The author concludes that "Western medicine might gain much and lose little if the asking prices of aspirin and bicarbonate of soda, for example, were adjusted upward to create an aura of quality that would engender confidence in the curative value of these useful products."[20]

Differential Role Perception

In every society, people learn the behavior that is appropriate to them and that they may expect from others, in an infinite number of situations in which they find themselves. Differing perceptions of role behavior frequently cause difficulties in intercultural settings, because the members of each group are faced with behavior which they do not expect or do not believe to be appropriate to the setting, and in turn they are unsure as to what may be expected of them.

A widespread example is that of the patient-physician interview when the former comes from a background in which the

[19] Communicated by Dr. Fawzy Gadalla.
[20] Marriott, 1955, p. 255.

folk medical curer has given the dominant image of what to expect from a healer. Usually such curers, regardless of the part of the world from which they come, differ from scientifically trained physicians in that they do not ask for a case history. Often they divine the nature and cause of the complaint in some mystical or magical fashion. Also, they work in a leisurely fashion; they are expected to have unlimited time to be with the patient. Furthermore, they are thought of as friends who are not preoccupied with immediate payment. Since their curing ability sometimes reflects supernatural power, a gift of superior forces, they are not expected to take financial advantage of someone else's need. Instead, at a later time, when the patient is well, he may give a present to the leader in appreciation of his services.

When patients with this image of the role of the curer find themselves in a physician's office, they are often puzzled, offended, and perhaps rebellious. "Where does it hurt?" asks the physician. "Tell me how you feel. How long has this gone on? Have you been afflicted in this way on other occasions?" and so on. The patient perceives this questioning to mean that the physician is not well trained or not very smart. If the folk curer, he reasons, does not need to ask questions, why is it that a physician who claims far greater knowledge must ask them? Further, the patient is disturbed because this new curer seems anxious to hurry him along, to get him out of the office. Perhaps, too, he has been offended because the nurse asked about immediate payment. The patient may lapse into sullen silence, and the interview stalls.

The physician, on the other hand, is used to treating patients who expect to be asked questions, who realize that the doctor is busy and has little time, and who assume payment for services rendered is just. Such a physician is puzzled by the behavior of the patient from a different cultural background, and he may become angered and irritated at his mute subject. At best the patient appears stupid, he reasons, and at worst he is downright uncooperative. Culturally-determined behavioral expectations— the differential perception of roles—have produced a near-hopeless situation.

Anthony Barker, in a beautifully written account of medical-mission practice among the Zulu, describes this situation.

> Real difficulties arise from the patients' conception of a correct approach to the doctor. In Europe it is accepted as the patient's duty to put his doctor in possession of any relevant facts about his symptoms, their intensity and duration, the history of any previous attacks of the same nature, and any other information which the doctor may require to guide his examination and arrive at a diagnosis. Among African patients such communicativeness is considered to be mere weakness, giving away far too much and leaving no opportunity for the doctor to demonstrate his skill for which he is being paid. Such complaints as are made frequently owe more to a sense of the picturesque and a respect for tradition than to the literal Anglo-Saxon truth.[21]

On the other hand, in many instances physicians have been so successful in selling the superiority of their techniques that, unwittingly, they have created new but incorrect perceptions in the minds of their patients about the nature of modern medicine. In most parts of the world the wonder-working hypodermic needle has come to be associated with good medical practice. If people go to a physician they expect an injection, and if they do not receive it, they suspect that the physician is deceiving them or that he is not a competent medical man. The prescription of oral medicine or of different diet does not meet their expectations for modern medicine.

The belief in the efficacy of the hypodermic is so firmly established in some places that round-about measures must be taken to give proper treatment. In the new Dominion of Nigeria the

21 Barker, 1959, p. 65.

injection is as popular as elsewhere. Dr. Adeniji Adeniyi-Jones
tells me that, when internal medicine is indicated, he sometimes
has found it necessary to give patients a simultaneous injection
of a saline solution. "We attack the illness in two ways," he
tells them. "Medicine goes into your stomach through the
mouth, and into your body with the injection. When the two
meet inside you they react powerfully and cure the disease."
This explanation usually satisfies patients.

In the same country, pre-penicillin treatment for yaws not
infrequently was accompanied by inflammation where the injection was given because of poor antiseptic measures. This
infection came, in the minds of patients, to be a part of the
cure, proof that the medicine was in fact doing its job. When
the far superior penicillin treatment was introduced, public
confidence was lost because there was no accompanying infection. Eventually it became necessary to add an irritant to the
penicillin, to produce a mild local reaction following the injection. Then the patients' expectation was met; the reaction was
proof that the treatment was valid.[22]

Differing Perception of Purpose

In a slightly different sense, differing perception of purpose
or goals of programs between planners and technicians, on the
one hand, and recipient peoples, on the other, may hinder
change. There have been occasions when technicians felt that
their work was going well and that their programs and goals
were understood and approved by the people with whom they
worked, and then, for no apparent reason, people appeared to
lose interest or seemed unwilling to follow all the way through.
Such cases often are due to the expectation of recipient peoples
for fewer or different services; when their minimum expectations are met they are quite happy and see no need to ask for
more. For example, in a fine public health center in an area of

[22] Communicated by Dr. Adeniji Adeniyi-Jones.

Pittsburgh, with a mixed Negro, foreign, and low-income white American population, patients came willingly a time or two for immunization and other tangible services, but they failed to return for routine examinations. Research revealed that the mothers were entirely satisfied with the attentions they received, but these limited services were all they expected or wanted, and they saw no reason to continue to come for advice they didn't think they needed.[23]

Erasmus describes a similar experience in Haiti. A group of small landowners were provided with irrigation water on a block of about 50 acres. They harvested a much improved rice crop and were delighted with the results. Next an attempt was made to improve the land still further by contour leveling across property boundaries, but this was unsuccessful. "The owners, already satisfied with their increased production, could not see how leveling would result in sufficient further increase to justify the price they would be required to pay."[24] As in Pittsburgh, with minimum expectations satisfied, patrons saw no need for additional services.

COMMUNICATION PROBLEMS

In the process of communication someone initiates action in the form of symbols which usually are verbal or visual or a combination of both. Someone else interprets these symbols in accordance with a culturally determined understanding of what they mean. When both parties are in basic agreement as to the meaning of the symbols, successful communication results. To the extent that people share a common language and culture, their communication is made easy: it will be recalled that facilitation of communication is one of the basic functions of culture. People who speak the same language "agree" upon the

[23] Communicated by Miss Mary Fox Arnold.
[24] Erasmus, 1952, p. 22.

meaning of the sounds and sequence of the verbal symbols that make up language. They perceive them in the same way, and consequently they are able to understand each other without difficulty. Visual symbols function in the same way. Common gestures such as "come," "go," or "wait" are communication devices which are mutually understood by members of the same culture. To most Americans a dancing and singing beer can on a TV screen means, not that someone has perfected a remarkable new can, but that someone wants to tell us that this is good beer.

Members of distinct cultures may make use of the same or similar symbols, but usually the meanings that are attached to these symbols are different. Consequently, when members of one culture are exposed to the symbols of another culture, these symbols are either misinterpreted, or not understood at all. For example, the French name "Jean" is recognized by literate Americans as a printed symbol for a name. The Frenchman pronounces it (approximately) "John," and thinks of a man. The American pronounces it "Jeen," and thinks of a woman. The same symbol, but with different meanings, results in faulty communication. In Mexico the thumb and forefinger of the hand held closely together and slightly vibrated tells the observer to "wait just a minute." To the untutored American, recently arrived in Mexico, this symbol is meaningless.

Language Difficulties

Verbal communication problems which exist between speakers of different languages are apparent to all. What is not always fully appreciated is that serious difficulties may exist between people who presumably speak the same language, for in a large and complex society the total range of linguistic symbols and associated meanings is so great that no one person can master them all. Consequently, the members of subgroups within societies utilize specialized vocabularies and ways of expressing themselves which facilitate communication among themselves, but which are not fully comprehensible to nonmembers. American teen-age slang probably in some measure is unintelligible to most parents. Again, members of professions and trades, such as doctors, lawyers, college professors, carpenters, plumbers, electricians, all use specialized words and expressions. It becomes so much second nature to speak in one's subdialect that it is easy to forget that these professional "shorthands" often are not effective devices to communicate with people who are not members of the group, even though they are members of the same culture and speak the same basic language. Again, some professionals confuse a complicated jargon with profundity and try to impress others with their mastery of a field by concealing their meaning with a welter of words. It is easy to slip into a professional lingo, almost without knowing it, and a periodic review of how one is expressing ideas is salutary for most of us.

A brief news item in the *San Francisco Chronicle,* on February 20, 1956, offered a good example of poor communication. The story, datelined London, read as follows: "During the worst weather of the century the British Automobile Association offered this comment on road conditions: 'Never since the motor car became an integral part of the social fabric has road paralysis on this scale been experienced before.'" The *Chronicle* headed the article "That is to say, road conditions are plain lousy!"

Medical personnel are among the worst offenders with respect to poor communication. Clark reports the case of a physician in a maternal-and-child-health clinic in a Spanish-speaking community in the United States who gave routine weaning instructions to a young mother with limited command of English: "Apply a tight pectoral binding and restrict your fluid intake." The physician was especially sympathetic to her Spanish-speaking patients and realized they presented special problems. Yet it had never occurred to her that her routine speech habits were actually a function of a highly specialized profession and that a good many educated American women would have to think twice before they understood her.[25]

Social science research in medical programs in Latin America indicates that poor communication between physicians and nurses, on the one hand, and health center clinic patients on the other, sometimes prevents maximum efficiency. In 1952 I attended a "mothers' club" meeting in Temuco, Chile, in which an intelligent and well-trained public health nurse talked to about twenty expectant mothers on the problems of pregnancy. Previously a physician had advised them to "walk three kilometers a day," and the nurse repeated this instruction. I asked, and received permission, to interject a question: "How far *is* three kilometers?" This precipitated a lively argument. Some mothers said nine blocks, others twenty-seven, and a few eighty-one. No agreement was reached. The mothers had learned their lesson, but in the real sense, there had been no communication, because these instructions were meaningless. These women simply were not trained to think in terms of distance as an educated person would. If this important instruction had been phrased as "walk to the plaza and back," or "to the market and then to the church," or to whatever specific places known to them would give the approximate desired exercise, real communication would have existed.

Isabel Kelly noted a similar occurrence in Mexico. In a maternal-and-child-health clinic, the Mexican physician told the mother to nurse her child "every three hours." When the anthropologist asked the mother at what hours she would feed the child, she replied, "At six, seven, eight," and so on. The startled doctor repeated his instructions, but the mother still gave the same answer. Instructions in terms of time as defined by hours were meaningless to this woman. She had no clock, she was unable to tell time, and in her life experience it had never been

25 Communicated by Dr. Margaret Clark.

necessary to grasp the import of time as understood in hours.[26]

Demonstration Dangers

It is in part because of the recognized limitations in linguistic communication that visual symbols, in the form of demonstrations, posters, films, and the like are so important in developmental programs. Yet even here there are dangers that the meaning of the symbols to the initiator of the action will not be the meaning attached by the observers. In New Zealand a successful health education poster designed to encourage students to brush their teeth showed a whale jumping out of the water in pursuit of a tube of toothpaste. This poster was reproduced for use in Fiji. The response was immediate and overwhelming: Fiji fishermen sent a rush call to New Zealand for large quantities of this wonderful new fish bait![27]

As a part of the health program at Cornell University's Hacienda Vicos Peruvian project, an American color film teaching the transmission of typhus by lice was shown to the Indian workers and their families. The film was previewed by health personnel, who felt it would be understood by the local people, who had been plagued by lice all their lives. Selected members of the Indian community received special instructions about lice and how they transmit disease, in the hope that they could further explain the problem to their fellows. At the showing the physician explained, through an interpreter, the principal facts of transmission.

A week later members of the audience were asked questions to see how effective the health education project had been. It became apparent that the message had not gotten across and that the louse as a vector was not understood. First, the viewers said they had lice but, as in the case of the fly model on the Pacific Island (Chapter 7), they had never seen giant lice like

26 Foster, 1952, p. 12. (Kelly is reported in Foster article.)
27 Communicated by Miss Merle S. Farland, R. N.

those shown on the screen so they didn't see the connection. Second, they said they had never seen sick people like those shown in the film, who had a curious and unpleasant white and rosy color. Perhaps, they speculated, this was a disease that afflicted other kinds of people, but again they saw no connection with their own problems. Finally, since they were not familiar with movies, they did not perceive the episodes in the film as a continuum, but rather as a great many odd scenes with no visible relationship.[28]

In this example the health program, while not appreciably furthered, was probably not seriously hampered. On other occasions unsuccessful demonstrations, or demonstrations that are carelessly carried out, may actually prejudice the viewers. In programs of directed culture change a skillful demonstration is undeniably one of the most effective communication techniques. In agricultural work, for example, the extension agent will ask for the loan of a small plot of land which will be cultivated in a fashion considered to be superior to traditional ways and in which improved seed will be used. If the work is based on careful research, and if the agent knows the proper steps, the demonstration plot should produce a greater yield than adjacent fields cultivated with the old methods. Or the agent may request permission to fertilize a part of a field so that the results may be compared with the unfertilized area.

But if demonstration and other techniques are not skillfully carried out they may actually set back programs, thereby constituting barriers to subsequent change. Viewers perceive what actually happens and not what ought to happen. The need for workers in change programs is so great that not infrequently imperfectly trained people have been asked to do work for which they were not yet fully prepared. In 1955 I spoke with an East Pakistan peasant who complained that the local village worker was incompetent. It turned out that the worker had put

[28] Communicated by Dr. Carlos Alfaro.

140 · Traditional cultures

too much ammonium sulphate fertilizer on the peasant's bottle gourd plant and the plant died. In an area in West Pakistan a number of people vaccinated against smallpox subsequently died of the illness; investigation revealed that the vaccine had lost its potency because of lack of refrigeration. Vaccinators who came the following year found their task almost hopeless. In India in the same year I noted cases in which highly touted "improved" seed had not been thoroughly tested for the local area. It turned out that local soil and climatic conditions were sufficiently different from those of the experimental station that the "improved" seed proved to be inferior to the local variety. Here again the agricultural extension agent subsequently found farmers to be skeptical of his claim that he could help them increase crop yields.

These dangers are particularly great when local workers are under pressure from their superiors to show results for national targets. Dube tells of instances in which village level workers in India were under orders to do things which were clearly unsound. In some cases the seed sent to project headquarters obviously was inferior, and it was apparent that its use would not produce the desired and promised results. In spite of this the village level workers were under pressure to distribute it. Their misgivings were amply justified, and the harvest was very poor. "In the following year the VLWs found it difficult to sell more seed, though this time it was certainly excellent in quality."[29]

A demonstration can be successful, and the results can be as promised, and yet fail. In a chicken farming program among Mexican Indians the dangers of Newcastle disease were explained, the method of inoculation was demonstrated, and the birds in the demonstration area were protected. But a number of hens died of other diseases against which they had not been protected. This convinced the Indians that the advice about inoculation was worthless.

[29] Dube, 1958, p. 187.

LEARNING PROBLEMS

The adoption of new ideas and techniques means that people must learn (and often, "unlearn"). The psychology of learning has been well studied and described in recent years, but an awareness of the complexity of the process has not always been translated into action in developmental programs. On one level, Dube has pointed out how Indian village level workers have complained because they felt inadequately trained for some of the tasks assigned them.[30] Tasks which seem perfectly simple to one who has mastered them may appear very difficult, and perhaps not worth attempting, to people who have not had opportunity to master them. During recent field work in the Mexican village of Tzintzuntzan I was impressed with the importance of a combination of learning circumstances favoring the acquisition of new techniques. Two examples will illustrate.

About 1950 the local tax collector, an outsider, brought the first bicycle to the village. His assistant, a local youth, had as one duty tending the gasoline pump that provided water for the village. The pump was located about a mile away, on a good road. By foot the daily round trip meant an hour or more; by bicycle it could be accomplished in fifteen minutes. The young man quickly learned to ride the tax collector's bicycle and saved money to buy his own.

In a second case a local housewife took up the use of a simple home press that greatly speeds tortilla-making, an operation that in many Mexican homes requires two or three hours daily. Her niece had visited her for some months, bringing her press from a distant town, and taught the aunt the techniques. The aunt was delighted and soon acquired her own press.

In these two instances, the same combination of circumstances was present. First, there was the *continuing presence of a teacher,* over a number of days, to give instruction at the

[30] *Ibid.,* p. 184.

instant it was wanted: learning was not based on a quick and hurried demonstration or two. Second, the learners both *had the opportunity to try the novelty,* to practice on it without investing money. Their interest in no way threatened the basic security of their families or diverted funds to untested ends. Third, each had the opportunity *to convince himself of the utility* of the innovation before making a financial investment. They didn't have to make their payments on faith, on the say-so of someone else, but only after they had tried and seen the results. Fourth, the *cost of the novelties was in both cases within the resources* of the learners. If any of the four conditions had been absent, it is much less likely that the innovations would have been adopted.

I suspect that this, or a similar combination of favorable circumstances, will be found in many instances of successful mastery of new techniques, and, to the extent that such circumstances can be created, innovation will be promoted.

8 . . . . *Stimulants to change*

In the face of the imposing series of barriers to change presented in the preceding chapters, one may well wonder how advances can ever be made. Part of the answer was given in discussing barriers: look for ways to neutralize or get around them, or select areas for initial work where they are weak. For example, fear of novelty is a common thing, yet in any region there always seem to be progressive individuals and communities. If work is started in such villages and with such people, the chances for success are greater than if work begins with more conservative elements. My recent research in Tzintzuntzan, Mexico, where about two thirds of the families earn all or part of their living from pottery-making, shows that as a class potters are measurably more conservative than farmers or fishermen, who make up the remainder of the families. Although Tzintzuntzan has been a major target for UNESCO's Latin American Fundamental Education Training Center (CREFAL) in Pátzcuaro, developmental results have been modest and less impressive than those in some adjacent nonpottery towns. There is a good deal of evidence to suggest that the conservatism of Tzintzuntzan reflects a basic conservatism in the psychological make-up of potters in other parts of the world. As a rule-of-thumb guide to community development work, I would suggest that new community development programs avoid pottery-making villages as initial targets.

The strategy of planned development involves not only identification and neutralization of barriers to change, but also the identification and utilization of a series of positive factors—likewise cultural, social, and psychological—which constantly oppose the forces of conservatism and which may be thought of, for lack of a better expression, as stimulants to change. When in a particular society stimulants are few and poorly developed, the culture remains static; when they are numerous and strong, change comes about readily. Speaking of community development, Jackson states the picture clearly:

> When a village is faced with a suggestion of change, there exists a balance of forces. On one side of the scales are those forces which are against change—conservatism, apathy, fear and and like; on the other side are the forces for change—dissatisfaction with existing conditions, village pride, and so on. Successful community development consists largely of choosing those projects where the balance is almost even, and then trying to lighten the forces against change or to increase the factors making for change.[1]

An understanding of psychological motivations is basic to planned change, yet change depends on much more than the presence of adequate desire to try something new. Motivations for a general change may be strong, but unless the innovation fits local cultural, social, and ideological values, it will have a weak reception. The example of village water-supply systems will be recalled (Chapter 1). People usually are happy to have a convenient source of water, but unless a host of supporting factors exists the chances of a successful project are slim. Commu-

[1] Jackson, 1956, p. 30.

nity laundries with batteries of washtubs (Chapter 6) also illustrate how a social fit was worked out, whereby the small-group values of washerwomen were not disturbed but vastly greater convenience was provided.

As a general rule, then, we may say that to the extent that existing cultural and social values can be maintained in project planning, an environment is created in which a variety of individual and group motivations will operate—motivations which will ultimately determine the success or failure of a program. In some instances, of course, change is produced by fiat or decree: landlords may tell their tenants to do something, and they may have no choice but to obey. A government may decide that everyone will be vaccinated against smallpox, and troops can be utilized to ensure that the work is done. More often, however, planned programs of change are based on the assumption that true success comes primarily when people make decisions voluntarily. For this reason it is particularly important to understand the kinds of motivations that are most effective in inducing change. These motivations, of course, apply to all change situations, and not just to those that are planned. Successful workers, however, are those who understand motivation and cast their programs in such fashion that maximum utilization can be made of them.

MOTIVATIONS TO CHANGE

Motivations are of different types and generality. Some are "culture-bound," in that their presence or absence is a function of characteristics of particular cultures. For example, religious beliefs in some cultures offer motivations to certain kinds of change, but in other cultures these motivations are weak or lacking. In post-Reformation Protestant Europe the desire to find salvation through personal interpretation of the Scriptures placed a great premium on literacy. A religious motivation—the desire to read the Bible—thus helps explain the world's first mass literacy development. On the other hand, in Catholic Europe, interpretation of the Bible was reserved to the Church, and except for the priesthood the religious motivation for literacy was less pronounced. In 1955 in India I found that the desire to be able to read the sacred scriptures of the Gita, and hence to enjoy a more secure place in afterlife, motivated some people to learn to read, in a fashion reminiscent of early Protestantism.[2] In most of the modern world, however, it seems likely that—as in ancient Mesopotamia—commercial needs probably will be the single greatest motivating factor in literacy in the long run.

Again, competition and the competitive situation often are strong motivations for change. These are not, however, cultural universals, for in some societies it is considered bad manners to attempt to excel one's fellows. Ruth Benedict has pointed out that psychological intelligence tests given to Dakota Indian children were meaningless because of a cultural taboo against giving any answer in the presence of someone who did not know the answer. In other American Indian societies a person is trained never to answer a question or state a fact unless he is absolutely sure of himself.[3] Obviously, in such societies the competitive motivation will be of far less importance in bringing change than among native white Americans.

Other kinds of motivations seem to be universal or near-universal in that they cut across all kinds of societies and cultures and are found in some degree almost everywhere. These motivations include such things as the desire for prestige or for economic gain, the wish to comply with friendship obligations, and the like. In the following discussion no formal attempt is made to separate universal and culture-bound motivations, although, when the evidence is good, limitations to the appeal of certain types are pointed out.

2 Adams, Foster, and Taylor, 1955, p. 56.
3 Benedict, 1940, pp. 111,

Motivations are, of course, of very different intensities. In my experience two stand out far above all others, and these probably are responsible for the great majority of changes that have occurred and are now occurring. The first of these is the desire for prestige and higher status, and the second is the attraction of economic gain. Both motivations are related, since economic gain usually enhances one's status, but for analytical purposes it is simpler to consider them apart.

Desire for Prestige

In the modern world there appears to be a near-universal desire to emulate in some degree the behavior of people we feel occupy a higher position than we do. The savage is delighted with a black silk top hat and the middle-class American strives for a high-priced automobile. For both the urge is the same. Increased prestige is achieved through acquisition of or modification in certain visible symbols such as food, clothing, housing, material items, and speech patterns. Dube points out, for example, how the prestige factor is significant in bringing change to Indian villages. Modern Indian, as well as Western clothes, cigarettes, sun-glasses and tea are popular both because of their utility and because they possess great prestige value. Moreover, "those who have urban contacts seek to distinguish themselves from the ordinary village folk in their dress, manner of speech, food and recreations. Imitation of urban ways in the last decade and a half has come to be recognized as a distinguishing feature of respectable elements of the village population."[4]

Hoyt notes a similar development in Africa, where goods and services associated with prestige are in great demand among tribal peoples. "Very often the most prestige-carrying goods are something to wear, both because what is worn is conspicuous and because such goods, though not necessarily inexpensive, are relatively so compared with housing, house equipment, and

[4] Dube, 1955, p. 229.

vehicles. . . . Recently there has been a great run in British East Africa for dark spectacles, so much so that an African character wearing dark spectacles is used to typify a vain simpleton, the reason being that dark spectacles are desired for dress wear at social events after the sun has set."[5] In similar vein Hogbin has found that in Melanesia the prestige factor largely accounts for the use of corrugated iron roofs on the better homes, which is more durable, but less comfortable, than the old sago-palm thatch.[6]

In influencing food habits, too, the prestige factor cuts across cultural boundaries, often to the detriment of the health of the individual. In modern India, Jelliffe has noted that mothers of the lower socioeconomic groups in Calcutta increasingly spend money on highly advertised, patented, powdered carbohydrate foods which have prestige value, rather than on milk and other locally produced foods which represent better nutritional value for the same expenditures. He also points out how two species of fish are raised in the "pond-fish" programs of community development programs. Both are of equal nutritional value, but one is considered high class, while the other is low class and "snakelike." Relative demand is illustrated by the fact that the latter sells at about half the price of the former.[7] In Wales, writes Rees, "Bought food is considered more elegant than that which is home-produced, and the guest is frequently honoured with tinned salmon or *Spam*."[8] He tells how on one occasion a farmer's wife served him ham and eggs for supper, apologizing that she had nothing else in the house!

In the southeastern United States Cussler and De Give found that among rural peoples foods of prestige value, such as those that are purchased rather than home-grown and those thought to be preferred by the upper classes, are desired by lower-class

[5] Hoyt, 1956, p. 14.
[6] Hogbin, 1958, pp. 85-86.
[7] Jelliffe, 1957, p. 137.
[8] Rees, 1951, p. 29.

people. The authors conclude that prestige is much more important than health education and other rational programs in determining changes in dietary patterns.[9]

In health programs also the prestige factor often seems to outweigh other motivations in leading people to new habits. In Latin America and in India and Pakistan, I have noted that latrines frequently are installed not because of an appreciation of the desirability of environmental sanitation, but because they add an extra note of elegance to a man's home, and he thereby rises in importance in the eyes of his peers. In Egypt, modern medicine is making some progress because "In serious cases the doctor's help is usually sought besides the traditional cures, and it is becoming a sign of social prestige to bring him into the home of the sick."[10]

Friedl points out a similar phenomenon in Greece, where the rivalry between village families for prestige is promoting increased use of hospitals. "Hospital care is believed to be the sophisticated, urban way of caring for serious illness and childbirth. Hospitalization therefore can enhance family prestige." This point of view is stimulated by the visits of high-prestige urban relatives who stress the superiority of city doctors over their country counterparts. Hospitalization in nearby cities and towns is the best way to enjoy the attentions of urban physicians. "The result is that childbirth and the care of serious illness at home has come to be associated with low social position and low income, hospital care with high social position."[11]

In many newly developing countries the traditional status of nurses and midwives has been very low; they have been looked upon as menials, often of lax moral standards. Consequently, with developing health services in these countries, it is often difficult to recruit educated and intelligent girls for this work.

[9] Cussler and De Give, 1952, pp. 36-37, 91.
[10] Ammar, 1954, p. 79.
[11] Friedl, 1958, p. 26.

In some places the prestige factor has in part overcome this problem. When I visited El Salvador in 1951 the head of the new School of Nursing was a daughter of one of the most important families in the country, and she had been well trained in the United States. The prestige of her status was such that other girls who would have been reluctant to enter nursing were drawn into the profession. Similarly, about 1954 a two-year school for midwives was established in Kabul, Afghanistan. It was hoped that with a corps of well-trained women better pre- and postnatal practices, as well as delivery conditions, could be introduced into the country. Because of extreme restrictions of purdah, even women of the upper classes usually could receive no scientific medical attention. The Minister of Health described the need for this program to the Prime Minister, who enthusiastically replied. "I'll ask my daughters if they don't want to take the course." Two of them did, and at the time of my visit in 1957 one was director of the school. The prestige of the Prime Minister's approval, as evidenced by his willingness to allow his daughters to take the training, attracted girls from other families of high status, and the program is rated as highly successful. By contrast, a French-style Faculty of Nursing was established about 1940 in the University, but the traditional low prestige attached to nursing in France has carried over. The school has had difficulty in attracting competent candidates and must draw them from the lower-middle classes, where education is minimal.[12]

Desire for Economic Gain

In earlier chapters examples were given showing how social and cultural factors have caused people to forego economic gain: the Peruvian fisherman, the Sioux Indians, and the maize-growers in the American Southwest. Yet in the final analysis these attitudes appear to be a delaying or holding action, rather

[12] Communicated by His Excellency Dr. A. Zahir, Minister of Health.

than a definitive barrier. Sooner or later the economic pull seems certain to outweigh other factors. Demonstration techniques, especially in agricultural extension programs, capitalize on this fact. In 1955 in the Philippines I was shown extensive rice fields planted with improved methods. A few successful demonstrations a year earlier had convinced farmers to cultivate hundreds of acres with the new techniques.

There is convincing evidence to show that the taste factor is significant in discouraging some new crop varieties. But when we examine case histories of the introduction or attempted introduction of new food crops, it becomes apparent that when the crop is grown for the market, rather than for subsistence, there is no problem of taste, consistency, or cooking qualities, and wives do not veto their husbands' initiative. This distinction is made clear by Dube. In the Indian village he studied, acceptance of improved wheat for home consumption was unenthusiastic because of undersirable taste, even though its agricultural merits were recognized. But improved varieties of sugar cane were quickly taken up by the same farmers, because, as cash crops, they brought much high prices at mills. People remembered the old sugar cane variety with nostalgia for its superior taste and allegedly better food value, but this was not a staple, and the pull of the market won out.[13]

Erasmus has analyzed a number of instances in Latin America where attempts were made to induce rural populations to cultivate vegetable gardens for home consumption. He found that vegetable growing generally was taken up by farmers living near cities or towns, or along reliable communication routes leading to them, but that otherwise, if the farmer found no market, the programs failed after aid was withdrawn. But, once farmers grew vegetables for the market they invariably increased their consumption of them so that, indirectly via the

[13] Dube, 1956, p. 20.

pull of the market, nutritional goals were achieved.[14]

In Greece the hard-headed and skeptical Macedonian farmers were reluctant to try the new crops and improved methods of cultivation recommended by Near East Foundation technicians. The big problem was to get the first farmer to try the improved practice. Fortunately most demonstrations were successful, and when these men were seen to have had such a successful year, the trick was turned. ". . . when an improved practice resulted in more cash in hand, the problem of pushing the practice was solved, for then the peasants would clamor for the very instruction about which they had been skeptical before."[15] A generation later, after World War II and long after the termination of Near East work, a survey was carried out in five villages to determine the long-range effect of this pioneer developmental project. It was found that "practices with obvious direct economic results" had been more completely adopted than practices with less obvious or more indirect results.[16]

These last three examples illustrate two important lessons. First, programs designed to persuade farmers to grow new or improved crops will have a better chance if the produce is destined for the market rather than for home consumption. And, second, once people begin to grow new crops for the market, they are almost certain to begin to consume them at home. Tastes are not absolutely rigid; we all have to learn to like olives.

Mair finds developments in African land tenure suggest that economic forces ultimately override those of such values as tradition and religion. The modern African's actions increasingly are determined by his perception of economic advantage and not to "an abstract theory of the sacredness of land which inhibits their recognition of its economic potentialities.

14 Erasmus, 1954, p. 150.
15 Allen, 1943, p. 261.
16 Beers, 1950, pp. 281-282.

. . . there are not many recorded cases where someone who was invited to dispose of land for a profitable consideration has invoked such principles as a ground for refusal . . ."[17] She suggests as a generalization of wide application that "the conservative force of tradition is never proof against the attraction of economic advantage, provided that the advantage is sufficient and is clearly recognized. In the case of land it is abundantly clear that the emotional and religious attitudes towards it which are inculcated by native tradition have not prevented the development of a commercial attitude."[18]

Competitive Situation

People often are spurred to innovation by the motivation of competition. This may be observed between individuals, between groups, and between villages. Nationalism, too, involves feelings of competition between nations. Competition may be thought of as a basic ingredient in the prestige motivation, since successful competition usually leads to greater prestige for the winner. In 1955 in India I noted a case in which a rival threatened the established leader by building the first latrine in the village. Only by building a bigger and better latrine was the latter able to maintain his position.

In developmental programs the importance of competition generally has been recognized, and efforts have been made to utilize this motivation in bringing change. Erasmus found that in Latin American 4H programs results were better when young people worked separate garden plots in competition with each other, rather than working the same land cooperatively in such a way that they could not compare results.[19] Agricultural and livestock fairs, to which people bring their best produce and animals, often have stimulated interest in programs in these

---

[17] Mair, 1957, p. 46.
[18] *Ibid.*, p. 52.
[19] Erasmus, 1954, p. 152.

fields. In the Nad-i-Ali area of the Helmand Valley in Afghanistan such fairs, accompanied by judging of orchards, gardens,
and fields, with prizes in the form of agricultural tools, have
been very successful. Cassel reports that among the Zulu annual
garden competitions, accompanied by the establishment of a
small market for the sale of surplus produce, constituted a successful technique.[20]

Tannous believes that in the Near East competition between
families or parties within the community may be effectively
employed to promote change. He found that in one village two
societies tried for several years to excel each other in play production and welfare work. "In most cases it was found that
when one family adopted a new agricultural technique successfully, the other families felt challenged to do the same."[21]

In some parts of the world—Africa and Oceania, for example
—intervillage competition appears to be one of the strongest
motivations to change. Keesing tells how, in Samoa, first under
the Germans and then under the New Zealanders, a number of
improvements were promoted in this way. Roads and paths
were built, and safe water supply systems were installed in most
villages. Environmental sanitation work was carried out by
means of "emulation between villages," and individual competition between mothers, families, and villages promoted child-
welfare work, especially through women's health committees.
In mission schools, rivalry between villages proved to be an
important, if not sustained, motivation to study for examinations.[22]

In Nigeria when straightforward appeals to progress and development failed "apathy could often be broken down by arousing a spirit of competition or emulation between neighbouring
communities by playing up local rivalries."[23] In the same area

20 Cassel, 1955, p. 26.
21 Tannous, 1944, p. 8.
22 Keesing, 1934, pp. 298, 304, 382-383, 417.
23 C. deN. Hill, 1957, p. 21.

Jackson points out how the village community attracts the warmest loyalty from its members, and "when one village acquires for itself some amenity that its neighbors lack this is a matter for intense pride." This causes envy among neighboring villages, which often strive to keep up. Thus he feels that encouraging competition between villages is a very useful developmental technique.[24]

The same motivation is found in India. Dube notes that the desire to build up the reputation of one's village is often instrumental in causing acceptance of projects. "A village which built a new school, constructed a public building, or paved all its lanes could earn a reputation in the vicinity for being 'progressive.' Competition between individuals, families, kin-groups, castes, and villages was also at the back of many programmes."[25]

But competition is not a sure incentive to greater effort. Dube describes a cattle show in which substantial and useful prizes created interest and in which the judging was entirely fair. Still, many people were disappointed. "Some felt that all villages entering cattle in the show should have been rewarded in some way or the other for their co-operation: a village would not lose face if even one of its residents got a prize. In one case it was found that the leaders of the village which had secured a large number of prizes were half apologetic, for their very success was viewed by others as a mark of selfishness."[26] The same results were noted in crop competitions. Winners were not stimulated to maintain their lead the following year. In one instance a winner said he did not want to be selfish and that others were now entitled to win. Dube found little evidence that anyone adopted new practices or took extra care of his crops in order to win a prize.

Competition can also be dangerous in that it leads people to spend money for prestige symbols that they do not really need. In rural Greece, Friedl found that urban-inspired competition for prestige "often encourages spending beyond the boundaries of economic wisdom, quite on the 'keeping up with the Joneses' pattern." For example, clothing which is not suited to the country and which wears out rapidly is sometimes purchased in preference to garments better suited to country tasks. On the other hand, the competitive urge is not all bad, she finds, for it has produced such improvements as sanitary latrines and increased willingness to accept hospitalization.[27]

The competitive motivation seems ultimately to rise, in newly developing nations, to the national level, where it takes the familiar form of nationalism. The nationalistic spur often is important in bringing about change. Neisser describes how the desire "to take a feather out of the white man's cap" by learning to read and write was an important aid in educational work in Nigeria,[28] and in the same country Jackson speaks of the "spiritual discontent," stemming from the African's belief that Europeans regard him as inferior, which motivates many people to excel.[29]

A conscious appeal to nationalistic feelings has, in many situations, promoted change. Tannous tells how in the Near East the evoking of the "glorious past" stimulates the *fellāhīn* to improve agricultural practices. He found that showing lantern slides of Arab monuments still standing in the Middle East, lecturing on the Arab contribution to world civilization, and giving a laudatory description of their country's ancient successful agricultural practices contributed significantly to extension work.[30] Among the Zulu, where diet had deteriorated over the years, the aims of a comprehensive health program were fur-

27 Friedl, 1959, p. 35.
28 Neisser, 1955, p. 355.
29 Jackson, 1956, p. 36.
30 Tannous, 1944, p. 8.

thered by pointing out to people the values of the old diet, and by stimulating their pride in past ways and their desire to maintain former standards.[31]

In India the speeches of community development leaders often contrast the country's present problems with its high position in antiquity, and villagers are asked to help restore this former glory through hard work. If the United States and Russia, they are asked, could build up their national prosperity from lowly beginnings, why could India not do the same?[32]

Obligations of Friendship

In much of the world friendship patterns are more carefully worked out and balanced than in the United States. Disinterested friendship often plays small part in the daily relations between people. The mere fact of the recognition of the friendship means that the partners assume mutual obligations and expect reciprocal favors in return. Pitt-Rivers' classic account of friendship in the Andalusian village of Alcalá points up the nature of relationships that will be encountered when a technician—or an anthropologist for that matter—enters a folk or peasant community and establishes contact with local people. Friendship, says Pitt-Rivers, in such cases is based on a "spirit of contract." Friendship is the free association with a person of one's choice: it implies mutual liking, but it also involves mutual service. "To enter into friendship with someone means putting oneself in a state of obligation. This obligation obliges one to meet his request, even though it involves a sacrifice on one's own part. One must not, if one can help it, say 'no' to a friend." In Alcalá, a friendship is established through a favor which expresses one's *simpatia,* or mutual liking for a person. If the favor is accepted, then the bond is established, and one is then entitled to expect the return of favors.[33]

31 Cassel, 1955, p. 24.
32 Dube, 1958, pp. 109-110.
33 Pitt-Rivers, 1954, pp. 138, 139.

If friendship is looked at in this light, rather than in the more casual American way, many of the reasons for cooperation on the part of villagers will be understood. In 1955 I found, in asking villagers in India why they had accepted certain community development projects, that the frequent answer was, "to please the village level worker." The villagers were not necessarily convinced of the desirability or utility of the action, but they had come to feel indebted to the VLW, and the obligations of friendship, as they understood them, required them to help their new friend. Similarly, Dube discusses the instructions of village level workers to "fraternize" with villagers. "Fraternization involved establishing friendly relations, and friendships, according to village norms, involve a series of mutual and reciprocal obligations. Hospitality must be returned in one form or the other, and one must support one's friend." Factional dangers were present in the villages Dube studied. "The members of the friendly group would support the officials not because they are convinced about the utility or efficiency of the programs sponsored by them, but simply as their part in the obligations of friendship."[34]

In the UNESCO-sponsored fundamental education project (CREFAL) in Pátzcuaro, Mexico, a great deal of the cooperation encountered in one village can be explained by the fact that one of the specialists previously had worked there as an anthropologist, and the friendship ties that had developed between him and many villagers obligated them to participate in a number of activities which, if they had been left to their own judgment, they would have rejected. The same fact of friendship was the principal motivation for seven of the eleven Peruvian housewives in the village of Los Molinos who heeded the advice of Nelida, the health educator, and decided to boil drinking water regularly.[35]

[34] Dube, 1957, p. 136.
[35] Wellin, 1955, p. 83.

Play Motivation

The significance of the play motif in the processes of invention and discovery is well known. Most scientists—frequently as a form of relaxation—like to play with their data, to arrange facts in new combinations, or to pursue a line of investigation for no other reason than that it is fun. Sometimes important new ideas emerge from this play process. Play also is an important factor in culture change, but unfortunately it has not been well documented. Perhaps it is best seen in the United States, where we often try a new tool or gadget just for the fun of it, out of curiosity. But this love of play does not seem to be culture-bound—it can be expected to crop up on any cultural level. The Trumai Indians of central Brazil are among the most primitive of all peoples, yet when they were visited by the anthropologist Buell Quain in the late 1930's, they were tremendously interested in his belongings and made continual attempts to acquire them. "Adults as well as children whined in order to obtain objects from him. This attitude was manifested towards useful objects such as knives and axes, but they also pleaded and begged for articles having only curiosity value to them. . . . to be curious about an object was to want it."[36]

Among the South African Zulu, Cassel found that the curiosity of the women about how a fetus was nourished *in utero* led to much discussion in prenatal clinics, thus facilitating the use of posters and models showing the functions of the placenta and umbilical cord.[37] Dube reports that several items in the community development program he studied, such as new agricultural implements and improved techniques, were tried out of curiosity. "While a number of innovations were rejected because of their strangeness and people's lack of familiarity with them, some others were enthusiastically adopted because they

[36] Murphy and Quain, 1955, p. 41.
[37] Cassel, 1955, pp. 24-25.

were so novel."[38] And in Greece, Allen describes how improvements in farming not infrequently appealed to the Macedonian farmer as fads.[39]

I encountered an unusual example of the effect of the play motif in East Bengal in 1955. In one village to which I was taken nearly 80 percent of the families had built bore-hole latrines, all within the space of several weeks. I asked the American technician how he explained this. He assured me that the health lectures had been carefully worked out and given by his Pakistani associates, that the people had listened with care and been convinced of the desirability of building latrines. Such success had never before occurred in any environmental sanitation program with which I was familiar, and it seemed likely other factors were present. Investigation proved this to be true. In this part of East Pakistan there is a thick covering of rich alluvial soil, which permits the use of an auger for drilling the latrine pit. Four men can bore through as much as 20 feet of this soil in an hour or so, and the results are little short of miraculous. It turned out that the villagers were enchanted with this marvelous new tool, and all wanted to try their hand at it. They felt that the concrete perforated slab they had to buy to cap the hole was a small price to pay to enjoy an hour or two with this wonderful new toy. Competition between groups of men were informally organized, and records were set and broken in rapid succession. For several weeks this was undoubtedly the happiest village in the country. And, at the end of the time, a good job of environmental sanitation had been done—but not for the reason the health team thought!

Religious Appeal

Examples have already been given of how a religious motivation was instrumental in two areas in creating a demand for

38 Dube, 1958, p. 84.
39 Allen, 1943, p. 248.

reading. Conscious utilization of a religious motivation can sometimes be achieved if a developmental worker is familiar with the religious beliefs and sacred writings of the people among whom he works. In several villages of the Etawah Pilot Project in community development in India acacia trees were planted on an acre of wasteland near the villages, and carefully watered and tended so that the young trees were not destroyed by goats. How was this unusual cooperative undertaking achieved? "The land was solemnly dedicated by each village as a 'Krishna grove' *(Krishnaban),* so that there was real emotional attachment to it as a sacred undertaking, sacred to Lord Krishna." The villagers were determined that they would not "let Krishna down," as had happened in other communities.[40]

The same technique was used—by lucky accident—in Future Farmers of Greece clubs organized as a part of the Near East Foundation program in that country. In some villages as many as 9000 treelets were successfully planted. Although it was not a conscious part of the strategy of change, the village priest was always called upon to participate. ". . . in simple, Orthodox ritual [he] blessed the willowy saplings before the lads put them into the ground, while the villagers looked on approvingly."[41] This religious sanction was one of several conditions which favored the work.

In working with the *fellāhīn* of the Middle East good results often can be attained by the use of citations from the Koran, thus adding the supreme religious validation to the lesser authority of the technician. Expressions such as "Allah hath said in His exalted book," and "All those who love the prophet," and "He who is willing among you to honor his religion and Allah's book" seldom fail to arouse active response. In addition, the Koran contains a wealth of statements pertinent to literacy, health, and improvements in agriculture which can be cited to

[40] Mayer and Associates, 1958, pp. 215-216.
[41] Allen, 1943, p. 230.

clinch the truthfulness of an argument for innovation.[42] Examples of such statements, which can be used in health and developmental programs, are given by Dr. Fawzy Gadalla: for personal hygiene, "Cleanliness is a part of Islam"; to encourage dental hygiene, "If it were not hard upon my people I would have asked them to brush their teeth before each prayer" (i.e., five times a day); and to stimulate cooperation, "A Moslem to a Moslem are as the walls of a building supporting one another." Dr. Gadalla emphasizes the importance, in a Moslem country, of the worker introducing his task with the phrase "In the name of Allah." This shows that the technician is a good, religious man. When in practice in Egypt Dr. Gadalla always used this phrase before beginning an operation or an examination, and before giving an injection or dressing a wound.[43]

THE PROBLEM OF "FIT"

In studying examples of social and cultural change one encounters a series of factors which have contributed significantly to the introduction of new forms of behavior and which, although motivation obviously is involved, can better be illustrated under the heading above. These factors involve such things as cultural values, social forms, motor patterns, and economic reality.

Social Forms and Values

An innovation, to be successful, requires among other things a supporting social structure onto which it can be grafted. This simply means that in all societies traditional institutions have recognized roles; if new forms can be integrated or associated with these traditional roles, they have a better chance of being accepted than if there is nothing to tie to. A scientifically trained

[42] Tannous, 1944, p. 8.
[43] Communicated by Dr. Fawzy Gadalla.

physician, whatever his problems may be in working with people whose previous experience has been with folk medical curers, has at least one point in his favor: his role—that of a person who tries to make people well—is known and appreciated. The health educator, on the other hand, labors under the handicap that traditional societies make no provision for people with his function. Jackson illustrates this point clearly with an example from Nigeria. Here, as in much of the world, maintenance of new facilities is a major problem. When better and more sanitary village markets were constructed the improvement was kept up largely because there was a pre-existing system for cleaning the market after the day's sales; the social form to care for the new facility was there, and no new organization had to be set up. But when a new project such as a reading room was completed, which had no parallel in village life, it proved almost impossible to create a new organization to care for it.[44]

In the Lake Pátzcuaro region of Mexico the UNESCO-sponsored CREFAL fundamental education program has been successful in introducing chicken farming in a number of villages. The local people have kept chickens for centuries, and the White Leghorns have generally been recognized as superior birds. Here the fit between values, social forms, and economic possibilities has been good, and the program has been gratifying in results. Contrast this with a similar case in China several years ago: White Leghorns, from the standpoint of the poultryman the best bird for the area, were introduced as in Mexico. But the innovator was unaware of a tabu against raising and eating white birds, and consequently little progress was made.[45] It seems likely that a bird such as the Rhode Island Red might have been successfully introduced, since it would offer no fundamental conflict with local values: the fit would be adequate.

[44] Jackson, 1956, p. 101.
[45] Yan Hsin-Pao, 1949, p. 18.

Similarly, in parts of Mexico pigeons and doves are believed to bring bad luck in the form of illness, death, or desertion by one's spouse. Developmental programs which have tried to introduce these birds in such areas have not met with success.[46] But emphasis on chicken farming might well meet with the success accorded it in Pátzcuaro.

Motor Patterns

The motor patterns of a group fit the tools and activities which characterize daily life. Developmental programs usually involve new material items and new customs whose fit to urban or Western culture may be perfect, but which are not in perfect harmony with local ways. Examples have been given of barriers due to differences in motor patterns. To the extent that new tools and techniques can be adapted to pre-existing ways of using the body, the possibilities for successful introduction are multiplied. Often great ingenuity is displayed by native peoples in reworking the products of the machine age.

Firth tells how, in Tikopia, a Polynesian island outlier in Melanesia, steel tools replaced the aboriginal giant clamshell blades; when the Tikopians acquired the wood plane, instead of using it to smooth timber, they removed the blade and hafted it to an adze. The adze is the traditional woodworking tool, and they found the new blade a significant improvement over the clam shell.[47]

Many years ago Thompson described how Mexican farmers, who customarily use an ancient Mediterranean-type single-handled "scratch" plow, were known to modify American two-handled plows by removing one handle. The tool was easier to modify than the motor pattern. He also described how, to the astonishment of American and British railway construction gang foreman, Mexican peons, when furnished with modern

46 Kelly, 1958, p. 206.
47 Firth, 1956, p. 94.

wheelbarrows, removed the wheel and lifted the barrow proper to their backs, supporting and carrying it with a forehead tumpline! The Mexican, since the time of the building of great prehistoric pyramids, has moved earth by carrying it in a basket supported on the back in this fashion. Even today the tourist in Mexico City may see earth from the foundations of new skyscrapers being carried out of the ground in this fashion. The knack of handling a wheelbarrow is not something an adult picks up easily, so the willing railway workers, not wishing to displease their masters by rejecting their help, solved the problem by changing the tool to conform to their motor patterns.[48]

The lesson of adapting tools to prevailing body habits apparently has to be learned independently time after time. An American sanitary engineer once told me of a problem he had solved in Haiti. His work gang of Haitian laborers had been supplied with standard long-handled American shovels to dig a drainage ditch. The work went badly; the laborers seemed incredibly clumsy with their shovels, and frequently the handles got in the way, and inadvertently they knocked each other on the head. The sanitary engineer sensed the cause of the difficulty. Haitians customarily use short-handled tools which they grasp near the blade, bending over in a position that would be most uncomfortable for an American worker. The engineer cut the last two feet off each shovel handle and work progressed satisfactorily. Traditional motor patterns were now unhampered by excess handle.

It should be apparent that if motor patterns and postures of a particular culture are known, it is often possible to introduce important changes that do no violence to local ways. This is not a new discovery. Two hundred years ago British rifle manufacturers who sold to the Iroquois and other Indians of eastern North America discovered that the stocks of their products were wearing away at the top, and that customer resistance followed.

[48] Thompson, 1922, p. 52.

In the thick underbrush of the eastern woodlands Indians customarily dragged their long bows after them, one tip riding lightly on the ground, to avoid entangling them in thickets. For the same reason they dragged rifles along the ground, but because of their greater weight the wooden stocks eroded away. An ingenious manufacturer solved the problem by designing a special iron butt-plate that curved over and protected the part of the stock that came into contact with the ground and, presumably, he henceforth had satisfied customers.[49]

The lesson of the plow, first described by Thompson, has been learned by a great many agricultural experts in United Nations and Point Four programs. Often—but by no means always—light-weight one-handled mold-board plows are being introduced into those parts of the world where the traditional plow has but one handle, and in such instances a major factor of resistance is overcome. The technician on a foreign assignment who is willing to study local motor patterns and can find ways to modify new implements that he is introducing, sometimes finds that this simple operation spells the difference between success and failure.

Sequence

The particular instant at which an innovation appears in a change situation will have much to do with its acceptance or rejection. The success of an innovation, as has been pointed out, depends in large measure on the supporting circumstances that may exist, as well as the recognition by people of the need for the new thing. But in a period of rapid change, the number and strengths of the factors that improve the chances for acceptance of a specific item will fluctuate over the years. If the innovation appears at the point in time at which the supporting factors "peak," the chances for acceptance are excellent. If it appears in the "trough," rejection is likely. The skilled change

[49] Communicated by Dr. William N. Fenton.

agent is the one who can recognize when the time is ripe for the next step in his program and who has the patience to hold back until this time. However desirable an innovation may seem, there is no point in trying to force its acceptance at a time when all change indices say "no, not yet."

Literacy and adult education generally are thought to be basic desiderata in community development programs. Yet more often than not such activities have met with little success. In part the reason has been that they have been presented before people were ready for them. Richardson tells how the village reading rooms of the Near East Foundation's Greek program initially were failures. They simply had no meaning in terms of village life. But after the Future Farmers of Greece clubs were organized, with the stimulation of boyish interest in better husbandry practices, the ability to read and the ready access to sources of knowledge placed a premium on reading rooms.[50]

Usually the desire to read and write comes late in the development of peasant society. Villagers do not look upon literacy as an abstract thing that is good per se. It is something that takes time and hard work, and when it is achieved it has no meaning for most people. Berreman tells how, in a Himalayan foothill village, attitudes toward government school programs generally are not favorable. This attitude is due in considerable measure to the apparent absence of tangible benefits accruing to those people who have been educated in the past.[51]

Buitrón illustrates this point with an example from Chimborazo, Ecuador, where he arrived three months after a number of farmers had received certificates of literacy following an adult education campaign. When he asked them to write their names they were unable to do so; in three months they had forgotten even this elemental art *because they had no need to read*

[50] Richardson, 1945, p. 22.
[51] Berreman, 1959, p. 625.

or write. For this reason, writes Buitrón, before teaching anything we must be sure the new knowledge will fill a real need felt by the people, and if this is not the case, we must first create the need.

The group just described consists of landless hacienda wage employees. Buitrón contrasts them with another agricultural group which also weaves and sells cloth. The members of this group, in order to sell, must know Spanish as well as Indian languages, must learn schedules of buses and trains, read house numbers, learn accurately the value of money, and be able to make simple mathematical calculations in order to make change. "Among these people there is great need of literacy. They themselves understand and recognize this need, and without outside advice, send their children to school." Buitrón concludes that "those who believe that to eradicate illiteracy it is sufficient to augment the number of teachers, better their preparation, and create more schools, are completely mistaken."[52]

Jackson describes an illuminating example in Nigeria. During World War II an adult literacy campaign was very successful, but interest nearly vanished at the end of hostilities. People did not want to read and write for the sheer joy of intellectual mastery; they wanted to communicate with their young men who were away as soldiers. When the soldiers returned, there was much less felt need for literacy.[53]

Literacy becomes important only when villagers begin to see that those persons who are literate have extra advantages, or when they come to feel they are less likely to be cheated by city people if they can read. As standards of living are raised and there is increased travel and contact with the remainder of the nation, conditions become increasingly favorable for presenting adult education programs to rural peoples. But until this time arrives, slight success is the usual rule.

[52] Buitrón, 1960, pp. 169-171.
[53] Jackson, 1956, p. 21.

A similar pattern of recognized need is apparent in health programs. Public health work is based on the philosophy of prevention of the conditions that lead to illness, rather than on curing the sick. Yet the evidence indicates that in those parts of the world where curative facilities are not readily available, preventive programs have little meaning to people. The immediate needs of the ill must be met before they are interested in immunization and environmental sanitation, the importance of which, from their point of view, is pretty hard to see anyway. Experience shows that the prestige won by curative medicine is one of the most effective ways to sell preventive programs. At the right time in the sequence of a medical program, people will take on faith things that will not attract them at an earlier period.

Timing

The problems of sequence are long range. But another aspect of the likelihood of acceptance of innovation can be thought of as a function of the right time within the yearly cycle. This is particularly true when people's pocketbooks are involved. In the average rural community, for example, the amount of cash people have fluctuates widely during the year. At harvest time they are relatively prosperous. This is the traditional time for weddings and often for fiestas that involve big expenditures. It is a time when new clothing and household needs are looked after. If new material items or practices come to the attention of villagers at this time, they are much more apt to spend money on them than they would be a few months earlier, when the new harvest has not come in and the resources of the preceding year are nearly exhausted.

Villagers appear to understand perfectly well the psychology of timing. In Tzintzuntzan in 1959 a progressive man introduced a small tortilla bakery. This consisted of an oil-fired drum—a griddle—on which twenty-five or so tortillas could bake simultaneously. Four women using small hand-presses were able to maintain the supply of raw tortillas. *Nixtamal*—the dough— was purchased wholesale in a nearby town, and the finished product was sold at a price most people agreed was entirely reasonable. I asked many friends whether they thought the enterprise would be successful. Most agreed that the innovation met a real need, and that there would be many times when it would be convenient to buy ready-made tortillas. But they pointed out that two months before harvest time people had very little money to spend, and that it was a poor time to try to develop the new buying habits on which the success of the enterprise depended. One woman astutely remarked that the right time to have started the bakery would be during the major fiesta of the year, which occurred a couple of months after the harvest. At this time great numbers of friends and relatives come from other villages, often staying a week. Ambulant food vendors set up stalls in the plaza, and people are accustomed to buying a good many meals, both for the novelty and because the festive activities leave little time for preparing food for large numbers of guests. The combination of relative prosperity, a temporary pattern of buying cooked food, and the desire to save time for festivities, she reasoned, would all favor the tortilla bakery.

Middle-Class Receptivity

What is the socioeconomic position of people who seem to adopt new practices most easily? Well-to-do people, obviously, have the means to acquire many innovations inaccessible to their less-well-off neighbors. When it is a question of items of material culture, this group is often the most receptive. But frequently these people are basically conservative. They are content with their position, and if major changes in the way of life of their community occur, there is no certainty that they will continue to enjoy this advantage. Further, such people often have a deeper commitment to dominant local values than do less fortunate people. The reluctance of superior farmers in India to buy improved seed, because of fear of loss of face, will be recalled (Chapter 5).

The poorest people sometimes seem like good candidates for change. They have so little to lose, economically and socially, it is argued, that they are taking no great risk in adopting the new. Many developmental programs in such fields as agriculture and health have been directed toward this target group, both because of the philosophy of dire need and because of the belief that they will be receptive. But experience again shows that the lower socioeconomic groups are usually the poorest candidates for change. In 1951 I was told in Chile that the national public health service had, with great reluctance, come to the conclusion that the lowest 20 percent of the population could not effectively be reached at that time, and few efforts were directed toward them. This group did not have the education to understand health problems, and it did not have the economic resources to meet even the slim individual financial obligations required by patients.

Fear renders the poorest people incapable of trying new things. They know that their productive capacities, with traditional means, will provide a bare subsistence, but their margin of survival is so slim that they feel they cannot risk even a tiny amount to experiment with something that is new and untested. Marriott has described how in the village he knew in India a new wheat seed is not seen simply as a simple addition or replacement or improvement in the farmer's technology. He thinks of all the possible consequences that may result, and often concludes that even small alterations in his tightly knit technology may lead to disaster.[54] He cannot afford the risk of the unknown.

Mandelbaum states the dilemma well when he writes, "The

[54] Marriott, 1952, p. 266.

paradox seems to be that those who are in tightest economic circumstances, who have most to gain by adopting patterns leading to increased production, may be the most reluctant to do so, since they can least afford the slightest decrement of income which experimenting with new patterns may involve, if only temporarily."[55]

In my experience the most receptive people are those who are neither at the top nor the bottom of the local socioeconomic scale. They have enough so that they can gamble with limited experiments without unduly threatening their well-being, but their position is not so secure but that the attraction of greater income, as well as the possibility of satisfying other felt needs, is a strong motivation to action. Usually they do not represent vested interests that may be threatened by major innovations nor, on the other hand, are they sunk in apathy, believing that no real change is possible.

Authority

The extent to which the use of authority—or, to use a happy euphemism I have heard in India, "executive methods"—should be used in programs of planned change is debatable. Viewed as a social phenomenon that is a part of the dynamics of change, however, there is no doubt that it is an important factor in change. Many people would feel that there are situations in which the good of the majority at times requires the use of authority over the will and beliefs of the minority. Compulsory vaccination and chlorination of water have brought significant health improvements, over the protests of dissident minorities. In other cases the initial use of authority where it was possible has meant that the people so affected have voluntarily carried on after learning the advantages of a new custom.

The American potato has contributed enormously to the security of Europe, and yet its introduction was not spontaneous

[55] Mandelbaum, 1953, p. 6.

and unopposed. It was rumored that it poisoned the soil, that it caused diarrhea, and that it was otherwise harmful. Benjamin Thompson (Count Rumford), a royalist who left his native Massachusetts in 1776, became military adviser to the Duke of Bavaria. Noting the frequent crop failures of those days, he felt convinced that if local farmers would plant potatoes their lives would be less in jeopardy. But neither persuasion nor demonstration won converts. So, as head of the army, he ordered every soldier in the Duke's forces to plant potatoes, to care for, harvest, and eat them. The length of military service was sufficient in those days to give a soldier time to learn to grow potatoes and to develop a taste for them. "After the men returned to their farms and villages, potato crops appeared all over the country and the food of Europe gained greater security."[56]

In Mexico City during World War II it was found necessary to order a major change in the hours of businesses and stores. Formerly there was a three-hour siesta, which permitted everyone to return home, eat at leisure, and perhaps take a short rest before returning to the center of town. In order to conserve tires, gasoline, and motive equipment, the long dinner period was abolished in favor of *horas corridas* whereby businesses and stores remained open for the entire work day, with employees going out for short lunch periods or eating food brought from home. This meant that employees returned home at least two hours earlier than formerly. At first there was a great protest against this blow to Mexican culture, and it was hinted that *yanqui* imperialism was perhaps involved. But most people found they enjoyed their new evening freedom much more than the long lunch hours, and when at the end of the war it was suggested that the old-fashioned hours be restored there was a great outcry. People liked what had been imposed upon them by administrative decision.

It must be remembered that the usual American attitude to-

[56] Graubard, 1943, p. 5.

ward authority—that it must be legally achieved and judiciously exercised—is by no means universal. Power and authority for their own sake are respected in much of the world. A man may even be a tyrant, but his position is known, and his behavior is predictable. Awareness of this respect for power helps us understand why, in much of Latin America, the strong man, the *caudillo* who rules in arbitrary fashion, is often able to command a popular following. This is also true in other parts of the world. Ullah describes how, in a Punjab village in West Pakistan, "The social goal of life of an individual and thereby of a family is to be effective and powerful enough to be of help to friends and awe the enemies. Success of a family and an individual in life is measured by the extent of one's influence over other people. *A person who has no enemy, whom nobody fears and whom nobody obeys is a worthless person.*"[57]

Similarly, Ammar describes how, in an Egyptian village, the *Omda*, the leader, lost power compared to his predecessor, a domineering individual, because he was a pleasant and genial person. "But the people think of authority as necessarily involving an assertion of power and domination. . . . If one wields power, one must be powerful and forceful, the villagers say, otherwise one would not be respected and feared."[58]

Gibb and Bowen, speaking of the Arab provinces in the Ottoman Empire in the eighteenth century, make the same point: "The conception of authority implied in the minds of the subjects themselves an assertion of power accompanied by a certain measure of harshness and violence. ' 'Abd el-Ra'ûf Pasa (says the Christian chronicler Michael of Damascas) was mild, just, and peaceloving, and because of his exceeding justice the people of Damascas were emboldened against him.' " And in Egypt, quoting the Egyptian el-Cabartî, " 'If the peasants were administered by a compassionate *multazim*, they despised him and his agents,

57 Ullah, 1958, p. 171. (Italics mine.)
58 Ammar, 1954, p. 80.

delayed payment of his taxes, called him by feminine names, and hoped for the ending of his *iltizâm* and the appointment of some tyrant without fear of God or mercy for them. . . .' "[59]

These extremes can hardly be justified in the modern world. But it can logically be argued that the use of authority to achieve directed culture change should be a function of prevailing cultural expectations and administrative practices. This probably means that sometimes basic decisions must be made by persons in authority, decisions which in other societies might be handled through more democratic channels. I rather regret that, in the city in which I live, civic officials have not been able arbitrarily to fluoridate the water. Democratically expressed public opinion sometimes is a poor way to establish truth.

In concluding this chapter, the fact should again be emphasized that people accept, and are able to accept, innovations because of a variety of interlocking and mutually reinforcing reasons. Frequently the reasons for acceptance are quite different from those that motivate change agents. Dube speaks of how in India there is a tendency in cultures to reinterpret the proffered innovation in terms of the dominant themes and existing needs of the society. He points out that certain items in development programs such as renovation of wells, paving of village lanes, and the construction of soakage and compost pits have been accepted in a number of villages where there is very little understanding of their significance for the health of the community. "Their acceptance has been motivated by such diverse factors as 'they look new and good,' and 'with them our village will look like a town,' 'we must do what the government asks us to do,' 'that is all that we can show the important visitors from outside,' and 'other villages are doing it and so we must also do it.' "[60]

[59] Gibb and Bowen, 1950, pp. 204-205.
[60] Dube, 1956, p. 30.

9 . . . . *The technical expert: his problems*

The technical expert, trained in the methods and imbued with the values of his culture, uprooted and transplanted to practice in an exotic environment, is not a phenomenon new to the mid-twentieth century. Railway engineers, bridge and boat builders, cotton-mill superintendents, and colonial administrators went out in great numbers from Europe and the United States beginning in the nineteenth century, to ply their trades far from home. But the technical specialist, particularly as a government or an international servant, who participates in regional and national programs of planned change whose rationale is not economic profit for shareholders is a relatively recent development. Early in this century the Rockefeller Foundation began public health work in remote (to North Americans) countries such as Ceylon and Ecuador, and shortly after World War I the Near East Foundation initiated community development activities in Greece. Other similar programs appeared during the years between the two wars. But the major push is a post-World War II phenomenon. Never have medical personnel, agricultural scientists, educators, community developers, public administration specialists, and a host of others been sent to work in foreign countries on a comparable scale.

All of these specialists, obviously, are potential agents of change, and many work with a high degree of success. Yet there are others of equal ability and motivation who are much less effective and who, at times, unwittingly stir positive resentment against the programs they work in. The American technical expert—an engineer, an agriculturalist, an educator, or a medical man—is a well-trained specialist. He has had the advantage of first-class university training, and he has probably worked in a private or government agency where he has been able to make good use of his training. He is proud of the high professional and ethical standards of his field and his colleagues, and he has no doubt that he controls knowledge that can make the world a better place in which to live. The medical man knows the same germs cause the same illnesses, without regard to race or culture, and the educator knows that psychologically the learning process is the same for all people; both know they have the technical qualifications to attack these problems.

How, then, can these technical specialists be other than successful in planned culture change programs? Is it not, on the face of it, ridiculous to say such a thing? Yet if we examine the situation more thoroughly, we find that the very excellence of American professional training, the atmosphere in which it is carried out, and the underlying presuppositions on which it is based all conspire against producing the best international technical specialist. Let us examine this training, for a moment, to see what its implications are for international, intercultural work.

The first thing we note is that most professional training in the United States is designed to equip the student to live and work in his own society. Or, putting the matter in another way, it means that American society—like all other societies—is characterized by medical, engineering, agricultural, educational, and many other kinds of problems. These problems are all a function of American culture. Professional training, therefore, and quite rightly, is designed to teach people to meet the needs posed by these problems. There is no need to teach the average professional student to think first of identifying major problems and then working out solutions to these problems. The major problems are thought to be quite obvious; the need is to ameliorate, not to identify, them. The professional knows the kinds of questions his society will ask of him and the job demands it will make upon him. These are the tests he must pass successfully. Consequently, most professional training is designed in terms of *programs* rather than underlying *problems,* and the technician comes to judge himself by what he has to offer to the programs in which he participates. Professional training produces program-oriented specialists. Only rarely does it produce problem-oriented specialists.

However sound this approach is for professionals who will practice in the United States, it is seriously deficient in preparing people for work in other societies. Man is so much a product of his culture—he is so ethnocentric—that he assumes that the advanced programs and techniques which work in his society are equally fitted to less developed countries. The combination of fine technical training and an ethnocentric point of view leads to false and dangerous definitions of a good technical aid program and the role of the international technical specialist. The "good" program or the best technical assistance comes to be defined as the *duplication of American-style programs and projects in the host country.* The obvious corollary is that the best technical expert is the person who *most perfectly transplants an American-style program.*

Neither axiom nor corollary is true. In newly developing areas the answers to the major problems have not been worked out. The task of the technical specialist is not to reproduce a standard American product, but to know how to adapt the scientific knowledge and operating techniques of his country to the economic, social, educational, and political reality of the country in which he works. The successful technical expert is the one who has learned to be problem-oriented and not program-oriented.

The kinds of mistakes the program-oriented specialist makes are illustrated by the following examples. In the early 1950's in Iran American public health technicians insisted, in the face of visible evidence to the contrary, that defecation in the open air would produce flies (dry atmosphere quickly dries fecal matter and flies do not breed). The program approach to this health problem, which logically had to exist, was the latrine which, when installed in numbers, became a fly breeder and villages previously free became infested.[1]

Technicians also sometimes fail to distinguish between technical excellence and cultural values, as the following vignette shows:

> In my country [Iran] village public baths are pools of warm water. These pools transmit disease, and shower baths would be much more sanitary. Now without spending my time arguing about the goodness or badness of, or attacking or defending the ideas and behavior of my countrymen, you should know that they don't like to see themselves and others as naked as their innocent ancestors used to be in the jungle, and they will never retrogress, even for a few minutes in a public bath, to the way of living of prehistoric times. Because of this strong feeling men always wear something in public baths to prevent the lower part of their bodies from being seen by others. An American sanitary engineer built a public shower bath, in an Iranian village, but he didn't separate the stalls with partitions. I told him the design would not be acceptable because men would be ashamed to take off their clothes in the presence of others. He told me that they would have to accept it, because people are created alike and there is nothing to be ashamed of. Although

[1] Communicated by Mr. Garegin Saroukhanian.

perhaps he was right in his philosophy, the villagers did not accept his doctrine and the new bath house was little used. Moreover, they joked about the bath and the new ideology of human equality![2]

Obviously, the men's shower room in an American university gymnasium was the engineer's only answer to a bathing and health problem. He had learned a health program, but he had not learned to think in terms of problems.

For some technicians an overseas assignment is looked upon as an opportunity to execute a project with a degree of excellence that cannot be achieved at home because of the control or interference of boards of supervisors, or economic factors, or other reasons that usually temper professional enthusiasm. In 1957 in the Helmand Valley of Afghanistan I was shown irrigation works designed and built by American engineers and technicians to standards as high as could be devised on drafting tables. For all the technical excellence, however, serious problems were encountered in the local distribution of water to farmers' fields. American agricultural agents told me the degree of sophistication and responsibility needed by the farmer to operate and maintain the superbly designed gates, valves, and ditches was higher than could reasonably be expected of American irrigation farmers. Yet many of the Helmand Valley farmers had only recently been resettled from a traditional nomadic life. The project designers had had an opportunity to design and build a system which, for a variety of reasons, they could not have done at home. The fact that their project was not an answer to local problems escaped them.

It is only fair to point out that American technicians are not unique in frequent failure to relate a program to a problem. Almost anyone who is trained in the program approach may make the same error. In 1951 I accompanied a highly trained, pleasant, young Salvadorean visiting public health nurse as she

[2] Communicated by Mr. Mehdy Soraya.

made her rounds in the poorest areas of coffee plantations. Her instructions, which she had learned by rote from a translation of an American diet book, were to teach mothers to feed their children well, to emphasize oranges, eggs, meat, and milk. In house after house the advice was given, while unwashed, malnourished children played listlessly on dirt floors, and the mothers numbly but respectfully promised they would follow instructions. These mothers considered themselves lucky to have enough beans and tortillas to dull the pangs of hunger; the recommended diet was, to them, nothing more than words. The program, which to the nurse was synonymous with good role performance, was to teach American standards of diet; the problem was to devise a way, within economic possibilities, to introduce some slight improvement in the traditional diet.

On another occasion I accompanied an equally competent and well-trained Chilean nurse, in a lower-class neighborhood of a good-sized town. In one home, large by local standards and clean by any standards, the mother proudly displayed her fat and healthy youngest child, a baby of ten months. The baby had been immunized, and it was obviously well cared for and nourished. There was no health problem here and, it seemed to me, the nurse's only function should have been to pinch the baby's cheek and praise the mother for her fine care. But the nurse had learned a program, and she knew her role. "Did you give him a glass of orange juice this morning? Did he have his egg?" Did he have this, that, and the other thing, most of which he had not. The mother became first embarrassed and then angry. Finally she almost shouted, "When you have raised as many children as I have you will know something about child care." Inability to distinguish between a program and a problem—or in this case the lack of a problem—nullified the potential benefits accruing from continuing friendly relations between the nurse and the mother.

The kinds of difficulties that stem from program orientation are seen in much community development work. Since World War II a great deal of successful village developmental work has been achieved through programs variously labeled "fundamental education," "community organization," and "community development." Not all work, however, has been entirely successful. The bulk of community development efforts and the underlying philosophy are an outgrowth of American and British experience. The American pattern is one whereby people are stimulated to think and talk about their problems, to define their "felt needs," to come together for cooperative action, and through "self-help" programs, contribute to their material and spiritual well-being. Particularly in the South, community projects based on this philosophy and concept have been noteworthy.

When Americans participate in international community development programs, their concept of the problem and their program to attack the problem derive from the American model. Consequently, the concept of American-style community development and generally the attendant clichés as well have been exported, much as health, agricultural, and educational programs are exported. Many of the difficulties that have followed are due to the fact that a concept is as much a function of a particular culture as a tool or a health program; it cannot automatically be grafted to a foreign body. Let us examine, for a moment, some of the preconditions in the United States that were instrumental in defining the philosophy and methodolgy of community development:

1. Communities have the power to tax themselves.
2. Administrative organizations with the legal powers to take action are under community control.
3. Populations are basically literate.
4. Leadership patterns are well developed.
5. Since the time of the frontier there has been a tradition of

genuine cooperative work, and formal and informal social
devices such as the town meeting and proliferating committees exist to implement this cooperation.
6. However depressed a particular small area, it is a part of a
wealthy country which will, in times of need, funnel help
from other areas.
7. Technical services in health, agriculture, education, and the
like are highly developed and available.

In short, there is unlimited basic potential. The role of the
community developer is therefore that of a catalyst, someone
who can stimulate people to take stock, assess needs, decide
upon action, determine priorities, and get to work. This makes
sense in the American context. But let us look at the peasant
villages in newly developing countries where this philosophy is
being applied. Here are the corresponding characteristics commonly found:

1. The communities have essentially no power to levy taxes.
They are at the mercy of national or state governments for
all major and most minor developmental funds, including
building schools and paying teachers. Any project that costs
much money must be financed from outside the community.
2. Village government is truncated; only the most minor decisions can legally be made, and elected village leaders are reluctant to push beyond the modest limits of their authority.
3. Populations are not literate. People are often uncritical in
their judgments and rumors run rife.
4. Leadership patterns are poorly developed. Often the most
competent people judiciously avoid entanglement in leadership squabbles.
5. There is little tradition for cooperation; there are fewer
mechanisms for it; and people fear cooperation will enable
their fellows to take advantage of them.
6. Peasant villages are part of economically depressed nations;

they cannot count on the funneling of much help from other parts of the country.

7. Basic technical services are poorly developed, and sometimes lacking. Even if the community defines its needs, it cannot often get the outside support it wishes.

Hence, an American type of program based on the American philosophy often finds itself on rather barren ground. A community catalyst can go only so far. In fact, then, community development programs in newly developing areas pay lip service to the slogans of American community development—it becomes almost a religion—but "felt needs" usually turn out to be rather standard programs in environmental sanitation, medical services, agricultural extension, and education, which are recognized—correctly, I think—by national planners as the major needs of rural areas. It is not often that a "teahouse of the August moon" is built out of developmental funds because villagers insist it is their number-one need.

The point I am trying to make is not that community development is unsuccessful; it is good, and sometimes excellent, in spite of the natural handicaps under which it labors. The point is that a *conceptual* and *philosophical* cultural fit are essential in defining developmental programs, and that often highly competent technicians have not been prepared by their American training and experience to work out this fit.

When the American technician can discard his conceptual bias about what is good community development, he is in a position to put his skills to work. He will see that the first task is to consider the limiting factors in the total sociocultural-economic setting and to assess such resources as are available. He will then realize that the major decisions as to what can be done in a community must be worked out on a nonvillage level, as a part of over-all national social and economic planning. Perhaps the village worker will find he is less a catalyst and more a coordinator and explainer, one who helps villagers understand the role of substantive specialists in health and agriculture who formerly were not parts of traditional society. Perhaps his main task will be to prepare the ground so that the limited national services available can be most efficiently used on the local level. This will not be American-type community development, but it will be good community development because it is a function of the needs and possibilities not of the United States but of the local country.

Another source of difficulty to the technical expert lies in professional pride. Pride in the contributions one's profession makes to human welfare is a fine thing, but unalloyed enthusiasm for the magic in one's own field is equivalent to wearing blinders while navigating through shoals and uncharted seas. Good professionals come to feel that, although technological development is a complex thing that involves many diverse efforts, somehow the contribution of their field is the key element, and that if they can only do what they feel is essential, most of the other problems will fall into line. The health specialist feels, "If only we can bring good health to these people, they can work efficiently, have more to eat, be stronger, and enjoy their leisure in a way not now possible." Quite true. The agriculturalist feels, "If only we can get these people to raise more and better food they will enjoy better health, be able to work harder, and to enjoy their leisure." Also true. Educators feel, to a man, that the first thing to do in a newly developing country is to teach people to read and write; if you only make people literate, they argue, the remaining problems are not very difficult. And so on through the list of professions.

Professional compartmentalization—a function of American culture with its great division of labor—tends to be exported along with professional knowledge. Sometimes no harm results. But, as should be clear by now, technological change is a multilinear, not a unilinear, process, and each activity builds upon, draws from, and contributes to many other activities. When professional pride is combined with professional jealousy, the joint planning and operations that produce the most successful programs are difficult to achieve. Professional indoctrination, it seems to me, often makes it difficult for a well-trained person to appreciate fully the contributions that are made by specialists in other fields and to realize that the success of these specialists will enhance the value of one's own work.

The effectiveness of a technical specialist is dependent upon the extent to which he learns to think and work in terms of problems rather than programs. His effectiveness is also conditioned by the extent to which he is able to adjust to the ways of living and working of the host country. Everyone, when first stationed in a foreign country, experiences "culture shock" to some degree. In the words of the anthropologist Kalervo Oberg, who first popularized the expression, culture shock is a malady, an occupational disease of people who have been suddenly transplanted abroad. Culture shock is a mental illness, and as is true of much mental illness, the victim usually does not know he is afflicted. He finds that he is irritable, depressed, and probably annoyed by the lack of attention shown him by his local technical counterpart. Everything seems to go wrong, and the technician finds he is increasingly outspoken about the shortcomings of the country he expected to like. But it rarely occurs to him that the problem lies within himself; it is obvious that the host country and its unpredictable inhabitants are to blame.

Oberg defines the symptoms of culture shock as excessive preoccupation with drinking water, food, and dishes, fear of physical contact with servants, great concern over minor pains and skin erruptions, a hand-washing complex, fits of anger over delays and other minor frustrations, a fixed idea that "people" are cheating you, delay and outright refusal to learn the language of the country, an absent-minded faraway stare ("sometimes called the tropical stare"), a feeling of helplessness and a desire for the company of people of one's own nationality, and "a terrible longing to be back home, to be able to have a good cup of coffee and a piece of apple pie, to walk into that corner drugstore, to visit one's relatives, and in general, to talk to people who really make sense."[3]

The malady of culture shock is caused in part by communication problems and in part by gnawing feelings of inadequacy which grow stronger and stronger as the specialist realizes he is not going to reach all of those technical goals he had marked out.

> Culture shock is precipitated by the anxiety that results from losing all one's familiar cues. These cues include the thousand and one ways in which we orient ourselves to the situations of daily life: when to shake hands and what to say when we meet people, when and how much to tip, how to give orders to servants, how to make purchases, when to accept and when to refuse invitations, when to take statements seriously and when not. Those cues to behavior [which may be words, gestures, facial expressions, or customs] are acquired in the course of growing up and are as much a part of our culture as the language we speak. All of us depend for our peace of mind and our efficiency on hundreds of cues, most of which we do not carry on a level of conscious awareness.[4]

When a person enters a strange culture, these cues are removed; a series of basic props have been knocked out, and frustration and anxiety follow. "When Americans or other foreigners in a strange land get together to grouse about the host country, you can be sure they are suffering from culture shock."[5]

Immunity to culture shock does not come from being broadminded and full of good will. These are highly important characteristics of a successful specialist and they may aid in recovery, but they can no more prevent the illness than grim determina-

[3] Communicated by Dr. Kalervo Oberg.
[4] Oberg, 1955, p. 16.
[5] *Ibid.*, p. 16.

tion can prevent a cold. Individuals differ greatly in the degree to which culture shock affects them. A few people prove completely unable to make the necessary adjustment, and all technical aid missions of any size can point to skilled personnel who had to be repatriated because of inability to cope with local conditions. Other people get by with only a light touch of the affliction. Most of us go through a series of stages which represent a good, stiff attack of the illness, but from which full recovery is made. Oberg has outlined these stages as follows.

During the first, or incubation stage, the victim may feel positively euphoric. Probably he is staying in a good hotel or a staff guest house where food and sanitation approximate home conditions; the English language serves his pressing needs; the tourist sights are intriguing; the local people are courteous and helpful; and it is clear that a wonderful experience lies ahead. The new arrival notices colleagues who have been on duty a few months who seem grouchy and depressed and ill adjusted, and he may feel condescending about these poor fellows who have not yet made the adjustment that he, the new arrival, has accomplished, all in a few days.

During this period he finds a house, maids, schools for the children, perhaps a chauffeur, and moves into the new home, prepared to enjoy a scale of living he probably never knew at home. Then, wham! The Cook's tour is over, and the virus bites deep. There is maid trouble, school trouble, language trouble, house trouble, transportation trouble, shopping trouble —trouble everywhere. All the things about everyday living that were taken for granted at home now become insurmountable problems. The technician is now just another cog, as far as the bureaucracy to which he is assigned is concerned; he is no longer a novelty, and his national counterparts take him for granted. He is probably annoyed, too, because the gratitude he expects for his help is strangely lacking. This attitude is interpreted as indifference, or perhaps as an indication that the local people aren't friendly after all. At this stage the victim bands together with his fellow sufferers to exchange symptoms and to criticize the host country and all its citizens. The appraisal is derogatory, based on simple stereotypes which offer an easy rationalization for one's troubles. "These people can't plan," "They have no manners," "They ought to be taught how to get things done in a hurry," and so on, the complaining runs. At this period the cocktail circuit becomes a convenient crutch, an easy and uninhibiting atmosphere in which to get a load off the chest.

This second stage represents the crisis in the disease; if it is successfully weathered, the patient will be restored to health. Passing the crisis ushers the patient into the third, or recovery stage. He now begins to understand some of the cues which orient him and perhaps enough of the language so that his isolation is not complete. Little by little the problems of living are worked out, and it becomes apparent that the situation, although difficult, is not absolutely hopeless, as it seemed only a short time earlier. A returning sense of humor is helpful at this point; when the patient can joke about his sad plight, he is well on the road to recovery. By now, he almost imagines himself to be an authority on the country, and he can bolster his ego by talking in a knowing fashion before awed new arrivals. It helps, too, to realize that other people are experiencing the same depression and to be able to help them by holding out encouragement.

The fourth stage represents full or near full recovery. By now, if ever, the technician will have made a relatively good adjustment to the situation in which he finds himself. He comes to accept the customs of the country for what they are. He doesn't necessarily wax enthusiastic about all of them, but he doesn't chafe. From time to time he experiences strain in his working relationships, but the basic anxiety of not being able to live is gone. Presently the technician realizes that he is getting a great kick out of the new experience and that there can be real exhilaration in the overseas experience. But however perceptive, no one realizes fully the nature of his illness until he returns to the United States on home leave, or again to live in that country. It is almost embarrassing to realize how many shortcomings the good old U.S.A. seems to have and how frustrating and annoying so many experiences can be. Culture shock in reverse is much less serious than the original ailment, but it is surprising how many people can hardly wait through their home leaves to get back to the post which, only two short years before, seemed absolutely unbearable.

The difficulties that lead to culture shock are very real. A temperate-climate dweller has new health problems to face in the tropics, and food and water carry bacteria unknown at home to which an immunity must be developed. Business methods are different, and the corner shopkeeper may not agree that the customer is always right. Electric and water service may be cut at inconvenient times, and the telephone, even if it works perfectly, is a terrifying instrument when it carries a language foreign to the user. But these are usually minor difficulties. The environment remains the same, but the technician adapts himself to it; it is his changed attitude that has restored his health.

Culture shock is not limited to technical specialists on overseas assignments. Tourists all too frequently reveal the symptoms, and they respond like the stage-two technician: by griping and making unflattering comments about the country and its people. But there are two things that intensify culture shock for technical experts as against tourists and casual travelers. The tourist can always go home; usually he does before he has time to recover.

But the technician knows he is stuck for two long years, and the months ahead look like a life sentence. Not only this, but he has come to a foreign country with something of missionary zeal; the average technician is where he is because he feels he has something to contribute. But just at the time he is deepest in stage two of culture shock, he sees that he can't possibly accomplish in his two-year term the things he planned to do. The pace of the country seems slow; his counterparts seem uninterested; necessary materials are delayed; and budgets are held up.

The technician realizes, with horror, that he won't have much to show for his time. His self-esteem and his security are threatened, and the shock deepens. What will his professional colleagues back home—simultaneously his best friends and his most severe critics—think? In the final analysis our feeling of professional adequacy depends on how our colleagues evaluate us. We take pride in our ability but know that we must keep showing results if our reputation is not to falter. This means, unfortunately, that just at the time when we need maximum flexibility in coping with new conditions, security seems to lie in the course of maximum rigidity. The best technical expert, as pointed out, is the one who can appraise broad problems and decide on realistic courses of action. But program-oriented people need time and favorable conditions to learn problem-thinking, and this, while they are experiencing culture shock, is just what they don't have. In a strange and (apparently) hostile world, there is only one thing we can be absolutely sure of: we are first class, A-1 professionals. But how do we prove it? Obviously, we demonstrate it, to our own satisfaction if not that of others, by trying to duplicate the States-side job that we have so often done before. The one thing that is not relative, in an apparently topsy-turvy world, we feel, is that there is a right way and a wrong way to do the job, and cost what it may, we're going to do it the right way. So the American sanitary engineer in Iran builds a bang-up American-type shower and his colleague shows he knows how to cope with excreta-spawned flies, and the basic health problems remain untouched.

I recall a young American I encountered in a Latin American country, who appeared to be deep in stage two of shock. Slide rules stuck out of his pockets, pens and pencils were clipped to his lapels, his pockets bulged with tape measures, and he clutched drafting instruments in both hands. I knew immediately he was an architect. He was designing American-type small hospitals and health centers, utilizing expensive imported materials and construction techniques suited to American building methods. Local architectural styles were pleasing to the eye and functional to the task, building materials were inexpensive, carpenters and masons knew how to build with them, and—with a problem-oriented outlook—better and cheaper buildings could have been constructed. But the architect had learned ARCHITECTURE, and he was making a good fight to preserve his sanity by convincing himself that he had learned his lessons well.

How long does culture shock last? It depends on the individual. Resilient people are over it in three months. Not infrequently it goes on for a year. Few people, when first experiencing it, are well recovered in less than six months. A Brazilian health official once said, "It takes us a year to make a good consultant out of a North American technician,"[6] and this is a pretty good estimate of world-wide averages. A specialist begins to earn his keep after about a year of adjustment.

Does a case of culture shock immunize one against future attacks? Unfortunately, no. Future cases may be lighter and less frequent, but drastically different experiences can produce it time after time. In retrospect, I recognize at least three separate major attacks myself. On one occasion the primary cause, looking back, seems to have been loss of primary cues; on the other two occasions, fear of failing on the job I had undertaken set off the attack. On the most recent occasion I knew all about culture shock, but it was not until some months afterward, when I looked back on the experience, that I realized what accounted for my behavior.

[6] *Ibid.,* p. 15.

10 . . . . *The anthropologist at work: the conceptual context*

Technological development programs proceed more smoothly and are more successful when the cultural patterns of the participating peoples, the values and motivations of the innovators, and the social dynamics of the project setting are understood and utilized in planning and operations. If this hypothesis—an axiom to some of us—is accepted, the question remains, how do we gather and utilize the necessary information? There are some program planners and technical specialists who seem to know almost instinctively what they can and cannot do in a given situation, and this sensitivity is heightened through field experience. But these people are the exceptions; most program planners and field technicians do not have an innate feel for the social implications of guided change, nor are they fully aware of the possible consequences of their work. The ethnocentric blinders with which our culture provides us have to come off little by little. The sociocultural dimension in planned change is a little like grammar in language: it is there all the time, and basic, but it is not obvious until one's attention is called to it. Even when it is recognized, it is mastered only after hard study.

The theoretical viewpoints and the substantive data which can be used to teach the grammar of planned culture change are largely the result of social science research, particularly in the "behavioral" area of anthropology, sociology, and social psychology. In the British colonial service there have been administrators who have done superb work in studying the cultures of the people among whom they have worked. We have been proud to claim them as anthropologists. Usually, however, the administrator or technical specialist cannot make cultural studies in his spare time, even if he has the education that tells him what steps to take. This is especially true, of course, of the person whose overseas assignment is for two years and who, at the end of this period, returns home or goes to another country. The gathering and utilization of social science knowledge which can facilitate technical aid programs is a full-time job for specialists trained in the several fields concerned, just as successful public health work, community development, or agriculture is a full-time job for trained specialists. It is the responsibility of the social—or behavioral—scientist to gather the essential data and, working cooperatively with the technical specialist, see how these data can most profitably be utilized in the prosecution of the action program.

The role of the behavioral scientist in a developmental program can be thought of as one in which he makes formal utilization of the theoretical concepts, the research methodologies, and the factual data of his field to facilitate change in goal-directed projects. The words "formal utilization" are the clue to what is unique in the use of behavioral scientists, because through history men of great insight have utilized cultural, sociological, and psychological knowledge to achieve change in the behavior of groups of people. They were not making *formal* use of specific knowledge, but they knew what to do to accomplish their aims. Some of these examples make revealing reading for those of us who work in international development programs.

In the Spanish conquest of America, Christianity was successfully implanted in most areas because the Church was familiar with the strategy of directed culture change. Friars and priests learned the Indian languages to communicate with their charges and to study the pagan forms they wished to extirpate. They built churches on the former sites of Indian temples, and they encouraged the identification of pagan gods with the Virgin Mary and the saints. In these activities the Church was merely following the lessons it had learned in earlier centuries in Europe, when, during the spread of primitive Christianity throughout the Mediterranean, pagan deities often were transformed into new guise through the process of syncretism (Chapter 2).

One of the earliest specific examples of a sociocultural tactic for directed culture change is recorded by the Venerable Bede in *The Ecclesiastical History of the English People*. He tells of the reconversion of England at the end of the sixth century by missionaries sent from Ireland, and he reproduces a portion of a letter from Pope Gregory the Great to the abbot Mellitus in 597 or 598 which might serve as a modern text on how to utilize cultural and psychological knowledge to achieve one's ends.

When then God shall bring you unto our reverend brother Augustine bishop tell him, what I have of long time devised with myself of the cause of the English men. That is to wit that not the temples of the Idols, but the Idols which be in them be broken, that holy water be made and sprinkled about the same temples, altars builded, relics placed. For if the said churches be well made, it is needful that they be altered from the worshipping of devils into the service of God: that whilst the people doth not see their temples spoiled, they may (forsaking their error) be moved the more oft to haunt their wonted place to the honour and service of God. And for that they are wont to kill oxen in sacrifice to the devils, they shall use the same slaughter now, but changed to a better purpose. It may therefore be permitted them, that in the dedication days or other solemn days of martyrs, they maketh them bowers about their churches, and feasting together after a good religious sort, kill their oxen now to the refreshing of themselves, to the praise of God, and increase of charity, which before they were wont to offer up in sacrifice to the devils: that whilst some outward comforts are reserved unto them, they may thereby be brought the rather to the inward comforts of grace in God. For it is doubtless impossible from men being so rooted in evil customs, to cut off all their abuses upon the sudden. He that laboureth to climb up unto a high place, he goeth upward by steps and passes, not by leaps.[1]

Pope Gregory showed acumen in protecting himself against possible criticism within the Church by utilizing the rule, as valuable today as then, of justifying proposed change by citing religious precedent or authority:

So unto the children of Israel being in Egypt our Lord was well known. But yet he suffered them to do sacrifice unto him still in offering up beasts unto him, which otherwise they would have offered up unto the devils, as they were wont to do in the land of Egypt, that altering their intent, they should leave some, and also keep some of their old sacrifices: that is, that the beasts which they offered before, they should now offer still. But yet in offering them unto the true God, and not unto the devils, they should not be the same sacrifices in all points as they were before.[2]

More than a thousand years later a Spanish premier showed a comparable knowledge of culture and psychology in achieving a change which stymied the forces of law. On various occasions

[1] Hereford, 1935, pp. 56-57.
[2] *Ibid.*, p. 57.

in Spanish history the government, as an aid to crime detection, tried to prohibit men and women from covering their faces with cloaks, hats with turned-down brims, shawls, or scarves. In 1766 King Charles III, at the instigation of his unpopular Sicilian Premier Squillaci, dictated a Royal Order prohibiting soldiers and government employees from wearing the long cape and broad-brimmed hat, an order subsequently extended to the general public. The resulting furor is known in history as the Mutiny of Esquilache, and it resulted in banishment for the hated foreigner. His Spanish successor, the Count of Arandas, while in sympathy with the restrictions on dress, rescinded the order. He accomplished its purpose easily and painlessly by making the long cape and broad-brimmed hat the official uniform of the public executioner.[3]

In 1857 the Anglican missionary William Duncan began work among the Tsimshian Indians on the coast of northern British Columbia. He quickly realized he must understand not only the language, but also the culture and the system of interpersonal relationships that structured this society. His approach is particularly noteworthy because of its recognition of the problems of perception across cultural boundaries. He realized that there were aspects of Christian metaphysics which, if adhered to literally in preaching and services, might be interpreted by the Indians in a very different fashion from that intended. Since some of the religious practices of the Tsimshian involved cannibalistic rites, Duncan refused to introduce the sacrament of the Lord's Supper. He feared the distinction between symbol and substance would not be easy to impart. Further, since he was trying to eliminate the drinking of alcohol among his followers, he felt that giving them wine in a church service would confuse them and prejudice his work. Again, because of the strong Tsimshian emphasis on status and social classes and the outward symbols of position, all of which he dis-

3 Altamira, 1949, pp. 443-444.

approved, he refused to wear the vestments of an Anglican priest for fear he would encourage rather than discourage social differences. He likewise eschewed religious paintings and carvings, believing that the act or symbol would assume a talismanic virtue in the eyes of his followers.

Duncan's unorthodox ideas alarmed his superiors, and in 1877 he was replaced in his village by a regular clergyman with less cultural insight. Duncan's wisdom was demonstrated almost immediately. He had de-emphasized the concept of the Holy Ghost and the acceptance of direct revelation because of the importance among the Tsimshian of bodily possession by mythological spirits which caused the possessed individual to act in a rapturous and often inhuman fashion. Shortly after his successor began preaching a more orthodox Christianity, several converts became ecstatic, declaring they had witnessed miracles, had seen Christ on the cross, and had conversed with the Holy Spirit. The contagion spread to other settlements, and the Indians sang and danced. At the height of their ecstasy some offered to give the power of God, which they held in their cupped hands, to anyone who wished it, a direct transfer of the native pattern of inducing spirit possession in a cult initiate.[4]

A final example brings us down to the present time. During the Korean War in the early 1950's Indian troops supervised the repatriation of Allied-held Chinese prisoners. Those who wished to be sent home were separated out from anticommunist troops who wished to remain in South Korea. On one occasion an Indian major and several soldiers were seized by rioting anticommunist prisoners and held hostage inside the compound for ninety minutes. The flare-up subsided and the hostages were released after the Indian commanding officer, Major General S. P. P. Thorat, bravely entered the compound and asked the startled Chinese prisoners, "What sort of Chinese are you? Where is your hospitality? You have offered my men neither tea

[4] Barnett, 1942.

nor cigarettes." The surprised prisoners fell back and in a few minutes brought tea, cigarettes, and finally the major and his men. General Thorat said the prisoners' "sense of hospitality was touched" by his unexpected statement and they "looked at me completely flabbergasted."[5]

In contrast to these examples of proto-applied behavioral science, the modern anthropologist or sociologist working in a goal-directed program consciously utilizes the substantive data, the theoretical concepts, and the research techniques he controls. In a specific project the anthropologist—to draw from the author's field—tries to analyze the basic characteristics of the society and culture to which he has been sent, to understand the motivations and values of the members of the bureaucracy that is attempting the change, and to learn the patterns of interaction of the two systems. He brings a body of theory which provides the framework for his analysis. Using this theory, as well as the factual information he has or acquires, he attempts to predict what the total range of change will be if a specific program is successful or, conversely, he attempts to determine what minimum changes in an entire culture must occur before a specific project can succeed. He looks for the social and cultural barriers that inhibit change, suggests ways to neutralize them, and decides what motivations and other stimulants to change can most successfully be used in direct action, in aiding people to decide whether they wish to accept or reject proposed innovations. He hopes to help the members of the innovating group understand better the implications of its activities and the ways in which its organization and values bear upon the task at hand.

The anthropologist is gratified if his efforts contribute to a more successful program, but he wants more than this. If work in a goal-directed program does not permit him to learn new facts and draw generalizations about culture in general—in

[5] *Berkeley Daily Gazette*, September 26, 1953.

short, feed back into basic anthropological theory—he is not going to be fully satisfied. For the anthropologist has his own goals, which will be pointed out in Chapter 12.

But how, more precisely, does the anthropologist go about his task? How does he progress from the general to the specific? How does he translate broad cultural and social knowledge into the concrete terms that can be utilized in a program of international public health or community development? The first thing to note is that there are no precise rules for the application of anthropological knowledge in such situations. There are no do-it-yourself guides which tell what particular bits of theory or fact are significant for specific problems. Intuition, the ability to sense problems and mode of attack, is essential to the behavioral scientist who is to work successfully in an action setting. In all field work there is an artistic element which must be present if the results are to be significant. The effective applied anthropologist must be well grounded in social and cultural theory; he must command a substantial corpus of factual knowledge; and he must be sensitive to the widest possible range of stimulants in his field work.

With this caution in mind, it may be suggested that the anthropologist contributes three important things to any program: (1) a point of view, or a philosophy; (2) factual knowledge; (3) research techniques appropriate to the task.

The point of view is something like this: No culture is all good or all bad. Basically, all cultures are reasonably good; otherwise they would not have survived. The anthropologist is conditioned by training, and perhaps temperament, to look for the good in a society, goodness being defined in terms of the society's ability to satisfy the needs and aspirations of all its members without jeopardizing those of other societies. The anthropologist is not opposed to change, but he does not necessarily approve of change for its own sake. He believes that real progress is made when it springs from and builds on the good things already existing in a culture, rather than when it is defined in terms of an approximation of the American way of life.

Two examples will illustrate this point. In a seminar in the School of Public Health at the University of California we spent several sessions on the problem of diet in relation to culture. Students from foreign countries, studying nutritional problems, outlined for us the typical diets of their countries. Compared to National Research Council standards, the pictures were not encouraging. There were grave shortages of such foods as milk, citrus fruits, meats, and vegetables. In view of the economic limitations generally prevailing, most students felt that adequate diet in their countries was something that could not be attained for many years. Then, with the aid of Dr. Ruth Huenemann, Professor of Public Health Nutrition, and without direct reference to National Research Council standards, we looked for ways to improve the diets utilizing only those foods that grew or could easily be produced in each country. We quickly discovered that, although there were serious weaknesses in all diets, none was really bad. All could be greatly improved within the economic limitations of each country by building on what existed, rather than by trying to approximate the standards that had been developed for Americans in the United States. Viewed in this light, the members of the seminar felt that a seemingly hopeless problem became quite susceptible of solution.

The other example is told by Dr. Henry Renteln, who practiced medicine for several years after World War II in Iran as a member of a team of German physicians brought by the government of Iran to extend medical services to isolated villages and nomadic peoples. Dr. Renteln learned of a village in a high, remote area with a number of lepers. But when the villagers heard he was coming, they hid their leprous relatives in the hills, fearing they would be placed forcibly in a leprosarium. When the villagers learned that this was not the case, the lepers returned home. Then an interesting thing was discovered. Each leper had his own room in the house, which in itself is a luxury, and he stayed there practically in isolation. Although he was allowed out of his room and into the yard, he did not mingle with other family members. He received food in his own dish which he placed at the threshold of his room and which only he handled. In this primitive fashion the leper was physically isolated, but still he had the actual presence and emotional closeness to his family. Over the years the villagers had learned that the leper is only mildly contagious and does not have to be cast out. Here then we see how the villagers found a solution adapted to their needs, which offered relative protection to the healthy and which for the ill was more humane than casting them out or putting them in an institution.[6] The best control, Dr. Renteln felt, consisted in treatment built on the prevailing pattern of home care.

The factual knowledge the anthropologist brings to an action program is both theoretical and substantive. It consists of a body of general theory about society and culture, and particularly about processes of change—such as those described in earlier chapters—which have wide cross-cultural validity, and it consists of concrete data about the patterns of culture of the area in which the work is to be carried out. For example, the anthropologist who joins a public health or community development program in Latin America is first of all a general anthropologist. In addition, he presumably has read a long series of monographs and articles on Latin American culture, knows something about the history and geography of the area, and in general understands the basic characteristics of the societies and cultures of this area which set it off from Africa or Asia. To the extent that good basic anthropological research has been carried out previously in a project area, the anthropologist is able to proceed to specifics with just that much more dispatch.

[6] Communicated by Dr. Henry Renteln.

The research techniques the anthropologist brings to bear on field problems are the standard social science methods of interviews, schedules, censuses, and questionnaires. Of these the most important is what the sociologist calls the "open-ended" interview and what the psychologist calls the "depth" interview. It is an intensive rather than an extensive method. It is based on the assumption that detailed data from ten informants give more meaningful answers than superficial data from one hundred. Further, it is based on the assumption that the range of factors affecting a problem can never be fully defined in advance. The way to find out what is significant is to find informants who are willing to talk, to guide them gently, but for the most part to give them free reign. Only after the range of a problem has been explored in this fashion is it profitable to attempt to quantify data by means of a questionnaire. Is the problem the lack of public response to a new health clinic in a depressed area? The anthropologist's approach is to knock on doors or otherwise seek introductions to a small number of homes. Long hours of general conversation, guided but not forced in the direction of the clinic eventually will afford information on health beliefs and attitudes, authority patterns within the family, working schedules of the parents, economic problems, and a host of other factors that may be significant. Only after the potential breadth of the problem has been thus defined is it worthwhile to frame schedules and quantify responses.

In approaching a specific assignment, the anthropologist tries to do two things.

1. *To determine the relationship of the institution or elements involved to the total culture pattern.* Remembering that a culture is an integrated, functional unit, he tries to find out the nature of the phenomena he is studying, how they interlock with the remainder of the culture, and what their role and function are. In a health program, for example, he first asks what the concepts of illness and health are, and what role or

roles are played by illness. In a housing program he asks what the nature and function of a house are, what it means to its dwellers, how it relates to family structure, economic activities, hospitality patterns, and the like.

2. *To determine the patterns of interpersonal relations among all people who participate in a program.* This means a knowledge not only of the social structure of the group, but also of the new relationships that develop between the group and the organization that is trying to bring innovations from the outside.

The anthropologist begins by drawing upon his general knowledge. In a general way he is prepared to say what the range of functions of housing, of the family, of illness, of agriculture, of literacy may be in a sociocultural setting of a given type. But this general analysis will take him only so far. It must be followed up by field work to determine the specific and unique characteristics of a situation. Only then can recommendations safely be made.

This process can be illustrated by a hypothetical project designed to improve substandard housing. The anthropologist begins by asking very general and perhaps obvious questions: what is the nature of housing in this area, what is the function of a house, what are the purposes of housing thought to be by the people? Some of the general answers that come to mind are: a house is for shelter; it is a place to store food and feed a family; it provides bathing and toilet facilities; it affords privacy; it is a place for family interaction in work and recreation; perhaps it gives aesthetic satisfaction; perhaps it is a device to achieve prestige; perhaps religious functions are met. These answers, and many others, can be worked out in a moment. But if we really want to understand what a house is, and what its social, economic, and other functions are, we must study concrete examples and note the ways in which each room and facility are used, the time devoted to each, the motor patterns associated with the use of equipment and furnishings, the relationship of work to recreation areas, and a whole series of similar things.

If, in planning improved housing, the functions, use, and attitudes of the people are not well understood, the program will fall short of its goals. While doing field work in Round Valley, California, I discovered that the Indian Service had built homes for some of the Indian families. These were typical, small, rural American farmhouses, reasonably comfortable and well built. But the Indians liked to carry on many more activities outdoors than do American farmers: cooking, perhaps sleeping in good weather, and so forth. These houses were not a function of Indian attitudes and needs, and most of them had become pretty dilapidated through neglect.

The manner in which general appraisal of a problem in housing can be worked out in the field is illustrated by an analysis directed by Isabel Kelly. In Mexico the Ministry of Health and Public Assistance, through the division of Rural Medical Services, wished to improve housing in a number of ejido communities in the La Laguna region of the northcentral states of Coahuila and Durango. Ejidos are rural communities holding communal lands distributed following the Mexican Revolution that began in 1910. Sometimes lands are farmed communally, but more often plots are distributed on an individual basis for each farmer to work as he wishes.

Dr. Kelly and her Mexican associates carried out the major work over a period of seven months in the ejido of El Cuije, about 15 miles from Torreón. This settlement was found to consist of 57 *ejidatario* families (with land rights) totaling 356 persons, and about the same number of families without rights. The village was of irregular plan. Houses were adobe, with an earth floor; roofs were made of mud and reeds over beams; windows were small, with board shutters and no glass. Sanitary facilities were poor: only half of the houses had water taps in the patios, and the remaining families used public fountains. Latrines were completely lacking. Garbage and rubbish were simply thrown into the street. One house had a cold-water shower, but otherwise men bathed in irrigation ditches and women in tubs in their houses. Small domestic animals walked in and out of houses at will.

Since Dr. Kelly had lived in Mexico for many years and had studied Mexican culture in a number of local situations, and since her colleagues were Mexican, the group knew a great deal about basic Mexican culture. They were also imbued with the philosophy of building upon what already exists. But no anthropological research had been carried out in this particular part of Mexico, and no research directed toward housing problems as such had been recorded in any part of the country. Hence, a significant amount of research was necessary. During the first ten days the anthropologists visited homes, made friends with a number of people, and in a series of open-ended interviews began to block out the scope of the problem. They learned a great deal about the nature and functions of houses and the social uses to which they are put. These observations served as guide in working out a detailed questionnaire which supplied the statistical frame for analysis and recommendations. But it quickly became apparent that much more than a questionnaire on housing was needed, and ultimately the studies embraced data on farming techniques and attitudes, care of domestic animals, family budgets, nutritional problems, clothing, division of work within the family, traditional medical beliefs and practices, political and social organizations within the community, relations of the ejidatarios with the national government, and a whole series of similar things, which at first glance have little or nothing to do with housing. A solution to housing problems, it turned out, required knowledge of a great chunk of the culture.

The analysis of the fifty-seven houses studied revealed significant data. In forty-five the kitchen also served as dining room, in thirteen as living room, in ten as bedroom, and in six for crop storage. In those houses with living rooms the space was often used for sleeping, sometimes for eating, and sometimes for crop storage. Obviously, multiuse of rooms was a basic pattern to be considered in planning improved quarters. In furnishings, first priority was given by local people to at least one bed; this was found in all fifty-seven houses. Second priority was given to a wardrobe, found in 85 percent of the houses, and third priority to a dining-room sideboard, found in 75 percent. Sixty-six percent of the houses had radios, and 50 percent had sewing machines. Half the kitchens had kerosene stoves, and all had elevated adobe hearths, usually with hood and chimney. Other kitchen furnishings included the metate (grinding stone), water jars, a few shelves, pottery on the walls, knives and spoons, and the like. Kitchens usually presented a considerable state of disarray. Clothes were washed in irrigation ditches or in wooden tubs in the patios. All families had domestic animals, which not only had practical utility, but also served as savings (that is, they could be sold in time of emergency) and as items of prestige, especially in the case of horses. Maize was stored in temporary cribs erected in patios, and agricultural tools were thrown in any vacant space on the property.

In addition to the analysis of house composition and uses, all fifty-seven families were asked what they thought the ideal house should be, always given the economic limitations present. This showed how important it is to work with, and not to plan for, people. For example, the anthropologists thought that running water in kitchens would be indicated because of the convenience afforded, but wives were almost unanimous in preferring a tap in the patio. Faucets leak—this is a fact of life—and a leaky faucet in the kitchen could be a real problem. Again, it seemed to the anthropologists that permanent maize storage facilities would be desirable, but it turned out the people preferred the demountable type, since this afforded more yard space when supplies were depleted.

With all the data in, it was possible to make general recommendations to Rural Medical Services. In outline, these were as follows:

1. Houses should be oriented to face the southeast. They thus backed against the cold and wind of winter and the hot sun of summer afternoons.

2. Lot sizes should be 20 by 30 meters. This was recognized as smaller than desirable, but the people preferred a bit of crowding to encroaching on valuable agricultural land.

3. Traditional building materials should be used, because of economy and native knowledge of construction, but, with cement floors and larger windows on house fronts, better sanitary conditions would exist.

4. The minimum unit should consist of a kitchen-dining room, a living-bedroom, and an outdoor covered porch. This *corredor* would serve as a third room: it is ideal for much work, and in good weather some family members could sleep on it.

5. With respect to sanitary facilities, it was recommended that a single tap be installed in patios, for the reason indicated, and that water be distributed within the property with a hose. For washing and bathing, it first seemed desirable to combine a shower with a laundry room, since both required water and a drain, and times of use did not overlap. But it turned out that these facilities were in no way connected in the minds of the people. Further, women like to wash in the outdoors, under a shade, and not inside a small damp room. So in the final recommendation provision was made for a small shower room with a water tank on the roof, where water would be slightly warmed by solar action. Clothes were to be washed in a simple concrete tub under a shade. A pit latrine was recommended, with a simple septic tank for water drainage.

6. The kitchen plan was modified to provide more storage and shelf space, and counters of different heights were suggested to conform to different uses. For example, grinding with the metate requires, for comfort, a support at a height midway between the floor and the raised adobe hearth.

This basic design was flexible, in that additional rooms could be added as needed and as finances permitted; it utilized traditional materials and building skills; it met basic social needs; and it did no violence to any known values. Improved housing, designed on the basis of this kind of information, is much more apt to be successful than if the problem is thought of simply as an architectural and economic one.[7]

Several examples from the field of public health will further illustrate how the anthropologist goes about his task and how he analyzes the cultural, social, and interpersonal factors involved in specific situations. The most comprehensive of the studies to be considered was made by Margaret Clark in a Mexican American enclave in the city of San Jose, California. This study was planned as an experiment to see how social science knowledge might be utilized to make public health education programs among minority groups in the United States more effective, and in general to point up the problems and conflicts that exist which make medical and health needs among such people more difficult to solve than they are among native-born American whites. A committee, consisting of a professor of public health, the director of public health education of the state, the director of the county public health department in which the work was carried out, and three anthropologists, was set up to direct the work. The committee met regularly during the eighteen months of the study to hear progress reports, to make recommendations for further work, and to ensure the closest possible integration of health and social science interests.

It was recognized that health, illness, and the mechanisms to

7 Kelly, 1953.

restore one to health are intimately related to the entire culture of a group. Consequently, Miss Clark first devoted her efforts to making what is known in anthropology as a "community study," in which the basic patterns of life are outlined: social structure, economic activities, religious forms, relations of the group to local government agencies, basic attitudes and values, and the like. Only against this background, it was believed, could health problems be adequately analyzed. Next Miss Clark made a thorough study of the ideas about sickness and health. What is health? How is it defined? How is it maintained? Why do people fall ill? What is done to restore the sick to health? Who are curers and what is their training and techniques? What part does the family take in making decisions about medical treatment? In general, it was found that the answers to these questions fell in line with the broad patterns of folk medical belief and practice which, in recent years, have been well described in Latin America. But the Sal si Puedes group lives, and has lived for a long time, in an American setting, exposed to urban American health services and sanitary laws. It is gradually acculturating to an American way of life, although the progress is uneven and halting. This meant that knowledge about Latin American ideas of health and disease was useful in guiding research, but the significant answers came from the local field work.

One of the most important areas of data had to do with the manner in which illness was found to help stabilize social relations within the community through publicizing and punishing social offenses, providing a socially approved escape from censure for unsanctioned behavior, and dramatizing the acculturative situation. In one instance a young wife expecting her first child scolded her husband for returning home drunk. He beat her and put her out of the house in the rain. Her parents took her to the local curer *(curandera)*, who treated her so the unborn child would not suffer "fright illness" from the experience. Under normal circumstances this domestic spat would not have attracted attention. The husband had availed himself of a male prerogative: an evening out with the boys; and his wife had humiliated him by her scolding. Had she not been pregnant his beating would have passed unnoticed. But, because he endangered the life of his unborn child, the wife gained the support and sympathy of the community. Finally he saw the error of his action, apologized, and returned to his wife.

In another instance a woman with six children was faced with a prolonged visit by her husband's unemployed brother, his wife, and five children. With fifteen people living on the wages of a single laborer, the debt at the grocery store grew larger and larger and finally credit was cut off. With deeply engrained Mexican patterns of hospitality and mutual obligations between family members, she recognized her obligation to her husband's relatives. Yet she feared her children would not have enough to eat, and the crowded conditions of the house became almost unbearable. She began to suffer rapid pulse, shortness of breath, and sweating, symptoms that were defined as "fright" by the *curandera*. Now relieved of the obligation of caring for her brother-in-law's family by a socially sanctioned condition—illness—there was no alternative but that the visitors should move on. Had she remained in good health she would have been thought to be selfish and inhospitable if she had complained about her husband's relatives.

Illness may also be a protest against the acculturative situation. An elderly woman admitted to a hospital against her wishes was required to take daily showers after the acute phase of her illness was past. She objected, since her custom was less frequent tub baths, but her objections were ignored. While returning from her shower shortly thereafter she had an attack of "bad air," a folk-defined illness which, in her opinion and that of the family, was the result of the dangerous practice of daily showers. The illness gained her the sympathy of her family, who caused her to be released prematurely to be taken home for what they felt was proper care.[8]

Upon completion of her study it was possible for Miss Clark to make much more intelligible to county health personnel the reasons for the health behavior of Mexican Americans. Furthermore, she was now in a position to make a series of specific recommendations which, to the extent they could be carried out, should alleviate some of the problems plaguing workers in this intercultural health situation. These recommendations had to do with communication problems, economic problems, the conflict of modern medical practice and folk beliefs, problems relating to the definition of disease, to modesty, to hospitalization, and to differentially perceived medical roles.[9]

The importance of understanding the complex interpersonal relationships that exist in any setting is illustrated by Friedl in a brief article about a hospital in rural Greece.[10] Traditionally, she says, hospitalization has been viewed as desertion of the sick person by his family; in spite of this attitude, in recent years small private hospitals of from ten to twenty-five beds have sprung up in rural Boetia, and hospitalization is increasingly sought by villagers for childbirth and serious illness. The physicians who own the hospitals have been trained in Athens, and many have studied outside the country. Nurses, however, are local girls who have been trained by the doctors.

Dr. Friedl gives us a word-picture of a sickroom: an iron bedstead against each of the three walls away from the door, covered with linens brought by the woman who occupies the bed. In the center of the floor of the 12-foot-square room, five relatives of one patient are seated around a blanket on which are the remains of a picnic lunch. At the head of the bed of a young woman patient, the husband is heating macaroni over a burner

8 Clark, 1959, p. 198-202.
9 *Ibid.*, pp. 218-239.
10 Friedl, 1958.

on a small table, which he feeds to his wife when it is warm. The husband and daughter of the third patient stand by her bedside, watching the goings-on in the room. Two of the patients wear their own nightclothes, while the third is fully-dressed, lying on her bed.

The informality of such hospital treatment is a far cry from the modern hospitals of Athens and yet, Dr. Friedl reminds us, the technical and social patterns portrayed are almost ideally suited to the problem of introducing improved medical care to rural areas. "These hospital scenes and the patterns of hospital care they represent suggest a remarkable similarity between the treatment of illness at home and its treatment in a hospital. The same values and attitudes of Greek culture are demonstrated in both situations, and their reinforcement in a time of stress is not impeded by hospitalization."[11] The Greeks feel human companionship is an absolute good; on the other hand, solitude is unpleasant and to be avoided even when people are well. Therefore, when someone is in the vulnerable state of illness, it is particularly important that he be accompanied at all times by relatives. Since the family has such important social and psychological functions, ". . . the presence day and night of family members in hospitals fulfills the latent function of emotional support. Such support is essential for Greek patients, because they feel useless and unwanted whenever an illness prevents them from fulfilling their customary roles in the household."[12] The care by family members, the home cooking, and the crowded room—all anathema to a Western-trained nurse—all help to lessen the potential sense of isolation and strangeness of hospital surroundings. Dr. Friedl points out that these improvised hospital practices conform in many ways with recent social science recommendations for more flexibility in traditional American methods of institutionalizing hospital care.

[11] *Ibid.*, p. 25.
[12] *Ibid.*, p. 26.

"What careful analysis has pointed out as a desirable method for conscious, planned, and gradual change, has been evolved willy-nilly by these [Greek] doctors under the diverse pressures of their complex culture."[13]

The final example shows how the network of social relationships in the innovating organization affects a program, and how administrative changes may be reflected in the impact of a program. In a fine, large health center in Santiago de Chile, with a wide spectrum of curative and preventive services, the director decided that a well-planned program of health education was the next step to bringing better health to his area, the population of which for the most part was made up of families in the lower socioeconomic levels. According to the plan of the center, physicians, who were part-time employees usually spending two hours a day seeing patients, were expected to inculcate patients with the principles of hygiene and healthful living during the period of the visit. For the most part, however, physicians saw their role as that of "control," routine checking of health as well as administration of curative services as needed.

Nurses were expected to supplement the preventive medicine of the doctors and carry out health education. This they did by seeing patients after the doctors, by explaining and reinforcing his instructions, and by visiting patients in their homes. Since physicians were of high social status and patients of low status, poor communication frequently existed, so the nurse's amplification of the doctor's instructions was a very important part of the visit to the center. Furthermore, regular clients were reassured when, upon visiting the health center, they would find their friend, the nurse who visited them in their homes.

Since the director was unable to obtain the services of regular health educators to carry out his enlarged health education program, he decided to accomplish this end by relieving his nurses of clinical duty and assigning them to full-time home visiting,

13 *Ibid.,* p. 27.

leaving only one nurse for the irreducible minimum of clinical duties. The director thought of this change as primarily an administrative shift and a "technical modification" in the nurses' duties. Nevertheless, it produced rather significant changes in patterns of relationships between patients and center personnel. Health education in the clinics suffered, since the physicians, who were in any case largely uninterested in this aspect of their work, were now not buttressed by nurses. Contact between doctors and nurses became primarily dependent upon patient records, and this meant that desirable follow-up attentions often were delayed, in some instances for months.

The nurses generally were pleased with the new arrangement; perhaps in part they appreciated being out from under the immediate control of the physicians, who felt the nurses' role was supplementary to their own. On the other hand, they recognized that patients came to the center with less confidence than before. When they no longer found the nurse on duty who was their friend, who knew them in their homes, they felt strange and uncertain as to how to proceed. Further, without the intermediary function of the nurse the doctor's instructions were less well understood, sometimes his instructions were not met with the previous degree of confidence, and sometimes patients left without bothering to fill prescriptions.

At the time the study was made it was still too soon to tell whether these losses were balanced by the gains from more intensive home visiting. It is clear, however, that the social structure of the health center was a vital element in the combination of factors that make for an efficient organization, and that what appeared to be a routine administrative change had implications far beyond the point envisaged by anyone.[14]

[14] Simmons, 1955.

11 . . . . *The anthropologist at work: stages of analysis*

The role of the anthropologist, and other behavioral scientists, in technological development programs can also be examined in terms of a sequence of events. A technical aid project has an inception, a planning period, an operations period, and, perhaps, a stock-taking or evaluation period in which lessons learned are analyzed for future guidance. The theoretical stand of the anthropologist assigned to such a program is the same at all stages, but the kinds of things he does and the kinds of answers he gives depend on the particular point in the sequence at which he finds himself. For purposes of illustration, the work of the anthropologist at these four stages will be described under the headings of (1) prestudy, (2) planning, (3) on-going analysis, and (4) evaluation.

PRESTUDY

When a developmental project is anticipated, data must be gathered so that planning can be done intelligently. The amount of research an anthropologist must do at this point will depend in large measure on the amount of basic cultural research that has previously been carried out in the area concerned. If an anthropologist assigned, let us say, to a public health project already has a good idea of the social structure of the area involved, the economic patterns, the value system, the folk medical beliefs and practices, he can direct himself immediately to the specific subjects that presumably will prove important in the proposed project. His task will be to draw upon the corpus of unspecialized sociocultural data available, decide what specific information is lacking, and then attempt to fill in these gaps. Prestudy of a few weeks, and sometimes less, will then give the answers that are needed.

If, on the other hand, relatively little is known about the culture and society of an area, to give the same degree of help the anthropologist will need many times the research, for he will have to work out the broad patterns of life before he can answer specific questions. This is why basic anthropological research is so very important if efficient use is to be made of anthropologists in goal-oriented programs. What is already known constitutes scientific capital; it forms a plateau of sociocultural knowledge which permits more rapid work than does a take-off from a sea-level plain. A behavioral scientist can work much more effectively in a technical aid program in, say, Mexico or India, than in Afghanistan or Viet Nam, simply because so much basic research has already been done in the former countries, whereas in the latter countries almost no work has been done. Generalized basic research—research not directed toward specific problems—is also very important because, until work is begun on a developmental project, it is not possible to recognize all the significant factors.

The necessity of encouraging and supporting basic behavioral science research is, unfortunately, something that most government officials understand only with difficulty. They want specific answers to specific questions—and quickly. Their position is not hard to understand; they are prisoners of the annual budget. Results must be shown to justify continued support, and funds earmarked for work which may not pay off for several years seem a less attractive investment than those which may show quick returns. Still, if the best behavioral science support is to be given to technical aid programs, much more basic research must be sponsored by the organizations that administer such activities.

It should be clear, then, that the nature of anthropological prestudy will depend on the amount of previous anthropological research. If little has been done, then a prestudy will, by necessity, be undifferentiated from basic research. If much has been done, a prestudy will focus almost immediately on the goals of the proposed project. The work of Isabel Kelly and her colleagues described in the last chapter stands midway between these two poles. Initially she believed that housing in El Cuije could be studied almost excluding other aspects of culture because of what was already known. This turned out to be true only in part, since El Cuije is in a subcultural area of Mexico that had been largely overlooked in earlier studies. Consequently, the seven-month study embraced farming techniques, family budgets, work patterns within the family, political factors, and many other items that proved significant to the immediate task at hand. At the same time, from the very beginning, this research was specifically pointed toward housing, and little attention was given to such things as folklore, music, religious practices, and death observances which, however interesting, had little to do with project goals.

A prestudy of a different type is described briefly by Barnett. Woleai, a group of twenty-three islets ringing a large lagoon, located midway between Truk and Palau, was used as a Japanese air base during World War II. Coconut and breadfruit trees were cut down to make room for military installations, the women were evacuated to other islands, and the men put to work. At the end of the war the islets were largely denuded, much valuable land had been covered with coral and concrete, and agricultural possibilities were greatly reduced compared to the prewar period. As the people returned to the islands, it was clear that the American administration was faced with an assistance and welfare problem.

In 1950 a survey team was sent to study the situation and make recommendations. The anthropologist was to report on social, economic, political, religious, and educational conditions and to determine the inhabitants' needs for assistance. He found that the common hardships experienced by the natives had produced a community with a high degree of integration, and that they had shown realism in working out means of food production and distribution. But, although they had defined their basic need as more food, it appeared that they were not really facing starvation. The anthropologist therefore recommended against handouts of rice and canned goods which, he felt, would only raise their future expectations. He expressed the belief that some cash income—which had existed in Japanese times—was the most pressing need of the islanders, and that this should be obtained by efforts to improve agriculture and introduce other foods that the natives could raise themselves.[1]

PLANNING

With general background knowledge and, ideally, a prestudy directed toward specific problems, an anthropologist should be able to predict in broad outline the probable consequences of any proposed detail. Conversely, he should be able to explain the minimum preconditions for success in innovation, or to point out the unforeseen problems that will constitute barriers.

[1] Barnett, 1956, pp. 94-95.

In planning activities the anthropologist is making use particularly of his concept of culture as an integrated unit, in which one dislocation or change will affect and be affected by a whole series of other factors. In an Indian village the Western technical aid agent may feel that composting of cow dung will go a long way in solving problems of field fertilizing. The anthropologist, in working on plans for the village, will point out that manure has many uses which compete for the limited amount available. It is used as fuel in cooking, and its slow-burning characteristics make it particularly important in the preparation of ghee, a clarified butter used in a variety of foods. Manure is important in the mud used in house plastering, and a little is even used in the hubble-bubble pipe, around which male social gatherings center. Consequently, less than half of the dung produced by village cows remains available for fertilizer.[2]

One of my engineering colleagues once described an ingenious compost pit he had developed. Food refuse, green stalks, leaves, and almost any other vegetable matter could be thrown into the pit, where enough gas was generated to operate a simple burner adequate for the cooking needs of an average family. He saw this as a potential device to reduce the pressure on deforested lands in newly developing countries. But the refuse that would go in the pit also had traditional uses: as fertilizer, animal fodder, and the like, so that even if the device could be produced at low cost, it is by no means certain that it would meet wide acceptance.

Although anthropologists have been used more often in planning than in prestudy activities, there are remarkably few examples on record that show exactly what has been done. Isabel Kelly and her colleague, the Mexican anthropologist Hector García Manzanedo, report on one instance. They were asked by the head of the section of Experimental Studies of the Mexican

2 Marriott, 1952, p. 265.

Ministry of Health and Public Assistance to examine the Mexican Government's antimalarial program—a part of the current world-wide attempt to stamp out malaria—and to make recommendations for more efficient operations. This research was done without field work on the basis of the two anthropologists' wide general knowledge of Mexico. First they examined maps showing the infected areas, and then they superimposed these on maps showing the distribution of the Indian population of the country. This revealed that many of the areas of high infection were also areas of dense Indian population, often with many monolingual groups representing a number of different languages. This suggested that in parts of the country there would be far greater problems—and consequently greater costs—of communication on a per capita basis than had been anticipated by the medical planners.

Malarial control requires taking blood samples, and the anthropologists pointed out that there is widespread reluctance among many Indians, and often among rural mestizos as well, to permit this operation. Sometimes this opposition is based on the belief that the blood can be used for witchcraft directed against the victim through the processes of sympathetic magic, in which any evil done to something from the body will react in the body itself. In other areas the opposition stems from the belief that blood is a nonrenewable substance and to the extent that any is lost, a person loses strength and sexual vigor. In such areas the anthropologists suggested that withdrawal of blood possibly might be accomplished only through force. On the other hand, they pointed out, in parts of Yucatan and Quintana Roo withdrawal for diagnosis is a part of traditional therapy, and in these regions, they suggested, there is apt to be less resistance.

Based on observations where earlier malaria-control work had been done, they knew that insecticides often cause the death of small chicks, bees, and even cats, and that these deaths have aroused much antagonism. They warned of the need to explain very carefully the effect of DDT and to take measures to reduce to a minimum harmful side effects.

They also studied the administrative layout of the project and noted that the thirteen major zones of operation had been established largely on the basis of population. Each zone was to have essentially the same number of workers and the same plan of attack. Some of the zones were relatively homogeneous in population and offered no special problems. But those that included many different Indian groups, often in remote and isolated areas, obviously would require more workers, and workers with special talents for dealing with Indian groups. The anthropologists therefore suggested that the antimalaria organization seek the cooperation of the National Indian Institute, which already had developmental centers in a number of Indian areas. They felt that the "cultural promoters" already at work, who had gained the confidence of the Indians (and many of whom were Indians themselves), would be invaluable in aiding the antimalaria campaign in these areas.[3]

ON-GOING ANALYSIS

Potentially this is the setting in which the greatest scientific advances may be made and which should therefore be the most gratifying to the anthropologist. It is the situation in which the anthropologist has, or should have, the opportunity to test his hypotheses by seeing whether his predictions come true. It is the setting in which the anthropologist may have the opportunity to see, immediately and first hand, the consequences of innovation, and hence to study, under near-laboratory conditions, the whole process of acceptance or rejection of new elements. He talks with informants, notes their attitudes and their reactions. He can find out, with little effort, just *why*

[3] García Manzanedo and Kelly, 1955.

people do or think what they do. Competent technicians some-times do the same thing. Nevertheless, the average technician rarely has time for extended questioning, even if he knows the techniques and has a mind for it. The anthropologist, in this situation, provides the eyes and ears for the project. His sensi-tivity to developments can make possible modifications in plans, while there is still time to change, and experimentation with new or altered ideas.

The anthropologist is apt to be the first person to spot bar-riers as they develop, and he should be in a position to suggest ways to overcome them. He is in a position, too, to suggest ex-periments with alternate techniques and to measure and eval-uate the relative effectiveness of methods tried. In health educa-tion, for example, will a major emphasis be on movies, film strips, or the use of puppets? The best methods in a given area cannot be determined until several are tried out. The anthro-pologist can set up controlled experiments and give rather good answers to questions like this. The answers, in turn, have both theoretical and practical significance far beyond the immediate problem. One learns about basic motivations in this way; one can study perception as conditioned by society and culture; one can see more clearly the nature and means of the communica-tion process in the society.

A specific instance illustrates this situation. The Division of Health Education of the Department of Public Health of Cali-fornia wondered about the most effective·way to reach Spanish-speaking mothers in maternal-and-child-health clinics. Should the small pamphlets and sheets usually printed in English for English-speaking mothers be translated into Spanish? The best guess was that separate Spanish sheets would be much appre-ciated. But research revealed that a group acculturating toward American life is often sensitive about its language problems, that some mothers were offended by the suggestion that they might not be able to speak English. The conclusion was reached that the best thing would be a bilingual publication, which would not emphasize the ethnic differences of Spanish-speaking people, but which they could easily read in their native language.[4]

An unlimited number of experiments suggest themselves to anthropologists working as members of on-going programs. For example, how difficult would it be to introduce in Afghanistan the Mediterranean horn-tied yoke as a substitute for the traditional yoke that rests on the animals's massive hump, so that animal castration could successfully be pursued and livestock upgraded? (See Chapter 5.) Only an experiment would tell whether what appears to be an answer is in fact feasible.

The building of sanitary latrines sounds like a simple task, hardly necessitating experimental work. Yet public acceptance of latrines is far from automatic. Recent research in India points out how complex the problems are and how experimental work can give correct answers. The work was carried out in 1956 by the Rural Health Section of the Planning Research and Action Institute of Uttar Pradesh. After study of previous programs it was noted that there were two categories of problems: the physical design of the latrine itself and the human factors motivating people to install and use latrines. For sanitary reasons a "water-seal" design to be flushed by pouring water from a hand container was deemed most desirable. Physical factors included such elements as foolproof operation, low initial cost, and use of local materials. Human factors included a design adapted to people's beliefs and habits regarding the disposal of excreta, minimum odor, minimum cleaning required, elimination of danger of splashing while in use, the smallest amount of water possible to flush, and design so that composted faeces could be recovered. In the initial experiment eleven different designs were tried, and villagers were asked their reactions. Three subsequent experiments were carried out, in which the most promising models were refined, each time following the

4 Clark, 1959, p. 221.

comments of villagers. Finally, a design was worked out which appears to meet both physical and human requirements.[5]

The use of the term "experiment" in this sense upsets a great many anthropologists. It connotes "manipulation" of people and this must certainly mean an invasion of rights. Somehow it seems to imply the same thing as making rats run through a laboratory maize. The argument seems to me to be specious. The kinds of experimentation I have in mind are duplicated a hundred times a day in American life. Traffic experts experiment with traffic flow, one-way streets, limited parking. Good teachers experiment with their students by trying alternate forms of examination, different ways of giving courses. Industrial firms experiment with new products and different forms of packaging. But most of us would not feel that these activities represent invasions of basic rights. The only violation of basic rights that I have seen in developmental programs are those in which people have been asked to put up money for ventures that were not fully tested; in some cases a great deal has been lost. This is most regrettable and should be guarded against, but it does not change the fact that in most situations important experimental work, usually on a completely voluntary basis, can be carried out with valuable results both for science and for the goals of the program.

Program administrators sometimes think of anthropologists primarily as trouble-shooters. They "know the local culture" so that when something goes wrong, they can be sent in to pull the fat out of the fire. R. N. Adams tells of an instance in which he was cast in this role in a health program in Guatemala. The Institute of Nutrition of Central America and Panama (INCAP) was carrying out nutritional and health research work in several Indian villages near Guatemala City. Food supplementation was provided for school children as a part of a program to determine how the local diet, which appeared deficient in pro-

[5] PRAI, 1958.

tein, might be improved. In addition to being fed, children were given periodic physical examinations, which involved X-rays and blood withdrawal. In order to promote the best possible relations with villagers a Guatemalan social worker was employed to work in homes, and a clinic was established in each village with a full-time nurse, on the frequently sound assumption that catering to the health needs of all villagers would win friends for the program. At first the work went well, but then villagers in one community began skipping appointments, rumors circulated that the project was politically oriented, parents said their children were being injured, and hostility reached a point were continued work seemed doubtful.

At this point Adams was asked to analyze the problems. After limited research he decided tentatively that three major problems existed: poor communication among INCAP personnel; a disturbed national political situation which had local repercussions that adversely influenced the work; the rather extensive social work program designed to win friends which was, in fact, producing more trouble than aid.

Personal dislikes between some of the members of the field team had adversely influenced the communication that is vital in a program of this type. Since the social worker's activities had least to do with the basic program, she was placed under Adams's administrative direction, and in addition, he became a principal channel of communication between the other members, until certain changes had been made and a more congenial group of workers had been assembled. The important point here, says Adams, is that prior to investigation the field team placed the blame for lack of much Indian support on the Indians; "actually, the trouble lay within the organization of the field team itself, and the Indians were little more than uncomfortable bystanders in the affair."[6]

With respect to political factors, the problem lay in the exist-

[6] R. N. Adams, 1953, p. 11.

ence of two major national factions: a progovernment group, thought by many to be communist-led, and an anticommunist group. The Indians, as Catholics, were anticommunist. In August, 1951, the entire field team including Adams, found that they were being called communists, an identification based on the belief that INCAP, actually an international organization, was an organ of the government. This is a common situation in which anthropologists and action teams find themselves in Latin America, but Adam's handling of it here is unusual.

> The solution to this problem was crude but evidently effective. It involved tracking down the sources of the rumor that INCAP was communistic to its specific sources, and then having fairly strong conversations with the individuals concerned. There was nothing particularly gentle in our dealing with these individuals: we told them frankly that they had been lying, that they were spreading insidious misinformation about a reputable group of people, and that they were actually aiding the communists by doing this. At the same time, the field personnel visited the homes of everyone we had considered to be friends until that time, and the nature of the gossip was discussed openly.[7]

The third problem, that of the undesirable effects of the social work program, seems to run contrary to frequent experience in which one good program bolsters another. This program included bringing in a breeding boar to improve local stock, setting up a municipal chicken coop to demonstrate improved poultry husbandry methods, holding social evenings, and other such activities. Unfortunately these activities caused friction between villagers. The schoolteachers felt the boar belonged to them, whereas the local men who had fed it felt they should sell it for profit. The members of the committee that had helped with the municipal chicken coop believed they had the right to the eggs, which they sold for their own profit,

[7] *Ibid.,* p. 11.

rather than distributing them among potential chicken raisers. And often the social-evening movies would not arrive or the equipment would break down, leaving the people in an irritable mood. The clinic, too, caused problems; the doctor's visits were poorly timed or unpredictable, and services did not correspond to people's expectations. With the withdrawal of the social welfare program and the reduction in the clinic's services, sources of irritation were removed which facilitated concentration on the nutritional program.[8]

But still other problems remained, these centering around folk medical beliefs. Investigation revealed that opposition to blood withdrawal was based on the belief that blood is non-regenerative, that each person has only so much for an entire life, and to the extent that it is lost, the individual is permanently weakened. "One informant told the anthropologist that the villagers simply could not understand why doctors who claimed to know how to make people well went around intentionally taking the blood of little children, thus making them weaker. Weakness made one more susceptible to illness, so that blood-taking was the reverse of what doctors should be doing. This informant concluded that doctors could not know very much about making people well."[9]

When the nature of opposition to blood withdrawal was found, steps could be taken to counteract it. In part this involved determining the minimum amount of blood needed for the test and exercising care to make sure that no more than this was taken. In part it meant taking of only a few samples at a time, so that the psychological impact of a mass bloodletting was avoided. But it also meant capitalizing on folk belief. Since blood was considered to indicate strength or weakness, it followed that the condition of the blood could be used as a measure to determine a person's health and resistance to illness.

[8] *Ibid.*, p. 12.
[9] R. N. Adams, 1955, p. 447.

Accordingly, the workers started to explain how the blood withdrawal in small quantities permitted the doctors to tell about the health of the child and to take necessary steps should the child's blood prove to be sick. This explanation, thoroughly drilled into people, was accepted, and when, after an interval of more than two months, blood was again withdrawn, there was little opposition.[10]

As in this instance, an anthropologist in the role of a trouble-shooter often can be very helpful. But trouble-shooting is at best a stopgap measure. More and better prestudy and planning should usually make it possible to eliminate this role.

EVALUATION

This is one of the most important types of work that has been done by anthropologists working in goal-directed programs. The technique is to study a specific program through its history, utilizing documents and, when possible, interviewing the people who have participated, in order to extract lessons from the experience that can be fed back into improved planning for future work. The anthropologist often faces a special problem here. Human problems in technological change have not, in the past, always received the attention due them; consequently, many praiseworthy projects have foundered. An ex post facto analysis therefore frequently turns out to be a summary of what went wrong and not of what went right. This puts the anthropologist in the role of the carping critic, which doesn't endear him to the administrator who feels—correctly—that the anthropologist has not had to face the practical problems of running a project, and that if he had, he might be more tolerant. It is unfortunately true that most of the readings in the field of applied anthropology are analyses of failures or partial failures. Yet, from the standpoint of scientific research,

10 *Ibid.,* p. 448.

failure or success of a particular project is incidental; the important thing is whether lessons can be learned that will spell success in the future. The example of evaluation here summarized illustrates one major attempt to use behavioral scientists in program appraisal and shows, I hope, some of the helpful lessons that emerge from this type of work.

Beginning in 1944 the Smithsonian Institution sent visiting professors in the social sciences to Latin America to teach and to participate in making basic studies of rural culture. Sixteen volumes ultimately were published on many aspects of Latin American life. None of this work was pointed directly toward specific problems, but, with other Latin American research, it provided an excellent jumping off point for action work. This opportunity came in 1951 when the United States Public Health Service asked five Smithsonian professors—four anthropologists and a sociologist—to participate in a major evaluation of the first ten years of public health work carried out by the Institute of Inter-American Affairs in cooperation with host country health departments.[11] Health centers, a cornerstone of the ten-year program, were selected as the major focus of research, but hospitals and environmental sanitation also received attention. No standard questionnaires were sent from Washington; each scientist was asked to use his judgment as to how to approach the assignment. The sociologist (Simmons) emphasized such things as problems of social structure, status hierarchies in the medical profession, and conflicts stemming from different role perceptions. One anthropologist (Oberg) with long government experience stressed the administrative problems a United States government bureaucracy has in orienting its personnel (incidentally, in so doing he developed the concept of culture shock) and in working with host country counterparts. A second anthropologist (Kelly), historically and ethnographically oriented, emphasized the nature of folk medicine

[11] Erasmus, 1954; Foster, 1952, 1953; Oberg and Rios, 1955; Simmons, 1955.

and folk curing, the rural-urban dichotomy as reflected in behavior patterns, mothers' problems in meeting demands of their husbands, and the like. The other anthropologists (Erasmus and Foster) concentrated on economic factors and basic patterns of change. Some social scientists would criticize the obvious lack of research design. But this initially flexible approach outlined the scope of the problem. Preliminary findings were exchanged, basic problems were defined, and agreement was reached on how comparative data from seven countries could be obtained.

Two major problem areas were identified: (1) the quality and nature of interpersonal relationships, particularly between patients and public health personnel but also among public health personnel themselves; (2) the whole complex of beliefs, attitudes, and practices associated with health, prevention of disease, disease, and curing—in the broadest sense, "folk medicine."

It was found, for example, that health center patients often felt a lack of tact and diplomacy on the part of medical personnel. Part of the problem stemmed from ideas of class and status widespread in Latin America, where people below one's station in life are thought not to merit the same consideration shown toward one's equals or superiors. But in other instances apparent rudeness was completely unconscious and resulted from the desire of a nurse or health educator to do a thoroughly professional (and impersonal) job. The experiences of the Salvadorean and Chilean nurses (Chapter 9) will be remembered. The concept of proper role behavior of health center personnel, when executed, created in the patients a feeling of coldness and lack of sympathy. Again, patients complained because of very long waits in health centers, and because visiting hours were scheduled for bureaucratic reasons, and not to meet the needs of the client group. Finally, mothers often were antagonized because health centers would not accept sick children or would take sick children only if they had previously been enrolled. In newly developing countries low-income mothers are not particularly aware of the distinction between curative and preventive medicine—a distinction that is a function of the needs as well as the vested interests of professionals in industrialized countries. Consequently, when health centers which they had been told existed to improve health conditions refused to help them in their hour of need, mothers often took a dim view of the preventive services whose goals were foreign to their ways of thinking.

This research highlighted the fact, already recognized in some but not in all countries, that a successful American public health project cannot simply be transplanted to another country with different health levels, economic potential, and population groups. In Chile the decision had been made to accept sick children when they were brought to a health center. This won the confidence and approval of mothers, and, with their felt needs taken care of, they often were willing to accept preventive services even though they did not fully appreciate their nature. On the other hand, Mexico City health centers, initially operated in a strict United States fashion, turned away sick children not previously registered. Compared to Chile, these centers showed a high percentage of turnover of cases, and preventive work was much less successful. The lesson learned, and now generally accepted, is that in newly developing countries public curative medical programs are necessary to win the confidence and good will that makes preventive programs successful.

Among the significant things revealed by folk medical research is the fact—now documented in many other parts of the world—that peoples with little exposure to modern medicine dichotomize types of illness: there are those that a physician obviously can treat, such as pneumonia, yaws, malaria, and others that yield quickly to wonder drugs; and there are those that the physician cannot treat, because either he does not know about them or he denies that they exist. These often are folk-defined illnesses believed to be caused by magical or other forces: the evil eye, "bad air," "fright," and the like. The help of the physician is sought in the first instance but not usually in the second. After all, if a father knows his child has been "eyed" and the doctor says there is no such thing, it is asking a lot to believe that the right medical aid has been obtained.

Research in folk medical beliefs highlighted a basic problem that faces all medical personnel who work in newly developing countries or in areas where many of their clients have had limited exposure to modern medical practice. That is, to what extent, if any, should medical personnel cater to folk medical belief? Should all medical practice be carried out in the clinical terms that characterize an American city, or should changes be made in practices that violate folk belief, however superstitious such belief may be? Here are examples of the kinds of problems that are met.

Peasant peoples in much of the world believe that a ritual disposal of the placenta is essential for the well-being of mother and child. Frequently this means burying it under the home hearthstones. We know that expectant mothers and their families often resist hospitalization because of fear that harm will come if the placenta is otherwise handled. Do we simply assume that people will have to learn that their views are superstitious, or do we make arrangements to deliver the placenta to the family for traditional disposal? The latter solution is repugnant to some medical people, yet it has been successfully used on many occasions. In prenatal health centers with delivery facilities recently opened in northwest Argentina, initial reaction to hospital delivery was antagonistic. After the practice was adopted of giving the family the placenta for traditional disposal, attendance increased 20 percent to 50 percent in several centers. Dr. Carlos Canitrot believes this decision was instrumental in increased utilization of services.[12] In northern

12 Communicated by Dr. Carlos Canitrot.

Nigeria it is believed that the family must have not only the placenta but all blood lost during delivery as well. In order to attract patients for hospital delivery, sheets and bedding must be washed and the water given the family along with the placenta.[13] In El Salvador and other parts of Latin America, country people share an old Spanish belief: delivery takes place more easily if the mother wears or has under her bed her husband's hat, or if she wears his shirt or jacket. If catering to this superstition induces more expectant mothers to avail themselves of hospital services, should permission be given to the mother to do what she wants?

There is no easy answer to these questions. Many medical people working under such conditions increasingly believe that we can break out of our own medical folklore and superstition and cast at least some of our services in terms of local cultures. Harmless herbal teas, for example, may make it possible to persuade mothers to give water to infants with diarrhea which they would not give if instructions simply called for lots of boiled water. And if a group believes that three (or four) is a lucky number, medicine might be prescribed every three (or four) hours, or three or four times a day, or even in small units of three or four. If a hospital diet is in conflict with folk beliefs about the proper food for certain conditions, modifications might be made without injuring the dignity of medicine. Postpartum diets usually are strictly prescribed in peasant societies, and fear that they will be required to eat foods they know are harmful to them sometimes prevents otherwise willing women from seeking hospitalization for delivery. If research reveals that orange juice is proscribed but tomato juice is permissible, certainly it would seem that tomato juice should be served.

There is no single answer as to how far one should go in catering to folk beliefs. In 1957 lightning struck a palm tree in the yard of a tuberculosis sanitorium in Tucson. Because of the

[13] Communicated by Dr. Adeniji Adeniyi-Jones.

significance of lightning in their religion, Navaho Indian patients were greatly upset, and two left the sanitorium. The culturally sensitive hospital administrator brought a Navaho medicine man with his ceremonial paraphernalia to carry out the "sing" that normally would be done on the Reservation to counteract the danger brought by the lightning. The medicine man's words and songs were piped to all wards on the intercom, so that each Navaho heard the ceremony and his own personal blessing. After this there was no further talk of leaving the hospital, and a health crisis was averted.

But there is also evidence on the other side. As a part of the Smithsonian health research, Charles Erasmus interviewed a number of mothers in a fine new maternity hospital in Quito, Ecuador, which had had immense success after a very short time. The mothers all criticized the hospital for forcing things upon them that conflicted with their beliefs: wrong food, open windows admitting fresh air, daily baths, compulsory fingernail cleaning, and a host of other routine acts which they insisted endangered their and their infants' health. But when Dr. Erasmus asked why they came to the hospital, they replied that they had noticed babies born in the hospital were lots healthier than those born at home—so culture appeared, in this case, to fly out the window as a barrier to acceptance of new medical practices.[14]

This particular example, and other findings of this Latin American evaluation project as well, confirmed what agricultural extension agents long ago learned: a striking demonstration is one of the most effective ways to change behavior. This is not too difficult in agriculture. If part of a field is planted and cultivated according to tested scientific procedures, the advantages usually are obvious in a few months. But there is no comparable way to demonstrate the absence of smallpox, whooping cough, or diphtheria, which peasant mothers are quite willing to

[14] Communicated by Dr. Charles J. Erasmus.

believe may not come anyway. Educated people interpret the statistics and can be convinced, but this type of logic is not widespread in the world. The fact is that preventive medicine's values are almost impossible to demonstrate within the limits of preventive medicine practice itself. But much curative medicine gives immediate and convincing results. A man who sees leg ulcers caused by yaws disappear by magic after one or two injections of penicillin knows that a physician can do wonderful things.

One of the things we have learned in evaluation studies is that preventive medicine can capitalize on the dramatic successes of curative medicine. When participating in the Latin American health program evaluation, I was struck to see, in the city of Temuco, Chile, that there was widespread cooperation from mothers in a BCG antituberculosis vaccination campaign. Six months earlier a serious whooping cough epidemic had threatened. Vaccine was flown in, children were vaccinated, and the threatened epidemic was quickly cut short. Mothers told me that this showed them that doctors knew what they were doing when they said vaccinations would prevent illness, so when the doctors asked their help in the BCG campaign, they were quite happy to cooperate.

Many major technological development programs, such as India's Community Development Programme, now make use of social scientists in evaluation work, in order to feed knowledge back to planning to permit increasingly successful projects. But much remains to be done. One of the most serious shortcomings of evaluation work is that almost no comparative, cross-cultural analytical work has been undertaken. A wealth of experience lies buried in official reports and hidden in the minds of workers who have neither the time nor the training to write up their knowledge for the use of others. It sometimes seems as if the sociocultural dimension of planned change must be discovered, and its rules worked out independently, in every new project. There is very little mechanism to make available to new personnel the accumulated wisdom of earlier programs.

From 1916 to 1922 the Rockefeller Foundation carried out an antihookworm campaign in Ceylon. The history of this pioneer venture in cross-cultural technical aid has been superbly described by Jane Philips.[15] To me the most fascinating, and disheartening, thing about this program is that almost all the problems which later public health projects faced were encountered in Ceylon. The social and economic implications of technical aid were discovered, and many of the correct answers were worked out. Yet until Dr. Philips searched the records and talked with participants, no major effort appears to have been made to make this experience available to all health workers. Here are the kinds of things that were learned in Ceylon over forty years ago.

Barriers to change exist in the suspicion of government, rumors, the fact of free services, the low economic margin which makes it difficult for a coolie to lose a day or two of work, folk medical beliefs in conflict with western medicine, and differing concepts of the role of the curer. It was learned that preventive services were little understood by people who had pressing curative needs, and the importance of a broad medical (and social and economic) program became apparent when people were irritated by having their hookworm treated but not their leg ulcers and other more painful ailments. The common cultural misconceptions of technical workers were discovered when they applied their values in an exotic society, and the Americans experienced shock and annoyance at the lack of gratitude that greeted their humanitarian efforts.

One doctor, for example, identified himself with the planters, and became so involved in factionalism and the struggle for prestige that he finally resigned. Some of the field directors tried to express the American idea of democracy in an outgoing,

[15] Philips, 1955.

warm-hearted man-to-man approach which was misunderstood by people who were used to and expected a degree of authoritarian behavior from educated people. The Americans learned that, regardless of how friendly they were, in some degree they always were classed with the European masters. It took time for them to learn that dignified behavior was expected of them, tempered with the use of authority.

The lessons of the integrated nature of culture and the processes of culture change were hard to learn. The program planners intended to make a vivid demonstration of the scientific method which would eradicate hookworm in a small area, and thus set an irresistible example to the people to work cooperatively in solving other health problems. Not until 1924, near the end of the program, was it officially recognized that hookworm control had to be intimately related to other health work and to social conditions as well. When the Rockefeller scientists realized they could not eradicate hookworm in a given area because of all the factors that converged on any single illness, they shifted their emphasis to a permanent government control program and to the fundamentals of rural health work in general.

The subsequent work of the Rockefeller program was guided by the practical lessons learned in Ceylon, and the direction of policy was adapted to a growing realization of the interrelation of health and social and economic problems. But, until Dr. Philips made her study, this invaluable experience was not generally available as a guide for contemporary health workers; it was known only to relatively few people. Similarly, the equally valuable experiences of today's technical experts are, for the most part, going unexploited, because of lack of interest and the absence of a mechanism to collect, appraise, and set forth in usable form the lessons of contemporary international work.

12 . . . . *Technical aid and social science: some problems of teamwork*

If, as I strongly believe, social scientists, and particularly anthropologists, should play a more active role in technical aid programs, what should their role be? Two main problems arise: (1) the definition of the kinds of work an anthropologist should do, and (2) the nature of the administrative relationship between the anthropologist and the action team. Regrettably, except in rare instances, no good answers have been worked out for either problem. The history of anthropological participation in developmental programs is pretty much one of frustration, misunderstanding, and lack of good communication between administrators and scientists. On comparatively few occasions has the anthropologist felt completely satisfied with the way in which his role has been envisaged by administration and with the types of research he has been asked to do. And on equally few occasions has the administrator felt that he has had the kind of support and aid in solving his problems that he had hoped for from the anthropologist. This has been true, in spite of many honest and serious attempts to reconcile differences and to work together.

There is no easy answer to the problems of team work, but if the causes of difficulty are better understood, then more effective cooperation should result. The basic problem, it seems to me, arises from the fact that the anthropologist and the administrator are members of rather distinct subcultures with very different values and goals. We can properly speak of the "cultural chasm" (to use Saunders' felicitous phrase) between the two fields, just as we can speak of the cultural chasm as a barrier to efficient interaction between members of truly distinct cultures. The value system, the aims, the methods of work, and the goals of the administrator are vastly different from those of the anthropologist, and consequently, to the extent that either —in a working relationship with the other—is forced out of his comfortable subcultural mold, he will feel frustrated and dissatisfied with the arrangement.

The nature of the cultural chasm separating the anthropologist and his fellow social scientists from administrators and technical specialists can perhaps be seen more clearly if we think of the former as members of a *discipline* and the latter as members of a *profession*. The underlying assumption that characterizes academic disciplines is that the search for knowledge represents the highest value. The work of this kind of scientist is exploratory: he wants to find out, to know; he wants to order knowledge in meaningful patterns; he wants to build theory. As a scientist, he is not immediately concerned with the goodness or badness of his discoveries, nor with their immediate practical utilization.

The practice of professional work, on the other hand, draws upon the scientific knowledge of many disciplines, reworking this knowledge so that everyday problems can be solved. A profession differs from a discipline in that its activities are immediately goal-oriented. The existence of, let us say, a public health organization means that health problems have been defined, that it has been deemed desirable to solve these problems, and that a bureaucracy has been created to work toward their solution. A basic value judgment is implicit in all work: health is better than illness and every effort should be made to banish the latter. In other words, an academic discipline stresses theoretical research, whereas a profession stresses goal-directed action. The two aims are by no means mutually exclusive, but they are different, and when the two aims are pursued in a common project, a reconciliation of interests is essential.

An important difference in the two fields has to do with ego gratification. In neither is money the principal source of satisfaction, for the monetary rewards of both behavioral scientists and technicians are modest. Each looks for basic satisfaction in the esteem in which he is held by his disciplinary or professional colleagues, according to the standards set by each field. Public health personnel, for example, feel gratified when they know that their efforts have raised the level of health in their jurisdiction and that this success is recognized by their colleagues. Behavioral scientists, on the other hand, feel gratified when they feel that they have made new contributions to basic science, that they have formulated new and sound theories, and that these contributions are recognized by *their* colleagues. The distinct way in which professionals and research scientists achieve status in their fields obviously has an important bearing on how they view their roles and what they hope to accomplish in any cooperative program.

Obviously, if either a professional specialist or an anthropologist is asked to do work which impedes his striving toward recognition by his peers, he is not going to be a very happy person. An anthropologist on an applied project may delight the professionals with whom he is working; by satisfying the needs of administration he becomes a "good anthropologist."

But the chances are he is not satisfying himself, and he fears he will be overlooked by the members of his discipline whose approbation he seeks. To explore this problem further, let us see how both administrators (and technical specialists) and anthropologists conceive their roles and what they expect of the other in any joint work.

Looking at the problem first from the standpoint of the administrator, we see that he is charged with the achievement of ends, of goals that have been determined and for which an administrative organization has been created. As a good administrator he will, quite properly, utilize all the material and human resources at his disposal that will help achieve these goals. The personal convenience and likes and dislikes of the members of his staff, although something to be considered, are secondary to his primary task of getting the job done. Furthermore, he is operating within a budget, which usually must be defended annually, and the likelihood of continued support for his program depends on evidence of progress. If an anthropologist can contribute something within this framework, he will be a useful addition. More specifically, here are the kinds of things the administrator wants from an anthropologist.

1. Specific data pointed toward concrete problems: Are the inhabitants of a Pacific atoll well governed and content? How can we persuade farmers to utilize improved seed? Why do mothers drop out of prenatal health clinics? Why won't villagers cooperate for common ends? The administrator wants answers to these and a hundred similarly specific questions. He is not interested—or thinks he is not interested—in the basic cultural patterns of a rural area, because these are not specific. The problems most administrators see are of a day-to-day operational nature. When R. N. Adams was first sent to a Guatemalan village (Chapter 11) it was simply to find out why a nutritional research project on school children was arousing parental hostility. No thought had been given to basic social and cul-

tural analysis preceding the initiation of the project so that wise planning might have prevented the hostility. The administrator's definition of his cultural needs means that, most frequently, he thinks of the anthropologist as a trouble-shooter. He is someone who, from his encyclopedic knowledge of queer customs, ought to be able to dredge up an immediate answer to a puzzling and threatening problem.

2. Even when the administrator appreciates the cultural implications of developmental work, he needs pertinent information in readily digestible form. That is, reports must be written simply, with a minimum of sociological jargon. They must be of such nature that the administrator does not have to wade through mountains of incidental data which, however fascinating, do not have the answers for which he searches. Even if he had the inclination, the average administrator does not have the time to read all the anthropological information that may be available on the area in his charge.

Sir Philip Mitchell, former Governor of Kenya, and an early enthusiast for the use of anthropology in colonial administration, speaks tellingly to this point:

> There was, especially during the nineteen twenties and thirties, a spate of special reports and investigations; at one time, indeed, anthropologists, asserting that they only were gifted with understanding, busied themselves with enthusiasm about all the minutae of obscure tribal and personal practices, especially if they were agreeably associated with sex or flavoured with obscenity. There resulted a large number of painstaking and often accurate records of interesting habits and practices, of such length that no one had time to read them and often, in any case, irrelevant, by the time they became available, to the day to day business of Government.[1]

This common shortcoming (for action programs) of traditional reports is also recognized by some anthropologists. Forde,

[1] Mitchell, 1951, p. 57.

for example, writes that many of the African anthropological studies which should have been of considerable value in framing and implementing policy were not appreciated by administrators, since they were embodied in lengthy studies or specialist papers. "While from a scientific point of view these represented a great advance in the functional analysis of native institutions, they often assumed a knowledge of, and primary interest in, theoretical problems, and the relevance of their results to the immediate and even long-term problems of administration was not always brought home."[2]

3. The administrator needs information promptly. He cannot wait to get information from traditional anthropological channels of publication. Even short articles rarely appear in less than two years from the time of completion of field work, and full monographs often are delayed ten or more years. Given the nature of his assignment, it is unreasonable to expect an administrator to devote much attention, not to say money, to research which at best will be of help to his successor or successor's successor. He must have information promptly. Often this means verbal reports, perhaps at weekly staff meetings, and it certainly means periodic memoranda which may serve as a basis of justification to his superiors for some of the decisions he makes. Clearly the frequently confidential nature of these memoranda precludes publication.

The administrator has other, more general, conditions that must be fulfilled if he is to be happy in his relationship with the anthropologist. He must believe that the anthropologist knows something about the nature of administration, the inherent limitations and handicaps under which any program functions and which limit the course and degree of action that the administrator can take. He must feel that the anthropologist is sympathetic to the goals of his program as well as to the people toward whom a program is directed. The administrator

[2] Forde, 1953, p. 850.

cannot be expected to risk his reputation by taking the evaluation of the anthropologist, unless the anthropologist, too, is in some degree involved.

For the anthropologist there are also certain conditions that must be fulfilled in some degree if his work in the applied field is to be satisfying to him.

1. Wherever the limits may have been set, he must feel that he is allowed to make a study that is technically sound and professionally respectable. This does not necessarily mean that he insists on a full year to make a basic ethnographical study, although the general anthropological complaint certainly is lack of time in which to do adequate work. It does mean working under a policy in which the anthropologist is not at the beck and call of the administrator, to be pulled off one project and set to work on another, because a more recent and hence more urgent crisis has arisen. Given the administrator's frequent role concept of trouble-shooter for the anthropologist, this is a great danger. In other words, if the anthropologist is to work well, he must be a great deal more than an answer-box. He must feel he is doing good and original work in which he can take pride.

2. The anthropologist must feel that a reasonable part of his field research will become available to his profession and that it will be read by his colleagues. He needs the approbation of other anthropologists, their recognition that he is contributing to the field, if he is to be a first-class anthropologist. It is not enough to have the satisfaction of knowing that his administrative superior is pleased with his work. The administrator achieves distinction by success in reaching the goals of his organization; the anthropologist achieves distinction by a creditable list of scientifically sound publications.

3. The consequences of (1) and (2) are that, on other than short-term consultation jobs, the anthropologist must feel that the administrator knows something about the organization of his discipline, its values and goals, and that he has the sympathy

and support of the administrator in achieving personal ends, within the framework of bureaucratic limitations. Practically, this means that the administrator must take at least a middle-range view of anthropology; he must resist the temptation to assign the anthropologist to a new task each week, and he must ask himself if a series of quick answers are in fact of more value to him than fewer but more profound analyses. It also means—and this is the most difficult of all things to achieve—that it must be recognized administratively that writing, not only of reports but of articles and even monographs, is a major part of any job-description for anthropology. Further, it must be recognized that some of the things that will be written by the anthropologist are not immediately applicable to the ends of the program.

In my experience the biggest blind spot of administrators is inability to understand the principle of scientific capital, the accumulation of theory and fact, general and specific, that has been built up painstakingly over a period of many years. Anthropologists are able to give quick answers, and sometimes they do surprisingly well, because they can fall back on previously accumulated scientific capital; they can build on what is already known. Scientific capital is not something that is built up to an optimum level and then forgotten. Conditions change, new problems arise, new interests develop, so that the corpus of theory and fact must be continuously replenished if the needs of both theoretical anthropology and practical administration are to be met. The gain for both is long range, but it is just as real for the latter as for the former. This is, ultimately, the justification of government support for basic research. It is interesting to note that, in the United States, the principle is thoroughly understood by the Navy. The basic research on society and culture sponsored in Micronesia when that area was under military control stands as a monument to the foresight of Navy policy makers. By contrast, for all practical purposes, the principle of basic research was completely unknown to the policy makers of the International Cooperation Administration. The successor Point Four organization, the Agency for International Development, includes a research division called the Office of Development Research and Assistance. Time will tell whether the principle of basic research is better understood than in the past.

In view of the conflicting values and aims of administration and anthropology, and in view of the great variety in types of programs in which anthropologists may be used, it is clear that there is no one ideal administrative relationship. There are, however, certain minimum conditions which must be sought.

1. Both administrator and anthropologist must have a clear understanding of the philosophy underlying the work of the other and of the values and goals attached thereto. Not only must there be understanding, but also there must be acknowledgement of the importance and legitimacy of these values and goals.

2. There must be agreement on and understanding of the operational roles of both administrators and anthropologists in any program in which the latter are used. Each must understand the inherent limitations in the work of the other and expect neither special favors nor miracles.

3. The administrator must realize that he, his technical colleagues, and the whole sociocultural system within which his program is carried out are just as legitimate and necessary a research object for the anthropologist as is the analysis of the culture and society of the people toward whom the program is directed. This is not easy to grasp intellectually, and once grasped it is even more difficult to accept. When an anthropologist studies spontaneous change, his primary interest is directed to the group that is evolving. The stimuli that produce change are important, but they are diffuse and amorphous. But when an anthropologist studies directed culture change, he is as inter-

ested in the innovating group as in the client group. For, as should by now be clear, an understanding of the goals, values, and mode of operation of an action team has just as much to do with the success of a program as does the reaction of the recipient culture.

The professional worker in an action program has little difficulty in seeing that the culture of the group with which he is working will determine how people react to him in many ways. He can see that patterns of authority and concepts of role in the client group will affect the way in which he must direct messages or ask for cooperation. Tolerance and objectivity in studying others is not hard to achieve.

It is not so easy for a technician to accept the fact that an understanding of *his* attitudes, values, and motivations is just as important in successfully bringing about change. It is painful to realize that one implicitly accepts assumptions that have little validity beyond tradition and that one's professional outlook has been uncritically acquired. It is not easy for the technician to admit that the way he views his assignment and how he works is conditioned by such things as how he perceives his role in the bureaucracy to which he belongs, how he reacts to his supervisor, and how he deals with his colleagues and those who work under his direction.

Yet it should be clear that a technical aid mission can be looked upon as a society with a specific culture much as a village or an area is a society with a culture. It is composed of persons of both sexes, of different ages, organized in a hierarchy marked by power and authority, with well-defined roles and occupational specialization, with mutually recognized rights and obligations. This "technical" society shares common values, it engages in professional rituals, and it operates on assumptions that normally are not questioned. The cohesive and divisive forces found within it, the stresses and strains, and the unifying elements are similar to those in other societies. A technical aid mission can be studied in the same way that an ethnic group can be studied. It may be just as interesting, and it is certainly just as important in achieving maximum program efficiency.

Obviously, in much of the work he does the anthropologist will see his field as consisting of two interacting systems: the client group *and* the innovating group. Needless to say, he must also be aware of the points of view and the prejudices he himself brings and of the nature of his interaction with the two groups. Certain dangers are inherent in the examination of the innovating group. The anthropologist will have to question and observe technical specialists as they go about their daily chores. Unless this questioning is done with utmost tact, and unless the specialists have been well indoctrinated as to why it is being done, friction and hard feeling may develop. For some the mere fact that questions are asked implies that they are regarded as giving a less than satisfactory performance, especially in view of the fact that anthropologists often have been critical of technical workers. The anthropologist must phrase his questions so that they are as nearly free of value judgments as possible and so that they do not suggest a search for deficiencies in individual performances. When the members of a technical aid team recognize they are legitimate objects of study, and when anthropologists recognize the sensitivity of this kind of work and approach it with the same degree of caution used in making contact with a new tribe, the goals of both groups are more nearly met.

With these needs, limitations, cautions, and warnings in mind, what are the most effective ways to utilize anthropologists in technical aid programs? The precise working relationship in a specific situation will depend on the nature of the program, its duration, the status level of the participants, and a multitude of other factors. Anthropological thinking reflects a broader (and I think less realistic) spectrum of ideas about how the two groups can work together than does administrative thinking.

At one end of the spectrum is the anthropologist who feels he should do basic research and publish articles and monographs to be read and used by administrators as they see fit. The anthropologist may serve as a short-term consultant for specific problems, but he suggests no policy, passes no judgment, and fights to maintain his independence.

This position is attractive to the anthropologist for several reasons. He is his own boss, he does not have to worry about policy, he can be strictly impartial (although in fact he is usually pretty hard in judging the technicians in the area in which he works), and he can define his own problems. This kind of work has only one drawback, when judged for its practical utility: it rarely has any effect whatsoever, until it is interpreted and utilized by other anthropologists. The instance of the Smithsonian Institution's Institute of Social Anthropology is illustrative. The United States government supported wide-scale basic research in Latin American society and culture, ostensibly for practical purposes. But the work—sixteen volumes in all—was completely unknown to, and doubtless unusable by, those organizations that properly should have used it, and not until the anthropologists themselves participated in a public health evaluation project were the data of practical—as distinguished from scientific—value.

At the opposite end of the spectrum is the anthropologist who believes he should be a formal member of an action team; in extreme cases, even an administrator. He studies the people toward whom a program is directed, but he also studies the organization of which he himself is a member and the relationships between the two systems. He supplies technical information, and at times he implements it. For many anthropologists, this relationship is abhorrent. It partakes of social tinkering, and the anthropologist, enmeshed in everyday practical problems, is thought lost to his true calling. Wilson states this position well when he says "The conception of 'technical information' . . . is the key to the correct relationship between social scientists . . . and men of affairs. For human societies . . . have a hard reality which cannot be mastered without patience and objective study. It is the scientists' business to undertake that patient and objective study, it is the business of government and industry to make use of their results in the fashioning out of the present whatever future they desire."[3] Largely because of the extent to which this view is shared by other leading anthropologists, applied work is often viewed as second-class anthropology, without value as far as anthropological theory itself is concerned. Consequently, it is not easy to get the best anthropologists to serve in applied programs, until such men have made their reputations in basic research and theory building.

Fortunately this extreme position is by no means universal, and increasingly it is recognized that direct integration in an action team permits an anthropologist opportunities he would not have while working independently. The most important of these rewards is that, as a working member of a technical aid mission, an anthropologist can more effectively study the innovating organization. The anthropologist takes it for granted that he must gain the confidence of natives among whom he works; it is more difficult for him to see that this is equally true of the members of the bureaucracy. When he attends regular staff meetings with the others, is subject to the same series of frustrations and delays, is obviously one of the gang, and if, by chance, it is known that at some time in his life he has held administrative responsibility and been faced with budgetary and personnel problems, his problems of establishing rapport are minimized. In this setting the kind of work an anthropologist does is different from that in a basic community study. He spends less time with local peoples and more with the bureaucracy. But then, his problem is not just local people:

[3] Wilson, 1940, p. 46.

it is a pair of systems, studied as they interact.

The sympathy with which an anthropologist may view direct hire or maximum integration with a bureaucracy will depend on his experiences, and these are many. My own experiences with administrators have been generally agreeable as well as profitable, and perhaps for this reason I lean more toward close working relationships than do many anthropologists. But there are others who also recognize the limitations in the minimum integration conception. Barnett, speaking of a variety of reasons why anthropologists and administrators do not make contact, writes that "The essential difficulty in all these instances is that the research specialist is regarded as a stranger, often as an interloper, by regular government officials. He has no status within the organization, so his views can be treated like those of any other outside observer or critic."[4] When an anthropologist is a member of a team, by job definition he is expected to express opinions. He may be disregarded, but he is even more sure to be disregarded if he is a technical adviser who operates entirely on his own initiative, independently deciding what should be explored, and not being informed or appealed to on matters which the administration regards as problems.

In Department of the Interior policy in the Micronesian Trust Territory, direct representation of the social scientist's view on policy matters at the top level is regarded as essential, "and where it has not been looked upon with favor by a departmental officer, the absence of a consultative pattern is taken to be a major obstacle to the success of the experiment."[5] Barnett speaks of the ineffectiveness of the "free-lance anthropologist or the administratively isolated technical specialist," as well as of advisers and consultants who suffer from lack of familiarity with administrative processes and their day-to-day demands. "No one outside an activity can have the acquaintance with its require-

4 Barnett, 1956, p. 172.
5 *Ibid.*, p. 173.

ments that is a prerequisite for the preparation of readily adapt-able advice. . . . Policy determinants and operational rules may not be appreciated in recommendations by outsiders; and an unfamiliarity with internal power struggles and personal clashes often destroys the utility of a report simply because it has been phrased one way rather than another or presented to the wrong individual."[6]

Barnett, it should be noted, is not arguing for an anthro-pologist-administrator; in fact, he expressly rejects this in favor of a sharp demarcation between the two functions. He is point-ing out, and more clearly than it usually has been done, that the best scientific work may well be done with an administratively close relationship.

There are a few anthropologists, whose theoretical compe-tence is not in jeopardy, who admit they like to make value judgments based on their research and to do what they can to implement these judgments. One of the most convincing state-ments on this position is by Gladwin, who first did basic research under U.S. Navy-sponsored research (CIMA) on Truk, then served as anthropologist on the Civil Administration Unit, and finally took the position of Native Affairs Officer, in which capacity he was responsible for the political and economic af-fairs of the 15,000 natives of Truk and surrounding islands. While doing basic research Gladwin learned the language and acquired an unparalleled knowledge of the local culture, which has been described in a monograph that has achieved the status of classic in the field of culture and personality. Thus, he was well equipped to make decisions. Further, he was faced with no major ethical problem: the basically altruistic United States policy toward Micronesia was one to which he could whole-heartedly subscribe.

Gladwin obviously took satisfaction in feeling that he was directly helping the Trukese in his role as administrator. "It is

[6] *Ibid.*, p. 174.

my thesis, perhaps in self-justification, that, provided he has the opportunity to become adequately knowledgeable in the local culture and can develop adequate rapport, the anthropologist who wants to be useful in administration must himself become in some degree an administrator."[7] Gladwin found that ultimately he came to the point where he required another anthropologist to do most of the original field research and that his research subsequent to becoming an administrator was done on the run. But this he felt was compensated for by his unique competence to mediate between high-level policy and the immediate situation.

> The anthropologist, equally sensitive to American and to Micronesian values, can at least hope to achieve a balance between them which will do violence to neither. He is not only best qualified to do this, but also when he implements his own convictions he is, in the best American tradition, sticking his own neck out. If he fails, his failure will be weighed against his successes. But if someone else takes the responsibility for implementing the anthropologist's recommendations and they produce a fiasco, the result can be loss of faith in the anthropologist and a period, at least, of sharply reduced effectiveness. If the job is worth doing, the anthropologist must do it himself.[8]

My position is close to that of Gladwin. Decisions are going to be made that involve anthropological knowledge. Without quibbling as to whether he is acting as a citizen or a scientist in so doing, I think the anthropologist has a clear duty to society to participate in decisions in which, by training and experience, he is obviously an authority.

I would beg the question as to what is the best administrative relationship between anthropologist and technical aid program, and suggest that the task is to make sure that the representatives of both fields understand and appreciate the nature of the

[7] *Gladwin,* 1956, p. 64.
[8] *Ibid.,* pp. 64-65.

other's values and methods of work, and that for a specific assignment there is agreement on respective roles. A particular administrative arrangement then becomes secondary. In most cases a rather close relationship will be the answer, but this need not be a *sine qua non* for mutually profitable results.

13 . . . . The ethics
of planned change

Planned change is so much a part of our way of life that it perhaps seems odd to ask questions about the ethics of this kind of activity. Nevertheless, very genuine problems present themselves when we ask such questions as, "How far should we go in trying to help others?" and "What are our obligations, and what are the limits to these obligations?" Any program which has as a goal the changing of the way of living of people carries moral and philosophical implications. As we have seen, no single change, however desirable it seems to professional planners, can be evaluated solely in its own terms, for it carries consequences that may be good, bad, or both for the recipient peoples. Public health workers feel that health is better than sickness; this is all the justification they need. It is hard to quarrel with this simple statement. Yet the implications of "health is better than sickness" are not simple. At the Fifth World Health Assembly in Geneva a representative of the sister United Nations agency, the Food and Agriculture Organization, in addressing a plenary session, said in effect, "We can't keep up with you." Will four billion undernourished people be more desirable than two billion undernourished people? This is not an inevitable consequence of efficient public health, but there are competent judges who feel it is a very great possibility. I doubt that "health is better than illness" is an adequate moral justification in itself for this area of planned culture change.

Science cannot answer philosophical questions, but it can point out the consequences of decisions made on philosophical or ethical grounds. And it can provide the factual information and indicate the practical implications which can and should be known in making value judgments. It can point to its own limitations and perhaps suggest the nonscientific biases of its practitioners, who sometimes confuse these emotionally based opinions with hard logic. In brief, in defining our individual positions on the ethics of planned culture change we must utilize the scientific evidence at hand but recognize that emotional nonscientific elements inevitably will play a part in determining the stand we take.

In this final chapter I want to consider two levels, or kinds, of ethical problems. The first and more general is that just presented. It deals with the position to be taken by technical experts and program administrators in their everyday planning and working. It also deals with basic American national policy, the magnitude of a total aid program, and the range of activities to be included in this program. The second ethical problem is professional, and it reflects the nature of anthropological field work. The anthropologist is in much the same position as the physician, the lawyer, or the minister. He is privy to a great deal of confidential information which, if carelessly handled, might cause embarrassment and hardship to his informants. He simply cannot tell an administrator or a technical specialist all he knows about specific situations, however valuable that information might seem in solving practical problems. He might even have to conceal the identity of individuals actively working to sabotage programs. The best field work is done when informants realize that they can trust the anthropologist and that nothing he will say or write will endanger them. This is one of the reasons why good field work takes a long time; such trust is not developed overnight.

What should a reasonable ethical stand for a technical specialist or program planner include? It should include the willingness to understand the culture of recipient peoples, to look for the good in these cultures, to search for the reasons for traditional ways, to restrain excessive missionary zeal which leads to inability to see alternatives, and to take the time and trouble to prepare oneself, technically and emotionally, to work in a foreign society.

The enthusiasm of many technical specialists and of the equally numerous less well-trained professional do-gooders sometimes terrifies me. The blind ethnocentrism of many Americans, who have no doubt about the merit of their way of life and the desirability of helping other people enjoy it, takes my breath away. When I see an earnest American greeting a foreigner with a bone-crushing fraternity-type handshake, meanwhile fixing him with a beady stare, under the assumption that he thereby connotes sincerity, I blanche. A friendly smile, an extended right hand, a lapel label saying "Hello, my name is John Smith," and unlimited energy to pitch in and work are not enough to meet today's problems of international relations and technological development.

Much American technical aid has been received with appreciation and enthusiasm in host countries, and it has certainly helped produce noteworthy changes. But it has not all been successful, as readers of *The Ugly American* know. What does the proffering of technical aid mean? How does it look to potential recipients? The American sees it as obvious good will, an evidence of eagerness to help, to share good things with others, a symbol of generosity and selflessness, a gesture that cannot be misunderstood or misinterpreted. What does an offer of technical aid imply to potential recipients? It implies many things, such as potential modern imperialism, the danger of economic penetration, a shattering of traditional values, and it means also often-insensitive strangers taking the best houses and driving up the cost of living. Above all it says, in essence, "if you people will learn to do more things the way we do them, you will be better off." This is not a very flattering approach. Consummate sensitivity in proffering aid, mastery of economic, technical, and social facts needed to carry it out, and awareness of the limitations of such aid are absolutely basic to successful cooperative developmental work.

What should a reasonable ethical stand for an anthropologist or other social scientist working in technical aid programs include? It should include first of all a code of honor whereby the confidences of informants are not violated and whereby none of the actions of the anthropologist will affect adversely the peoples whom he studies. This code applies equally to villagers and to the members of the innovating teams whose activities the anthropologist will also want to understand. But an ethical stand for the anthropologist should also include recognition that peoples in newly developing countries often want to change more rapidly than he, the anthropologist, believes desirable, and that rapid and extensive change is not necessarily catastrophic. It should likewise include great sympathy for the innovators who work under great odds, in spite of which they accomplish notable things. Our toleration should not be restricted to native peoples; we must seek also to understand and work cooperatively with the members of technical missions.[1]

[1] In 1946 The Society for Applied Anthropology recognized the need for a formal code of ethics to guide the anthropologist working in an action program. A committee, headed by Margaret Mead, drew up a draft which was circulated and recirculated among the members of the Society for modification and refinement. The published code includes these basic points:

We recognize:

That the applied anthropologist must take responsibility for the effects of his

(Continued on page 262)

Anthropologists often lean over backwards in cautioning against almost any induced change. This position stems both from our belief about cultural relativism—that cultural forms are a function of a way of life and must be judged in terms of that way of life—and from our regret at seeing the good old days, when primitives were primitives, vanish. I often think that anthropologists—not infrequently political liberals—are, in basic personality structure, the most conservative of all academic and professional groups. After all, the primitive tribe, since the inception of our science, has been the raw stuff we study. However addicted to progress one may be in the abstract, it is sad to see these wonderful days slipping away. Then too, we anthropologists have seen, in the course of our field work, enough instances in which the well-intentioned efforts of developers have failed because of cultural blindness, so that we cannot avoid urging caution. This conservatism of anthropologists

---

(Continued from page 261)
recommendations, never maintaining that he is merely a technician unconcerned with the ends toward which his applied scientific skills are directed.

That the specific means adopted will inevitably determine the ends attained, hence ends can never be used to justify means and full responsibility must be taken for the ethical and social implications of both means and ends recommended or employed.

....

That the applied anthropologist should recognize a special responsibility to use his skill in such a way as to prevent any occurrence which will set in motion a train of events which involves irreversible losses of health or the loss of life to individuals or groups or irreversible damage to the natural productivity of the physical environment.

That the applied anthropologist must take the greatest care to protect his informants, especially in those aspects of confidence which his informants may not be able to stipulate for themselves.

....

To advance those forms of human relationships which contribute to the integrity of the individual human being; to maintain scientific and professional integrity and responsibility without fear or favor to the limit of the foreseeable effect of their actions; to respect both human personality and cultural values; to publish and share new methods and discoveries with colleagues; those are the principles which should be accepted and which should be known to be accepted by all those who work in the disciplines affecting human relationships.

Mead *et al.*, 1949.

has not been conducive to our best use as specialists; and the positive contributions we can and should make go unrealized, in part because of our own intransigence. As Margaret Mead says, "It is worth recognizing that the anthropologist has become—in fields like technical assistance and government of underdeveloped area peoples—the symbol of conservatism and pessimism, the specialist who states that most changes seen as desirable by the technician, the economist, or the administrator, will be very difficult, practically impossible, or, if practicable, destructive."[2] She further speaks of "the general occupational preference of anthropologists for the preservation of the past when it comes to the culture of native peoples. . . . measures which will stabilize an aboriginal people in a subsistence economy and therefore prevent them from any participation in world culture can be defended as 'preserving their culture.' "[3]

Anthropologists are not untouched by the spirit of Rousseau. A year's soujourn in a primitive tribe or a peasant village can be an exciting experience. The anthropologist is indoctrinated to see the good in all cultures, and not a few returned field workers have suffered in silence with a guilty conscience because they really didn't like the people they studied as well as they thought they should. Some peoples turn out to be positive stinkers, by almost any standards; it is not inconsistent to have sympathy for such people and to make real friends among them, and still recognize that a major cultural overhaul for them would be the best possible thing in the world. As Mead points out, primitive and peasant life is not per se beautiful and satisfying. It can be sordid, cruel, and unhealthy, a very poor device to allow its members to achieve their individual potentials.

People are often much more anxious to change, to abandon the old and take up the new, than anthropologists wish to admit. Dube, for example, points out how the rural Hindu ex-

[2] Mead, 1956, p. 98.
[3] *Ibid.*, p. 99.

presses verbal idealization of traditional patterns of village life, but that in spite of this *ideal* of traditional guides, there is in fact a "strong expectancy" of change.[4] People have seen or heard enough about the amenities of modern life that there has been a decided change in their level of expectation, and if these expectations are not at least partially met trouble will ensue.

Margaret Mead, in discussing her restudy of Manus (in the Admiralty Islands of Papua) after an absence of twenty-five years, points out that rapid change is not necessarily disrupting, contrary to frequently expressed anthropological dicta. She suggests as hypothesis just the opposite: that if change is desired by an entire group, if it cuts across an entire culture, and if all major areas of culture are simultaneously affected, there may well be less social disorganization and individual maladjustment than if changes occur piecemeal over a long period. "The possibility that we have over-rated the factor of 'cultural resistance' in the people who have seemed to be unwilling to be assimilated, and under-rated the resistance factors in the donor cultures, needs very serious re-examination."[5]

Sol Tax, in a sensitive article in which he discusses the kind of help he and his students have tried to give to the Fox Indians of Iowa in meeting modern conditions, expresses a scientific-ethical point of view that is subscribed to by many anthropologists, and which, by implication, he believes should represent the ethic of national policy in aid programs. Briefly, his position is that the Fox (and peoples in general) should be free to make the changes they wish. He speaks of "freedom for a community to choose its way of life," and of wanting to provide "genuine alternatives from which the people involved can freely choose"; and he says also that "what is best for them involves what they want to be."[6] It is hard to argue with this point of view and

[4] Dube, 1956, p. 29.
[5] Mead, 1956, p. 103.
[6] Tax, 1956, pp. 18-19.

yet, if subscribed to literally, it is potential dynamite. The point is that, however philosophically desirable it is for people to pick and choose, *they are in fact free to do so only within very narrow limits.* Neither the citizens of the technically most advanced civilizations nor those of newly developing nations are passing through a cafeteria line. All of the goodies of the modern world may be laid out before the hungry man, but they are not laid out so that he can pick and choose the dishes that please him, passing over those that do not appeal. The diner at the table of technological development is faced with a table d'hôte menu; he cannot order à la carte. When he selects an entree, the soup and salad are also going to come, and he will have to eat these, whether he likes them or not.

All societies are changing, and the members of single societies, as individuals and in groups, can make choices only within certain boundaries. It is the height of irresponsibility to lead the culturally hungry people of the newly developing countries to believe that they have complete freedom of self-determination. In this fashion aspirations are aroused that cannot possibly be met; political stability will not occur under such circumstances. It is the task of the social scientist—the anthropologist and his colleagues in other fields—to attempt to understand the broad patterns of social, economic, and political change, and *to determine what the degree of latitude in choice may be*. In helping peoples to develop, we must be sure to make clear to them *all* the consequences of their choices. This is true whether the level of cooperation is the prime minister's cabinet or a village community development project.

Theodorson points out that industrialization leads to new societal patterns *which cannot be rejected*. The machine, perhaps regrettably, is an expensive investment, and it cannot tolerate inefficient use; human labor in nonindustrial societies, on the other hand, is cheap. Willy-nilly, it will be molded to the machine's demands. It is unrealistic to ask for the benefits of the machine, but to be unwilling to pay its social cost.[7]

Staley has summed up the dilemma which faces new nations when he writes that they, like individuals, often want incompatible things:

> . . . they may want active industries and higher incomes but not real competition among businessmen or lower profits per unit of sales. . . . Underdeveloped countries may want fine highways and public buildings and a cradle-to-the-grave social security system, but not an honest tax system or a nonpolitical civil service or labor laws designed to encourage productivity and honest effort as well as to protect labor's rights. They may want good health, plenty of food, and a low death rate, but not a changed family system and a low birth rate.
>
> . . . The main pressures on the peoples of underdeveloped countries to change accustomed ways and make new choices among life's values are not intentional pressures, whether from the United States or any other source. Rather, they are impersonal pressures impinging from all sides out of a changing world environment. These the peoples of underdeveloped countries cannot escape. Their real choice is not whether to change, but how, how fast, and in what directions.[8]

Staley is speaking of the facts of change when he writes,

> To achieve successful development, underdeveloped countries have to reshape some of their fundamental social institutions. They also have to establish and learn to operate many new institutions unfamiliar to them but essential for modern productivity and free society. . . . The notion that old social institutions can be kept unchanged while only the mechanical side of modern industry is imported . . . may lead to complete frustration, or it may lead to a social monstrosity dangerous to the people of the country and to their neighbors.[9]

The task of the outsider, Staley believes, is not to tell people

[7] Theodorson, 1953, pp. 447, 481.
[8] Staley, 1954, pp. 390-391.
[9] *Ibid.*, p. 228.

what choices to make, but rather to point out to them the inter-relations between development, society, and culture so they will know what they are choosing. Further, he does not believe that industrialization must produce a carbon copy of Western social institutions; different kinds of social and political institutions can support an industrial economy, as is clear from the Russian example. But—and there can be no doubt about this—the social forms and cultural values of a traditional agricultural economy must be vastly modified wherever major technological change occurs, whether these social forms and cultural values are modeled after those of Western nations or are created especially by the newly developing nations to meet their own needs.

The ethic of helping people change their culture begins with a readiness to understand that culture, to recognize the good in it, and to know the reasons why it is what it is. This is not simply the morality of cultural relativism. It is not simply tolerance and broad-mindedness. It is basic wisdom for the technical agent. For in every culture there is a reason for each element. Sometimes the reason is no longer valid; change then will not be dangerous. Other times the reason is still valid, and change may spell disaster. Allen tells how in Greece an energetic salesman for a plow company persuaded peasants to buy shiny new moldboard plows. United States agricultural agents have tried to introduce similar plows in many parts of the world. Yet in this instance, the new and costly plows soon were discarded, and the farmers returned to the ancient scratch plow. "Investigations soon proved that the peasants were quite right to change back to their primitive instrument. They knew more than the aggressive salesman, and they knew more through instinct and experience than some of us did. For the soil in the particular locality was so thin that the modern steel plow did far more harm than good by turning up too much of the subsoil."[10]

10 Allen, 1943, p. 235.

Uneducated peoples may be wrong on technical matters; they
often are. But until we are sure they are wrong on a particular
point, it is unwise and morally wrong to try to "improve" them.
It is wrong to assume that a way, because it is modern, scientific,
and Western, is better than a traditional method. Margaret
Read reports to us the folk wisdom of an old woman in a village
in Central Africa: "You Europeans think you have everything
to teach us. You tell us we eat the wrong food, treat our babies
the wrong way, give our sick people the wrong medicine; you
are always telling us we are wrong. Yet, if we had always done
the wrong things, we should all be dead. And you see we are
not."[11]

The ethic of helping people change their culture includes
knowing what culture is, what its characteristics are, what it
means to a society, and what its processes of change are. It is
not enough to be a competent technician, morally fortified with
the unquestioned assumptions of goodness of one's profession.
One must be a *responsibly* competent technician, aware that
any technical improvement has social and economic consequences that may or may not be deleterious. The responsible
technician is the one who is able to help adapt scientific technology and methods to the ecological, social, and economic environment of the developing country, but who does not think
that good consists in leading others to do things as he does. It is
Staley again who gives a good example of what this means.
Hybrid corn, he points out, was developed in the American
Midwest. The strains developed there, however, did not do well
in Mexico, and it took years, using the Midwest methods, to
develop the many strains necessary for the different climatic
areas of Mexico. Yet the fundamental invention of corn-hybrid-
ization, and the principles and methods learned in developing
new strains, applied just as much to Mexico as Iowa.[12]

[11] Read, 1955, p. 7.
[12] Staley, 1954, pp. 229-230.

The ethic of helping people change involves restraint and caution in missionary zeal. It means that developmental personnel should be careful not to plan for people, but to work with them in searching for realistic answers to their problems. The helpful technical expert is the one who knows how to explain the range of alternatives possible in a given situation and to explain the probable consequences of each one. He encourages people to try new things when he believes they will solve problems and when they will not do excessive violence to a total way of life. He discourages them if they wish to try new things which seem incompatible with reality. But above all he leaves the decision to the people themselves; in the long run they, not he, are the ones who must be pleased.

Finally, the ethic of helping people change means taking the time to fit oneself, personally and humanly, to work in a foreign society. It means taking the trouble to learn about the cultural chasm that separates people, a chasm which, if unrecognized, can wreck the best of plans, but one which, if known, can usually be easily bridged. Successfully bridging the chasm means, in most instances, learning the language of the host country. It means learning and observing the rules of courtesy there present. It means learning to be humble, to be willing to learn, to believe things quite different from what one's previous experience has taught. It means sympathy and tolerance. It means a genuine and an unselfish desire to help, not in the well-meaning but bungling fashion of the monkey who tried to aid the fish, but in a realistic way based on full understanding of the nature of culture and culture change, and of the impact of advanced technologies on traditional communities. Above all it means awareness that the technical expert, the man who truly experiences the "dramatic discovery" of a conspicuously different culture, and who through his skill and sensitivity helps in some small way to solve its problems, is the person who gains most of all. He acquires riches of a very special kind which will bring him satisfaction throughout his life.

Bibliography

Adamic, Luis
  1934 *The native's return.* New York: Harper & Brothers.

Adams, Don
  1960 "The monkey and the fish: cultural pitfalls of an educational adviser," *International Development Review,* 2(2): 22-24.

Adams, Harold S., George M. Foster, and Paul S. Taylor
  1955 *Report on community development programs in India, Pakistan and the Philippines.* Washington, D.C.: International Cooperation Administration.

Adams, John B.
  1957 "Culture and conflict in an Egyptian village," *American Anthropologist, 59:225-235.*

Adams, Richard N.
  1951 "Personnel in culture change: a test of a hypothesis," *Social Forces, 30:185-189.*
  1953 "Notes on the application of anthropology," *Human Organization, 12(2):10-14.*
  1955 "A nutritional research program in Guatemala." In B. D. Paul, ed. *Health, culture and community.* New York: Russell Sage Foundation, pp. 435-458.

Allen, Harold B.
  1943 *Come over into Macedonia.* New Brunswick, N.J.: Rutgers University Press.

Altamira, Rafael

   1949   *A history of Spain from the beginnings to the present day.*
           Trans. Muna Lee. Toronto, New York, London: D. Van
           Nostrand Company, Inc.

Ammar, Hamed

   1954   *Growing up in an Egyptian village.* London: Routledge &
           Kegan Paul Ltd

Apodaca, Anacleto

   1952   "Corn and custom: the introduction of hybrid corn to
           Spanish American farmers in New Mexico." In E. H.
           Spicer, ed. *Human problems in technological change.* New
           York: Russell Sage Foundation, pp. 35-39.

Bailey, Flora L.

   1948   "Suggested techniques for inducing Navaho women to ac-
           cept hospitalization during childbirth and for implement-
           ing health education," *American Journal of Public Health,*
           38:1418-1423.

Banfield, Edward C.

   1958   *The moral basis of a backward society.* Glencoe, Ill.: The
           Free Press.

Barker, Anthony.

   1959   *The man next to me: an adventure in African medical
           practice.* New York: Harper & Brothers.

Barnett, H. G.

   1940   "Culture processes," *American Anthropologist, 42*:21-48.

   1941   "Personal conflicts and culture change," *Social Forces, 20:*
           160-171.

   1942   "Applied anthropology in 1860," *Applied Anthropology*
           (now *Human Organization*), *1*(3):19-32.

   1953   *Innovation: the basis of cultural change.* New York, To-
           ronto, London: McGraw-Hill Book Co., Inc.

   1956   *Anthropology in administration.* Evanston, Ill.: Row,
           Peterson and Company.

Beers, Howard W.

   1950   "Survival capacity of extension work in Greek villages,"
           Rural Sociology, 15:274-282.

Benedict, Ruth
1940 *Race: science and politics.* New York: Modern Age Books.
Berreman, Gerald D.
1959 *Kin, caste, and community in a Himalayan hill village.* Ithaca, N.Y.: Unpublished Ph.D. Dissertation, Cornell University.
Brown, G. Gordon
1957 "Some problems of culture contact with illustrations from East Africa and Samoa," *Human Organization 16*(3):11-14.
Buitrón, Aníbal
1959 "La investigación y el mejoramiento de las condiciones de vida," *CREFAL: Boletín Informativo,* nos. 26-27:6-9. (Pátzcuaro, Michoacán, Mexico.)
1960 "Problemas económico-sociales de la educación en la América Latina," *América Indígena, 20:*167-172.
Carstairs, G. Morris
1955 "Medicine and faith in rural Rajasthan." In B. D. Paul, ed. *Health, culture and community.* New York: Russell Sage Foundation, pp. 107-134.
1958 *The twice-born: a study of a community of high-caste Hindus.* Bloomington: University of Indiana Press.
Cassel, John
1955 "A comprehensive health program among South African Zulus." In B. D. Paul, ed. *Health, culture and community.* New York: Russell Sage Foundation, pp. 15-41.
Chance, Norman A.
1960 "Culture change and integration: an Eskimo example," *American Anthropologist, 62:*1028-1044.
Clark, Margaret
1959 *Health in the Mexican-American culture.* Berkeley and Los Angeles: University of California Press.
Cobarruvias [Covarrubias] Orozco, Sebastián de
1611 *Tesoro de la lengua castellana, o Española.* Madrid. (Reprinted in Barcelona, 1943.)
Coleman, James S.
1958 *Nigeria: background to nationalism.* Berkeley and Los Angeles: University of California Press.

274 · Bibliography

Cousins, Norman
  1961 "Confrontation," *Saturday Review*, *44*(12):30-32.
Crane, Robert I.
  1955 "Urbanism in India," *The American Journal of Sociology*, *60*:463-470.
Cussler, Margaret, and Mary L. De Give
  1952 *'Twixt the cup and the lip. Psychological and socio-cultural factors affecting food habits.* New York: Twayne Publishers.
Davis, Kingsley
  1951 *The population of India and Pakistan.* Princeton, N.J.: Princeton University Press.
Dube, S. C.
  1955 *Indian village.* London: Routledge and Kegan Paul Ltd.
  1956 "Cultural factors in rural community development," *The Journal of Asian Studies, 16*:19-30.
  1957 "Some problems of communication in rural community development," *Economic Development and Cultural Change, 5*:129-146.
  1958 *India's changing villages: human factors in community development.* London: Routledge and Kegan Paul Ltd.
Elder, J. P.
  1958 "A criticism of the graduate school of arts and sciences in Harvard University and Radcliffe College for those who took the Ph.D. at these institutions between 1950 and 1951," *Newsletter*, September 30. (Cambridge: The Harvard Foundation for Advanced Study and Research.)
Elkin, A. P.
  1936- "The reaction of primitive races to the white man's cul-
  1937 ture," *The Hibbert Journal, 35*(4):537-545.
Erasmus, Charles J.
  1952 "Agricultural changes in Haiti: patterns of resistance and acceptance," *Human Organization, 11*(4):20-26.
  1954 "An anthropologist views technical assistance," *The Scientific Monthly, 78*:147-158.
  1955 *Reciprocal labor: a study of its occurrence and disappearance among farming peoples in Latin America.* Berkeley:

Unpublished Ph.D. Dissertation, University of California.

Fejos, Paul
1959 "Man, magic and medicine." In Iago Galdston, ed. *Medicine and anthropology.* New York: International Universities Press, Inc.

Firth, Raymond
1956 *Elements of social organization.* 2nd ed. London: Watts & Co.

Forde, Daryll
1953 "Applied anthropology in government: British Africa." In A. L. Kroeber, chairman. *Anthropology today.* Chicago: University of Chicago Press, pp. 841-865.

Foster, George M.
1948 "Some implications of modern Mexican mold-made pottery," *Southwestern Journal of Anthropology, 4:*356-370.
1952 "Relationships between theoretical and applied anthropology: a public health program analysis," *Human Organization, 11(3):*5-16.
1953 "Use of anthropological methods and data in planning and operation," *Public Health Reports, 68:*841-857.

Friedl, Ernestine
1958 "Hospital care in provincial Greece," *Human Organization, 16(4):*24-27.
1959 "The role of kinship in the transmission of national culture to rural villages in mainland Greece," *American Anthropologist, 61:*30-38.

Friedmann, F. G.
1958 "The world of 'La Miseria,'" *Community Development Review,* no. 10:16-28. Washington, D.C.: International Cooperation Administration. (Reprinted from *Partisan Review,* 1953.)

García Manzanedo, Héctor, and Isabel Kelly
1955 *Comentarios al proyecto de la campaña para la erradicación del paludismo en México.* México, D.F.: Dirección de Estudios Experimentales en Salubridad Pública, Instituto de Asuntos Interamericanos. (Mimeo)

Gibb, H. A. R., and Harold Bowen
1950 *Islamic society and the west. A study of the impact of Western Civilization on Moslem culture in the Near East.* London, New York, Toronto: Oxford University Press, vol. 1, part 1.

Ginsburg, Norton S.
1955 "The great city in southeast Asia," *The American Journal of Sociology, 60*:455-462.

Gladwin, Thomas
1956 "Anthropology and administration in the trust territory of the Pacific Islands." In *Some uses of anthropology: theoretical and applied.* Washington, D.C.: The Anthropological Society of Washington, pp. 58-65.

Goswami, U. L., and S. C. Roy
1953 "India." In Phillips Ruopp, ed. *Approaches to community development.* The Hague, Bandung: W. Van Hoeve Ltd., pp. 299-317.

Gough, E. Kathleen
1952 "Changing kinship usages in the setting of political and economic change among the Nayars of Malabar," *Journal of the Royal Anthropological Institute, 82*:71-88.

Graubard, Mark
1943 *Man's food, its rhyme or reason.* New York: The Macmillan Company.

Greenfield, Kent Roberts
1947 "The Mediterranean way of life," *The Yale Review, 36*: 435-446.

Hamamsy, Laila Shukry
1957 "The role of women in a changing Navaho society," *American Anthropologist, 59*:101-111.

Hamburger, Adelaide
1954 "A família numa pequena comunidade paulista," *Sociologia, 16*:284-292. (São Paulo: Escola Livre de Sociologia e Política.)

Hereford, Philip, ed.
1935 *The ecclesiastical history of the English people* by the

Venerable Bede. Trans. Thomas Stapleton. London: Burns
Oates & Washbourne Ltd.
Herskovits, Melville J.
1948 *Man and his works.* New York: Alfred A. Knopf.
Hertz, Will
1958 "Mother India," *Oakland (Calif.) Tribune,* March 9.
Hill, Colin DeN.
1957 "Some notes on experience of community development in
southeast Nigeria," *Community Development Review,* no.
7:18-23. (Washington, D.C.: International Cooperation
Administration.)
Hill, W. W.
1944 "The Navaho Indians and the ghost dance of 1890," *American Anthropologist, 46:*523-527.
Hogbin, H. Ian
1958 *Social change.* London: Watts.
Hoselitz, Bert F.
1957 "Urbanization and economic growth in Asia," *Economic
Development and Cultural Change, 6:*42-54.
Hoyt, Elizabeth E.
1956 "The impact of a money economy on consumption patterns." In B. F. Hoselitz, ed. *Agrarian societies in transition.* (The Annals of the American Academy of Political
and Social Science, 305:12-22.)
Hunter, John M.
1959 "Reflections on the administrative aspects of a technical
assistance project," *Economic Development and Cultural
Change, 7:*445-451.
Hunter, Monica
1936 *Reaction to conquest. Effects of contact with Europeans on
the Pondo of South Africa.* London: Oxford University
Press.
Jackson, I. C.
1956 *Advance in Africa. A study of community development in
Eastern Nigeria.* London: Oxford University Press.
Jelliffe, D. B.
1957 "Social culture and nutrition: cultural blocks and protein

malnutrition in early childhood in rural West Bengal,"
Pediatrics, 20:128-138.

Keesing, Felix M.

1934 *Modern Samoa. Its government and changing life.* London:
George Allen & Unwin Ltd.

1941 *The south seas in the modern world.* New York: The John
Day Company.

Kelly, Isabel

1953 "Informe preliminar del proyecto de habitación en La
Laguna, Ejido de El Cuije, cercano a Torreón, Coahuila."
México, D.F.: Instituto de Asuntos Interamericanos.
(Mimeo)

1958 "Cambios en los patrones relacionados con la alimenta-
ción," *Boletín del Instituto Internacional Americano de
Protección a la Infancia,* 32:205-208. (Montevideo.)

1959 *La antropología, la cultura y la salud pública.* La Paz:
United States Operations Mission to Bolivia, The Institute
of Inter-American Affairs. (Mimeo)

King, Clarence

1958 *Working with people in small communities.* New York:
Harper & Brothers.

Kluckhohn, Clyde

1949 *Mirror for man.* New York, Toronto: McGraw-Hill Book
Co., Inc.

Kroeber, A. L.

1948 *Anthropology.* New York: Harcourt, Brace and Company.

Kroeber, A. L., and Clyde Kluckhohn

1952 *Culture: a critical review of concepts and definitions.*
Cambridge, Mass.: Papers of the Peabody Museum of
American Archaeology and Ethnology, Harvard University,
47:1-223.

Lange, Charles H.

1953 "The role of economics in Cochiti pueblo culture change,"
American Anthropologist, 55:674-694.

LeTourneau, Roger

1955 "Social change in the Muslim cities of North Africa," *The
American Journal of Sociology,* 60:527-535.

Lewis, Oscar
1951 *Life in a Mexican village: Tepoztlán restudied.* Urbana: University of Illinois Press.

Linton, Ralph
1936 *The study of man: an introduction.* New York, London: D. Appleton-Century Company.
1945 *The cultural background of personality.* New York: Appleton-Century-Crofts, Inc.

McCormack, William C.
1957 "Mysore villagers' view of change," *Economic Development and Cultural Change, 5:*257-262.

McDermott, W., K. Deuschle, J. Adair, H. Fulmer, and B. Loughlin
1960 "Introducing modern medicine in a Navajo community," *Science, 131:*197-205, 280-287.

Macgregor, Gordon
1946 *Warriors without weapons: a study of the society and personality development of the Pine Ridge Sioux.* Chicago: University of Chicago Press.

Mair, L. P.
1957 *Studies in applied anthropology.* London: University of London, The Athlone Press. (London School of Economics, Monographs on Social Anthropology, no. 16.)

Mandelbaum, David G.
1941 "Culture change among the Nilgiri tribes," *American Anthropologist, 43:*19-26.
1953 "Planning and social change in India," *Human Organization, 12*(3):4-12.

Marriott, McKim
1952 "Technological change in overdeveloped rural areas," *Economic Development and Cultural Change,* No. 4:261-272. (This subsequently became volume 1.)
1955 "Western medicine in a village of northern India." In B. D. Paul, ed., *Health, culture and community.* New York: Russell Sage Foundation, pp. 239-268.

Mayer, Albert, and Associates
1958 *Pilot project, India. The story of rural development at*

Etawah, Uttar Pradesh. Berkeley and Los Angeles: University of California Press.

Mead, Margaret
1956 "Applied anthropology, 1955." In *Some uses of anthropology: theoretical and applied.* Washington, D.C.: The Anthropological Society of Washington, pp. 94-108.

Mead, Margaret, Eliot D. Chapple, G. Gordon Brown
1949 "Report of the committee on ethics," *Human Organization, 8*(2):20-21.

Menéndez Pidal, Ramón
1950 *The Spaniards in their history.* Trans. Walter Starkie. London: Hollis & Carter.

Mitchell, Sir Philip
1951 "Review of *Native administration in the British territories in Africa,* by Lord Hailey," *Journal of African Administration, 3*:55-65.

Murphy, Robert F., and Buell Quain
1955 *The Trumaí Indians of Central Brazil.* New York: American Ethnological Society, Monograph no. 24.

Neisser, Charlotte S.
1955 "Community development and mass education in British Nigeria," *Economic Development and Cultural Change, 3*:352-365.

Norbeck, Edward, and Harumi Befu
1958 "Informal fictive kinship in Japan," *American Anthropologist, 60*:102-117.

[Oberg, Kalervo]
1955 In *Consultation in the Brazil-United States Cooperative Health Program 1942-1955.* Rio de Janeiro: United States Operations Mission to Brazil, The Institute of Inter-American Affairs.

Oberg, Kalervo, and José Arthur Rios
1955 "A community improvement project in Brazil." In B. D. Paul, ed. *Health, culture and community.* New York: Russell Sage Foundation pp. 349-376.

Opler, Morris E., and Rudra Datt Singh
1952 "Economic, political and social change in a village of

north central India," *Human Organization, 11*(2):5-12.

Paul, B. D., ed.
1955 *Health, culture and community. Case studies of public reactions to health programs.* New York: Russell Sage Foundation.

Philips, Jane
1955 "The hookworm campaign in Ceylon." In Howard M. Teaf, Jr., and Peter G. Franck, eds. *Hands across frontiers; case studies in technical cooperation.* Ithaca, N.Y.: Cornell University Press, pp. 265-305.

Pierson, Donald
1955 "Sickness and its cure in a Brazilian rural community," *Anais do XXXI Congreso Internacional de Americanistas,* São Paulo, pp. 281-291.

Pineda, Virginia Gutierrez de
1955 "Causas culturales de la mortalidad infantil," *Revista Colombiana de Antropología, 4:*13-85.

Pitt-Rivers, J. A.
1954 *The people of the sierra.* London: Weidenfeld and Nicolson.

Planning Research and Action Institute
1958 *Rural health; experiments on latrines for rural homes.* Lucknow: PRAI, Planning Department, Uttar Pradesh.

Read, Margaret
1955 "Culture contacts in education," *Education and social change in tropical areas.* London, Edinburgh, Paris, Melbourne, Toronto, and New York: Thomas Nelson and Sons Ltd., pp. 96-111.

Rees, Alwyn D.
1951 *Life in a Welsh countryside.* Cardiff: University of Wales Press.

Reichard, Gladys A.
1949 "The Navaho and Christianity," *American Anthropologist, 51:*66-71.

Richards, Audrey I.
1951 *Land, labour and diet in Northern Rhodesia. An economic*

study of the Bemba tribe. London, New York, Toronto: Oxford University Press.

Richardson, F. L. W., Jr.

1945 "First principles of rural rehabilitation," *Applied Anthropology* (now *Human Organization*), *4*(3):16-31.

Rosentiel, Annette

1954 "Long-term planning: its importance in the effective administration of social change," *Human Organization, 13* (2):5-10.

Runciman, Steven

1936 *Byzantine civilisation.* London: Edward Arnold & Co.

Sasaki, Tom, and John Adair

1952 "New land to farm: agricultural practices among the Navaho Indians of New Mexico." In E. H. Spicer, ed. *Human problems in technological change.* New York: Russell Sage Foundation, pp. 97-111.

Schneider, David M.

1955 "Abortion and depopulation on a Pacific island." In B. D. Paul, ed. *Health, culture and community.* New York: Russell Sage Foundation, pp. 211-235.

Sibley, Willis E.

1960- "Social structures and planned change: a case study from
1961 the Philippines," *Human Organization, 19:*209-211.

Silone, Ignazio

1934 *Fontamara.* Trans. Michael Wharf. New York: Harrison Smith & Robert Haas.

Simmons, Ozzie G.

1955 "The clinical team in a Chilean health center." In B. D. Paul, ed. *Health, culture and community.* New York: Russell Sage Foundation, pp. 325-348.

1959 "Drinking patterns and interpersonal performance in a Peruvian mestizo community," *Quarterly Journal of Studies on Alcohol, 20:*103-111.

Smith, Arthur H.

1899 *Village life in China: a study in sociology.* New York, Chicago, Toronto: Fleming H. Revell Company.

Solien, Nancie L., and Nevin S. Scrimshaw
1957 "Public health significance of child feeding practices observed in a Guatemalan village," *The Journal of Tropical Pediatrics, 3:*99-104.

Soustelle, Georgette
1958 *Tequila: un village nahuatl du Mexique oriental.* Paris: Université de Paris, Travaux et Mémoires de l'Institut d'Ethnologie, no. 62.

Spicer, E. H., ed.
1952 *Human problems in technological change: a casebook.* New York: Russell Sage Foundation.

1952 "Reluctant cotton pickers: incentive to work in a Japanese Relocation Center." In E. H. Spicer, ed. *Human problems in technological change.* New York: Russell Sage Foundation, pp. 41-54.

Spoehr, Alexander
1949 *Majuro: a village in the Marshall Islands.* Fieldiana, Vol. 39. Chicago: Chicago Natural History Museum, Publ. 641.

Staley, Eugene
1954 *The future of underdeveloped countries: political implications of economic development.* New York: Harper & Brothers.

Straus, Murray A.
1953 "Cultural factors in the functioning of agricultural extension in Ceylon," *Rural Sociology, 18:*249-256.

Tannous, Afif
1944 "Extension work among the Arab Fellahin," *Applied Anthropology* (now *Human Organization*), *3*(3):1-12.

Tax, Sol
1958 "The Fox project," *Human organization, 17*(1):17-19.

Taylor, Paul S.
1954 "Can we export 'the new rural society'?" *Rural Sociology, 19:*13-20.

Theodorson, George A.
1953 "Acceptance of industrialization and its attendant consequences for the social patterns of non-western societies," *American Sociological Review, 18:*477-484.

Thompson, Wallace.
1922 *The Mexican mind. A study of national psychology.* Boston: Little, Brown, and Co.
Ullah, Inayat
1958 "Caste, patti and faction in the life of a Punjab village," *Sociologus, 8:*170-186.
Verga, Giovanni
1955 *The house by the medlar tree.* Trans. Eric Mosbacher. New York: Doubleday Anchor Books.
Wellin, Edward
1955 "Water boiling in a Peruvian town." In B. D. Paul, ed. *Health, culture and community.* New York: Russell Sage Foundation, pp. 71-103.
Wilson, Godfrey
1940 "Anthropology as a public service," *Africa, 13:*43-60.
1941 *An essay on the economics of detribalization in Northern Rhodesia.* Livingstone, Northern Rhodesia: The Rhodes-Livingstone Papers, no. 5, part 1.
Wiser, Charlotte Viall, and William H. Wiser
1951 *Behind mud walls.* New York: Agricultural Missions, Inc.
Yang Hsin-Pao
1949 "Planning and implementing rural welfare programs," *Human Organization, 8*(3):17-21.

Index

DATE DUE

SEP 16 '66			
MAR 1 5 '67			
FEB 17 '68			
SEP 3 0 '69			
SEP 3 0 '69			
SEP 19 '72			
MAY 1 1 '76			
GAYLORD			PRINTED IN U.S.A.